The Institute of Chartered Accountants in England and Wales

MANAGEMENT INFORMATION

For exams in 2016

Study Manual

ICAEW

www.icaew.com

Management Information
The Institute of Chartered Accountants in England and Wales

ISBN: 978-1-78363-205-3

Previous ISBN: 978-0-85760-985-4

First edition 2007

Ninth edition 2015

British Library Cataloguing-in-Publication Data
A catalogue record for this book is available from the British Library

Printed in Great Britain by Ashford Colour Press Ltd, Gosport, Hants

Welcome to ICAEW

I am delighted that you have chosen ICAEW to progress your journey towards joining the chartered accountancy profession. It is one of the best decisions I also made.

The role of the accountancy profession in the world's economies has never been more important. People making financial decisions need knowledge and guidance based on the highest technical and ethical standards. ICAEW Chartered Accountants provide this better than anyone. They challenge people and organisations to think and act differently, to provide clarity and rigour, and so help create and sustain prosperity all over the world.

As a world leader of the accountancy and finance profession, we are proud to promote, develop and support over 144,000 chartered accountants worldwide. Our members have the knowledge, skills and commitment to maintain the highest professional standards and integrity. They are part of something special, and now, so are you. It's with our support and dedication that our members and hopefully yourself, will realise career ambitions, maintain a professional edge and contribute to the profession.

You are now on your journey towards joining the accountancy profession, and a highly rewarding career with endless opportunities. So, if you are studying for our Certificate in Finance, Accounting and Business (ICAEW CFAB) or our world-leading chartered accountancy qualification, the ACA, you too have made the first of many great decisions in your career.

You are in good company, with a network of over 26,000 students around the world made up of like-minded people, you are all supported by ICAEW. We are here to support you as you progress through your studies and career; we will be with you every step of the way, visit page ix to review the key resources available as you study.

I wish you the best of luck with your studies and look forward to welcoming you to the profession in the future.

Michael Izza
Chief Executive
ICAEW

Contents

Contents

ICAEW

1 Introduction

ACA qualification

The ICAEW chartered accountancy qualification, the ACA, is a world-leading professional qualification in accountancy, finance and business.

The ACA has integrated components that give you an in-depth understanding across accountancy, finance and business. Combined, they help build the technical knowledge, professional skills and practical experience needed to become an ICAEW Chartered Accountant.

Each component is designed to complement each other, which means that you can put theory into practice and you can understand and apply what you learn to your day-to-day work. Progression through all the elements of the ACA simultaneously will enable you to be more successful in the workplace and exams.

The components are:

- Professional development
- Ethics and professional scepticism
- 3-5 years practical work experience
- 15 accountancy, finance and business modules

To find out more on the components of the ACA and what is involved in training, visit your dashboard at icaew.com/dashboard.

ICAEW Certificate in Finance, Accounting and Business

The ICAEW Certificate in Finance, Accounting and Business (ICAEW CFAB) teaches essential skills and knowledge in the three key areas of finance, accounting and business.

ICAEW CFAB consists of the same six modules as the first level of our world-leading qualification, the ACA. This means, it can serve as a stand-alone qualification or as a stepping stone on your journey towards chartered accountancy.

You can find out more about the ICAEW CFAB exams and syllabus at icaew.com/cfabstudents.

To learn more about the ACA qualification and chartered accountancy, visit icaew.com/careers.

2 Management Information

The full syllabus and technical knowledge grids can be found within the module study guide. Visit icaew.com/dashboard for this and more resources.

2.1 Module aim

To enable candidates to prepare essential financial information for the management of a business.

On completion of this module, candidates will be able to:

- Establish the costs associated with the production of products and provision of services and use them to determine prices

- Select appropriate budgeting approaches and methods and prepare budgets

- Identify key features of effective performance management systems, select appropriate performance measures and calculate differences between actual performance and standards or budgets

- Identify and calculate relevant data for use in management decision making.

2.2 Method of assessment

The Management Information module is assessed by a 1.5 hour computer-based exam. 20% of the marks are allocated in one scenario-based question. This will be drawn from either syllabus area 1 (costing and pricing) or syllabus area 3 (performance management). The specific topics that may be examined on syllabus area 1 are: allocation, apportionment and absorption of overheads; activity based costing; absorption v marginal profits/losses; mark-up and margin (learning outcomes 1b, c and e). The specific topics that may be examined on syllabus area 3 are: calculation of variances; reconciling absorption and marginal costing profits/losses (learning outcomes 3 e and f). The remaining 80% of the marks are from 32 multiple choice, multi-part multiple choice or multiple response questions.

The thirty-three questions cover the areas of the syllabus in accordance with the weightings set out in the specification grid.

2.3 Specification grid

This grid shows the relative weightings of subjects within this module and should guide the relative study time spent on each. Over time the marks available in the assessment will equate to the weightings below, while slight variations may occur in individual assessments to enable suitably rigorous questions to be set.

Syllabus area	Weighting (%)
1 Costing and pricing; 5 Ethics	25
2 Budgeting and forecasting	25
3 Performance management	25
4 Management decision making	25
	100

3 Key Resources

Student support team

Our student support team are here to help you as much as possible, providing full support throughout your studies.

T +44 (0)1908 248 250
F +44 (0)1908 248 069
E studentsupport@icaew.com

Student website

The student area of our website provides the latest information, guidance and exclusive resources to help you as you progress through the ACA. Find everything you need (from sample papers to errata sheets) at icaew.com/dashboard.

If you are studying for the ICAEW CFAB qualification, you can access exam resources and support at icaew.com/cfab.

Online student community

The online student community provides support and practical advice – wherever you are, whenever you need it. With regular blogs covering a range of work, life and study topics as well as a forum where you can post your questions and share your own tips. ACA and ICAEW CFAB students can join the conversation at icaew.com/studentcommunity.

Tuition

The ICAEW Partner in Learning scheme recognises tuition providers who comply with our core principles of quality course delivery. If you are receiving structured tuition with an ICAEW Partner in Learning, make sure you know how and when you can contact your tutors for extra help. If you are not receiving structured tuition and are interested in classroom, online or distance learning tuition, take a look at our recognised Partner in Learning tuition providers in your area, on our website icaew.com/dashboard.

Faculties and Special Interest Groups

Faculties and special interest groups support and develop members and students in areas of work and industry sectors that are of particular interest.

Our seven faculties provide knowledge, events and essential technical resources. As an ACA or ICAEW CFAB student, you can register to receive a complimentary e-newsletter from one faculty of your choice each year throughout your studies.

Find out more about faculties and special interest groups at icaew.com/facultiesandsigs.

Library & Information Service

The Library & Information Service is ICAEW's world-leading accountancy and business library. The library provides access to thousands of resources online and a document delivery service, you'll be sure to find a useful eBook, relevant article or industry guide to help you. Find out more at icaew.com/library.

ICAEW

CHAPTER 1

The fundamentals of costing

Introduction
Examination context
Topic List

Summary and Self-test
Answers to Interactive questions
Answers to Self-test

Learning objectives

- Understand the concept of cost, and how cost information can be used for different purposes

- Understand different cost classifications and the meaning and use of fixed, variable, direct and indirect costs

- Classify costs as fixed, variable and semi-variable (or semi-fixed) and recognise where each can be used in decision-making

- Identify and explain ethical issues relating to the preparation, presentation and interpretation of financial information for the management of a business

The specific syllabus references for this chapter are: 1a, b, 5a.

Syllabus links

An understanding of how costs may be classified in different ways according to the purpose of the information being prepared is fundamental to this syllabus and underpins many of the learning objectives. It also has links to the Accounting syllabus in the context of understanding how costs are classified for the purposes of inventory valuation and profit measurement.

Examination context

Many of the fundamental aspects of costing covered in this chapter do not lend themselves easily to numerical objective test questions.

Therefore, you are more likely to see the majority of these subjects in narrative questions. For example, you might be required to pick out correct definitions or statements from a number of statements supplied in a question, or you might have to identify an appropriate cost unit from a number of suggestions for a particular organisation to use as the basis of its accounting system.

In the examination, candidates may be required to:

- Understand the purpose of a cost unit

- Classify costs as fixed, variable and semi-variable (or semi-fixed)

- Understand what is meant by the elements of cost

- Understand the difference between a direct cost and an indirect cost, between a controllable cost and an uncontrollable cost and between a product cost and a period cost

- Identify ethical issues relating to the preparation, presentation and interpretation of financial information

Knowing the various definitions is fundamental to answering questions in this area. For example it is essential to determine the 'cost object' in a question (ie the thing being costed), in order to determine whether costs are direct or indirect as regards that cost object.

1 What is cost accounting?

> ## Section overview
>
> - The management information system provides information to assist management with planning, control and decision-making.
>
> - In general terms, financial accounting is for external reporting whereas cost and management accounting is for internal reporting.
>
> - The financial accounting and cost accounting systems both record the same basic data but each set of records may analyse the data in a different way. Ultimately, financial results from both systems can, and should be, reconciled with each other.

1.1 The cost accountant

The cost accountant or a person having access to cost information should be able to provide the answers to questions such as the following.

- What was the cost of goods produced or services provided last period?
- What was the cost of operating a department last month?
- What revenues were earned last week?

Knowing about costs incurred or revenues earned enables management to do the following.

- **Assess the profitability** of a product, a service, a department, or the whole organisation.

- Determine appropriate **selling prices** with due regard to the costs of sale and target profit margins.

- **Put a value on inventory** (whether raw materials, work in progress, or finished goods) that is still held at the end of a period, for preparing a balance sheet of the company's assets and liabilities, and determining the cost of materials (goods) used or sold in a period.

These are all historical questions. The cost accountant also needs to provide information to help provide forecasts or estimates for the future, such as:

- What are the future costs of goods and services likely to be?

- What information does management need in order to make sensible decisions about future profits and costs?

- What financial resources will be needed to fund future growth or activities?

1.2 Cost accounting and management accounting

Originally cost accounting dealt with ways of accumulating historical costs and of charging these costs to units of output, or to departments, in order to establish inventory valuations, profits or losses and balance sheet items. It has since been extended into **planning**, **control** and **decision-making**, so that the cost accountant is now able to answer both sets of questions in Section 1.1 above. In today's environment the role of cost accounting in the provision of management information is therefore almost indistinguishable from that of management accounting, which is basically concerned with the **provision of information to assist management** with **planning**, **control** and **decision-making**.

1.3 Cost accounting systems

The managers of a business have responsibility for planning and controlling the resources used. To carry out this task effectively they must be provided with **sufficiently accurate** and **detailed information**, and the cost accounting system should provide this. Indeed, a costing system provides the foundations for **an organisation's internal financial information system for managers**.

Cost accounting systems are not restricted to manufacturing operations.

- Cost accounting information is also used in service industries, government departments and not-for-profit organisations, including charities.

- Within a manufacturing organisation itself, the cost accounting system should be applied not only to manufacturing operations but also to administration, selling and distribution, research and development and so on.

Cost accounting is concerned with **providing information to assist** the following.

- **Establishing inventory valuations, profits or losses and balance sheet** items

- **Planning** (for example the provision of forecast costs at different activity levels)

- **Control** (such as the provision of actual and standard costs (see Chapter 9) for comparison purposes)

- **Decision-making** (for example, the provision of information about actual unit costs for the period just ended for pricing decisions)

1.4 Financial accounting versus cost accounting

The financial accounting and cost accounting systems in a business both record the same basic data for income and expenditure, but each set of records may analyse the data in a different way. This is because each system has a **different purpose**.

- **Financial accounts** are usually prepared for stakeholders **external** to an organisation, eg shareholders, banks, customers, suppliers, HM Revenue & Customs and employees.

- **Management accounts** are usually prepared for **internal** managers of an organisation.

The data used to prepare financial accounts and management accounts are the same. The differences between the financial accounts and the management accounts arise because the data is usually analysed differently.

Financial accounts	Management accounts
Financial accounts detail the performance of an organisation over a defined period, including its cash flows and the state of affairs at the end of that period.	Management accounts are used to aid management to record, plan and control the organisation's activities and to help the decision-making process.
In the UK, limited companies must, by law, prepare financial accounts.	There is no legal requirement to prepare management accounts.
The format of published financial accounts is determined by law (mainly the Companies Acts), by Statements of Standard Accounting Practice and by Financial Reporting Standards. In theory the accounts of different organisations can therefore be easily compared.	The format of management accounts is entirely at management discretion: no strict rules govern the way they are prepared or presented. Each organisation can devise its own management accounting system and format of reports.
Financial accounts often concentrate on the business as a whole, aggregating revenues and costs from different operations, and are wholly historical.	Management accounts can focus on specific areas of an organisation's activities such as operating departments, individual sites or business streams. Information may be produced to aid a decision rather than to be an end product of a decision.
Most financial accounting information is of a monetary nature.	Management accounts incorporate non-monetary measures. Management may need to know, for example, tonnes of product produced, monthly machine hours, or miles travelled by sales representatives. These are often called 'Key Performance Indicators'.
Financial accounts present an essentially historical picture of past operations.	Management accounts are both a historical record and a future planning tool, linking to budgets and forecasts.

ICAEW

IAS 1 changes the titles of financial statements as they will be used in IFRSs.

- 'Balance sheet' will become 'statement of financial position'
- 'Income statement' will become 'statement of comprehensive income'
- 'Cash flow statement' will become 'statement of cash flows'

Entities are not required to use the new titles in their financial statements. Consequently this Study Manual may use these terms interchangeably.

2 Basic cost accounting concepts

Section overview

- A cost object is anything for which we are trying to ascertain the cost.
- Cost units are the basic control units for costing purposes.
- The term 'cost' can be used as a noun or as a verb.
- Costs need to be arranged into logical groups or classified in order to facilitate an efficient system for collecting and analysing costs.

2.1 Functions and departments

An organisation, whether it is a manufacturing company, a provider of services (such as a bank or a hotel) or a public sector organisation (such as a hospital), may be divided into a number of different **functions**, within which there are a number of **departments**. A manufacturing organisation might be structured as follows.

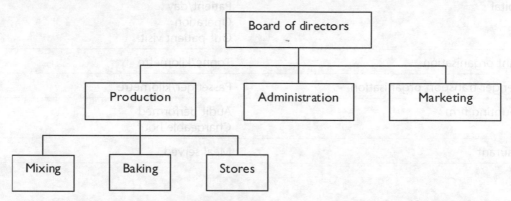

Suppose the organisation above produces chocolate cakes for a number of supermarket chains. The production function is involved with the making of the cakes, the administration department with the preparation of accounts and the employment of staff and the marketing department with the selling and distribution of the cakes.

Within the production function there are three departments, two of which are production departments (the mixing department and the baking department), which are actively involved in the production of the cakes, and one of which is a service department (stores department), which provides a service or back-up to the production departments.

2.2 Cost objects

Definition

Cost object: A cost object is anything for which we are trying to ascertain the cost.

Examples of cost objects include:

- A unit of product (eg a car)
- A unit of service (eg a valet service of a car)
- A department or function (eg the accounts department)
- A **project** (eg the installation of a new computer system)
- A **new product** or service (eg to enable the cost of development to be identified)

In the example above, cost objects could include:

- Individual chocolate cakes
- The administration function or mixing department

2.3 Cost units

Definition

Cost unit: **A cost unit** is the basic measure of product or service for which costs are determined.

Businesses are often interested in one particular cost object – the cost unit – and the cost per cost unit. Determining the cost per cost unit can help with pricing decisions, which you will study in more detail in Chapter 5.

Organisation	Possible cost unit
Steelworks	Tonne of steel produced Tonne of coke used
Hospital	Patient/day Operation Out-patient visit
Freight organisation	Tonne/kilometre
Passenger transport organisation	Passenger/kilometre
Accounting firm	Audit performed Chargeable hour
Restaurant	Meal served

2.4 Composite cost units

Notice that some of the cost units in the above table are made up of **two parts**, for example the patient/day cost unit for the hospital. These two-part cost units are known as **composite cost units** and they are used most often in service organisations.

Composite cost units help to improve cost control. For example, the measure of 'cost per patient' **might not be particularly useful for control purposes**. The cost per patient will vary depending on the length of the patient's stay, therefore monitoring costs using this basis would be difficult.

The cost per patient/day is not affected by the length of the individual patient's stay. Therefore it would be more useful for **monitoring and controlling costs**. Similarly, in a freight organisation the **cost per tonne/kilometre** (the cost of carrying one tonne for one kilometre) would be more meaningful for control than the cost per tonne carried, which would vary with the distance travelled.

Interactive question 1: Cost units [Difficulty level: Easy]

Identify which of the following cost objects would be suitable cost units for an hotel. Tick the boxes to indicate which would be suitable.

	Suitable cost unit		Suitable cost unit
Bar	☐	Conference delegate	☐
Restaurant	☐	Fitness suite	☐
Room/night	☐	Conference room/day	☐
Meal served	☐		

See **Answer** at the end of this chapter.

2.5 The concept of cost

The term 'cost' can be used as a noun when describing the amount of money incurred in producing a product: 'The cost to produce 100 units of product X last period was £3,400'.

Alternatively, 'cost' can be used as a verb, for example when describing the act of determining the amount of money incurred in operating a department: 'Please gather the information necessary to cost the quality control activity'.

You will rarely see the word 'cost' used alone. **Costs need to be classified in some way** so that they can be arranged into logical groups in order to facilitate an efficient system for collecting and analysing costs.

As you work through this Study Manual you will encounter many different types of cost, each of which has its usefulness and limitations in various circumstances.

2.6 Direct v indirect costs and cost objects

Direct costs are costs identified with a cost object. Indirect costs cannot be identified with a particular cost object. For example if a chair is a cost object then certain costs such as materials and the labour required to assemble the chair would be classed as direct costs for an individual chair. Factory rent could not be associated with an individual chair so would be classed as an indirect cost of the chair. However, if the cost object were the factory itself then the rent is a direct cost of the factory.

3 Cost classification for inventory valuation and profit measurement

Section overview

- The total cost of a cost unit is usually made up of three cost elements: materials, labour and other expenses. Each of these cost elements can be classified as direct costs or indirect costs.

- A direct cost can be traced in full to the cost unit that is being costed.

- The total direct cost (or 'prime cost') is the sum of the direct material cost + direct labour cost + direct expenses.

- An indirect cost (or overhead) cannot be traced directly and in full to the cost unit that is being costed.

- Types of indirect cost (or overhead) include production overhead, administration overhead, selling overhead and distribution overhead.

- Product costs are costs identified with goods produced or purchased for resale. These costs are allocated to the value of inventory until the goods are sold.

- Period costs are costs deducted as expenses during a particular period. These costs are not regarded as part of the value of inventory.

In this section we are only concerned with cost units (ie an individual job or unit of product or unit of service) as the cost object.

3.1 Cost elements

For the purposes of inventory valuation and profit measurement, the cost of one unit must be determined. The total cost of a cost unit of product or service is made up of the following three **elements of cost**.

- Materials
- Labour
- Other expenses (such as rent and rates, interest charges and so on)

Cost elements can be classified as **direct** costs or **indirect** costs as far as cost units are concerned.

3.2 Direct cost and prime cost

Definition

Direct cost: **A direct cost** is a cost that can be traced in full to the cost unit.

There are three types of direct cost.

- **Direct material costs** are the costs of materials that are known to have been used in making and selling a unit of product (or providing a service). Examples are components and packing materials.

- **Direct labour costs** are the specific costs of the workforce used to make a unit of product or provide a service. Direct labour costs are established by quantifying the cost of the time taken for a job, or the time taken in 'direct production work'. For example, the wages paid to an employee sewing buttons on a coat is a direct cost of that cost unit.

- **Other direct expenses** are those expenses that have been incurred in full as a direct consequence of making a unit of product, or providing a service, or running a department. For example, the cost of hiring a special machine for a job is a direct cost of that job.

Another term used to describe the total direct cost is prime cost.

Prime cost = total direct cost = direct material cost + direct labour cost + direct expenses

3.3 Indirect cost and overhead

Definition

Indirect cost (or overhead): A cost that is incurred which cannot be traced directly and in full to the cost unit.

Examples of indirect costs, where the cost object is a unit of output, might be the cost of supervisors' wages on a production line or cleaning materials and buildings insurance for a factory. These costs cannot be traced directly and in full to the cost unit in question.

Total expenditure may therefore be **analysed** as follows.

Materials cost	=	Direct materials cost	+	Indirect materials cost
+		+		+
Labour cost	=	Direct labour cost	+	Indirect labour cost
+		+		+
Expenses	=	Direct expenses	+	Indirect expenses
Total cost	=	Direct cost/prime cost	+	Indirect cost/overhead

3.3.1 Production overhead

Production (or manufacturing or factory) overhead includes all indirect material costs, indirect wages and indirect expenses **incurred in the factory from receipt of the order until its completion**, including:

- **Indirect materials**, which cannot be traced to units of the finished product.

  - Consumable stores, eg material used in negligible amounts or across several different products

- **Indirect wages**, meaning all wages not charged directly to a unit of product.

  - Salaries of non productive personnel in the production department, eg supervisor

- **Indirect expenses** (other than material and labour) not charged directly to units of production

  - Rent, rates and insurance of a factory
  - Depreciation, fuel, power and maintenance of plant and buildings

3.3.2 Administration overhead

Administration overhead is all indirect material costs, wages and expenses **incurred in the direction, control and administration of an undertaking**, including:

- Depreciation of office equipment
- Office salaries, including the salaries of secretaries and accountants
- Rent, rates, insurance, telephone, heat and light cost of general offices

3.3.3 Selling overhead

Selling overhead is all indirect materials costs, wages and expenses **incurred in promoting sales and retaining customers**, including:

- Printing and stationery, such as catalogues and price lists
- Salaries and commission of sales representatives
- Advertising and sales promotion, market research
- Rent, rates and insurance for sales offices and showrooms

3.3.4 Distribution overhead

Distribution overhead is all indirect material costs, wages and expenses **incurred in making the packed product ready for despatch and delivering it to the customer**, including:

- Cost of packing cases
- Wages of packers, drivers and despatch clerks
- Depreciation and running expenses of delivery vehicles

3.4 Product costs and period costs

For the preparation of financial statements, costs are often classified as either **product costs** or **period costs**. Product costs are costs identified with goods produced or purchased for resale. Period costs are costs deducted as expenses during a particular period.

Consider a retailer who acquires goods for resale without changing their basic form. The only product cost is therefore the purchase cost of the goods. Any unsold goods are held as inventory. The inventory is valued at the lower of purchase cost and net realisable value, which is the valuation basis stipulated in accounting standards, and included as an asset in the balance sheet. As the goods are sold, their cost becomes an expense in the form of 'cost of goods sold'. A retailer will also incur a variety of selling and administration expenses. Such costs are **period costs** because they are **deducted from revenue** without ever being regarded as part of the **value of inventory**.

Now consider a manufacturing firm in which direct materials are transformed into saleable goods with the help of direct labour and factory overheads. All these costs, even the factory overheads, are **product costs** because they are allocated to the value of inventory until the goods are sold (see Chapter 3). As with the retailer, selling and administration expenses are regarded as **period costs.**

4 Cost classification for planning and decision-making

Section overview

- Costs can be classified according to how they vary in relation to the level of activity.

- A knowledge of how the cost incurred varies at different activity levels is essential to planning and decision-making.

- A fixed cost is not affected by changes in the level of activity.

- A variable cost increases or decreases as the level of activity increases or decreases.

- A semi-variable cost is partly fixed and partly variable and is therefore partly affected by a change in the level of activity.

- The relevant range is the range of activity levels within which assumed cost behaviour patterns occur.

4.1 Cost behaviour patterns

A different way of classifying costs is in terms of their behaviour patterns. This means grouping costs according to how they vary in relation to the level of activity.

The level of activity can be measured in a variety of different ways depending on the circumstances. Examples of possible ways of measuring the level of activity are as follows.

- The volume of production in a period
- The number of items sold

- The number of invoices issued
- The number of units of electricity consumed

Planning and decision-making are concerned with future events and so managers require information on expected future costs and revenues. **A knowledge of how the cost incurred varies at different levels of activity is essential to planning and decision-making.**

For our purposes in this chapter, the level of activity will generally be taken to be the volume of production/output or sales.

4.2 Fixed costs

Definition

Fixed cost: **A fixed cost** is a cost that, within a relevant range of activity levels, is not affected by increases or decreases in the level of activity.

Fixed costs are a **period charge**, in that they relate to a span of time; as the time span increases, so too will the fixed costs. Figure 1.1 shows a sketch graph of a fixed cost.

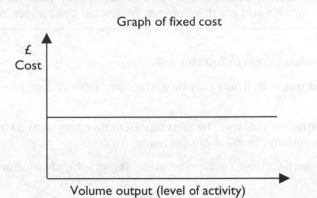

Figure 1.1: Fixed cost

Examples of fixed costs include the following.

- The salary of the managing director (per month or per annum)
- The rent of a single factory building (per month or per annum)
- Straight line depreciation of a single machine (per month or per annum)

4.3 Variable costs

Definition

Variable cost: **A variable cost** is a cost that increases or decreases as the level of activity increases or decreases.

A **variable cost** tends to vary directly with the level of activity. The variable cost **per unit** is the same amount for each unit produced whereas **total** variable cost increases as volume of output increases. Figure 1.2 shows a sketch graph of a variable cost.

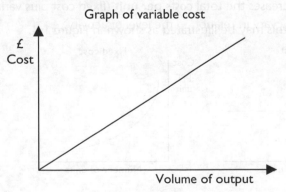

Figure 1.2: Variable cost

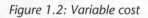

Examples of variable costs include the following.

- The cost of raw materials (where there is no discount for bulk purchasing, since bulk purchase discounts reduce the unit cost of purchases).

- Direct labour costs, which are usually classed as a variable cost even though basic wages are often fixed.

- Sales commission that is variable in relation to the volume or value of sales.

4.4 Semi-variable costs (or semi-fixed costs or mixed costs)

Definition

Semi-variable, semi-fixed or mixed costs: **Semi-variable, semi-fixed or mixed costs** are costs that are part-fixed and part-variable and are therefore partly affected by changes in the level of activity.

Examples of semi-variable costs include the following.

- **Electricity and gas bills**. There may be a 'standing' basic charge plus a charge per unit of consumption.

- **Sales representative's salary**. The sales representative may earn a basic monthly amount plus a commission based on the value of sales made.

The behaviour of a semi-variable cost can be presented graphically as shown in Figure 1.3.

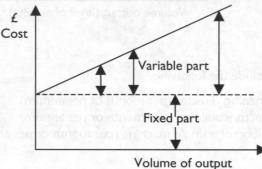

Figure 1.3: Semi-variable cost

4.5 Cost behaviour and total and unit costs

If the variable cost of producing a unit is £5 per unit then it will remain at that cost per unit no matter how many units are produced (within the relevant range).

However, if the business's fixed costs are £5,000 then the fixed cost **per unit** will decrease the more units are produced: for example, one unit will have fixed costs of £5,000 per unit; if 2,500 are produced the fixed cost per unit will be £2; if 5,000 are produced the fixed cost per unit will be only £1. Thus as the level of activity increases the total costs **per unit** (fixed cost plus variable cost) will decrease.

In sketch graph form this may be illustrated as shown in Figure 1.4.

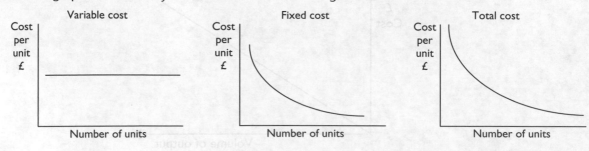

Figure 1.4: Cost behaviour

Interactive question 2: Fixed, variable or semi-variable cost?   [Difficulty level: Easy]

Tick the appropriate box for each cost.

		Fixed	Variable	Semi-variable
(a)	Telephone bill	☐	☐	☐
(b)	Annual salary of the chief accountant	☐	☐	☐
(c)	Cost of materials used to pack 20 units of product X into a box	☐	☐	☐

See **Answer** at the end of this chapter.

4.6   The relevant range

Definition

The relevant range: The relevant range is the range of activity levels within which assumed cost behaviour patterns occur.

For example, a fixed cost is only fixed for levels of activity within the relevant range, after which it could 'step up'.

The relevant range also broadly represents the **activity levels at which an organisation has had experience of operating in the past** and for which **cost information is available**. It can therefore be dangerous to attempt to predict costs at activity levels that are outside the relevant range (extrapolation).

For example, the rent of a factory is generally assumed to be a fixed cost. However, if the volume of activity increases beyond the relevant range then it may be necessary to rent an additional factory. The rent cost will then increase to a new, higher level. This is called a step increase in fixed cost and can be represented graphically as shown in Figure 1.5.

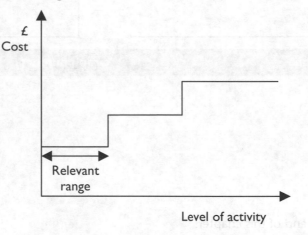

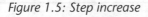

Figure 1.5: Step increase

Interactive question 3: Activity levels   [Difficulty level: Intermediate]

Select the correct words in the following sentence.

In general, as activity levels rise within a relevant range, the variable cost per unit will (a) **rise/fall/stay the same**, the fixed cost per unit will (b) **rise/fall/stay the same** and the total cost per unit will (c) **rise/fall/stay the same**.

See **Answer** at the end of this chapter.

Interactive question 4: Cost behaviour graphs [Difficulty level: Easy]

Match the sketches (1) to (4) below to the listed items of expense. In each case the vertical axis relates to total cost, the horizontal axis to activity level. Each graph may be used more than once. Write the graph number in the space provided.

(a) Electricity bill: a standing charge for each period plus a charge for each unit of electricity consumed.

(b) Supervisory labour, which is paid as a monthly salary.

(c) Sales commission, which amounts to 2% of sales revenue.

(d) Machine rental cost of a single item of equipment. The rental agreement is that £10 should be paid for every machine hour worked each month, subject to a maximum monthly charge of £480.

(e) Photocopier rental costs. The rental agreement is that £80 is paid each month, plus £0.01 per photocopy taken.

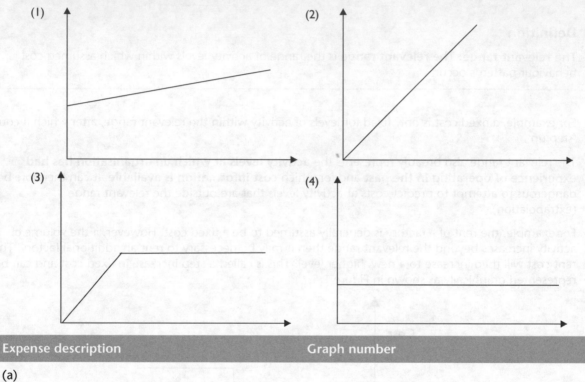

Expense description	Graph number
(a)	
(b)	
(c)	
(d)	
(e)	

See **Answer** at the end of this chapter.

5 Cost classification for control

Section overview

- For control purposes the most effective classification of costs is by responsibility, ie according to whether the costs are controllable or uncontrollable by a particular manager.

- A system of responsibility accounting segregates costs and revenues into areas of personal responsibility in order to monitor and assess the performance of each part of the organisation.

- A responsibility centre is a part of a business whose performance is the direct responsibility of a specific manager.

- An uncontrollable cost is a cost that cannot be influenced by a manager within a given time span.

5.1 Responsibility accounting

Allocating costs to products is not always useful for the purposes of control, as the production of a product, say, may consist of a number of operations, each of which is the responsibility of a different person. A product cost does not therefore provide a link between costs incurred and areas of responsibility. So costs (or revenues) must be traced in another way to the individuals responsible for each cost or revenue. This 'other way' is known as **responsibility accounting**.

Definitions

Responsibility accounting: Responsibility accounting is a system of accounting that segregates revenue and costs into areas of personal responsibility in order to monitor and assess the performance of each part of an organisation.

A responsibility centre: A responsibility centre is a department or function whose performance is the direct responsibility of a specific manager.

Managers of responsibility centres should only be held accountable for costs over which they have significant influence. From a motivation or incentivisation point of view this is important because it can be very demoralising for managers to have their performance judged on the basis of something over which they have no influence. It is also important from a control point of view that management reports should ensure that information on costs is reported to the manager who is able to take action to control them.

Responsibility accounting attempts to associate costs, revenues, assets and liabilities with the managers most capable of controlling them. As a system of accounting, it therefore distinguishes between controllable and uncontrollable costs.

5.2 Controllable and uncontrollable costs

Definitions

Controllable cost: A controllable cost is a cost that can be influenced by management decisions and actions.

Uncontrollable cost: An uncontrollable cost is a cost that cannot be affected by management within a given time span.

Most **variable costs** within a department are thought to be **controllable in the short term** because managers can influence the efficiency with which resources are used, even if they cannot do anything to raise or lower price levels.

A cost that is not controllable by a junior manager might be controllable by a senior manager. For example, there may be high direct labour costs in a department caused by excessive overtime working. The junior manager may feel obliged to continue with the overtime to meet production schedules, but his senior may be able to reduce costs by hiring extra full-time staff, thereby reducing the requirements for overtime.

A cost that is not controllable by a manager in one department may be controllable by a manager in another department. For example, an increase in material costs may be caused by buying at higher prices than expected (controllable by the purchasing department) or by excessive wastage (controllable by the production department) or by a faulty machine producing rejects (controllable by the maintenance department).

Some costs are **non-controllable**, such as increases in expenditure due to inflation. Other costs are **controllable, but in the long term rather than the short term**. For example, production costs might be reduced by the introduction of new machinery and technology, but in the short term, management must attempt to do the best they can with the resources and machinery at their disposal.

6 Ethics

Section overview

- What are the ethical issues relating to the preparation, presentation and interpretation of financial information?

6.1 Introduction

Cost accountants are often involved in the preparation and reporting of information to assist management with **planning**, **control** and **decision-making**. Such information may include **forecasts**, **budgets** and **variance analysis** which we will consider in detail in later chapters.

6.2 ICAEW ethical guidance for accountants involved in the preparation and reporting of information

6.2.1 Fundamental principles

The ICAEW defines a **professional accountant** as 'an individual who is a member of an IFAC member body'. A **professional accountant in business** is defined as 'a professional accountant employed or engaged in an executive or non-executive capacity in such areas as commerce, industry, service, the public sector, education, the not for profit sector, regulatory bodies or professional bodies, or a professional accountant contracted by such entities.'

The ICAEW provides ethical guidance that will ensure professional accountants in business **prepare** and **report information fairly, honestly** and **in accordance with relevant professional standards** so that the information will be understood in its context. The guidance is also designed to ensure that professional accountants in business take reasonable steps to maintain information for which they are responsible in a manner that:

- Describes clearly the true nature of business transactions, assets or liabilities
- Classifies and records information in a timely and proper manner
- Represents the facts accurately and completely in all material respects

The guidance can be found at icaew.com and much of this is dealt with in the certificate level Business and Finance syllabus.

The guidance is applicable to both members in practice and members in business (eg professional accountants involved in the preparation and reporting of information to assist management).

Fundamental Principle 1 – 'Integrity'

A member should behave with integrity in all professional and business relationships.

Integrity implies not only honesty but fair dealing, truthfulness and being straightforward. A member's advice and work must be uncorrupted by self-interest and not be influenced by the interests of other parties. A member should not be associated with information that is false or misleading or supplied recklessly.

Fundamental Principle 2 – 'Objectivity'

A member should strive for objectivity in all professional and business judgements.

Objectivity is the state of mind which has regard to all considerations relevant to the task in hand but no other. There should be no bias, conflict of interest or undue influence of others.

Fundamental Principle 3 – 'Professional competence and due care'

When providing professional services 'professional competence and due care' therefore mean:

- Having appropriate professional knowledge and skill

- Having a continuing awareness and an understanding of relevant technical, professional and business developments

- Exercising sound and independent judgement

- Acting diligently, that is:

  - Carefully
  - Thoroughly
  - On a timely basis and
  - In accordance with the requirements of an assignment

- Acting in accordance with applicable technical and professional standards

- Distinguishing clearly between an expression of opinion and an assertion of fact

Fundamental Principle 4 – 'Confidentiality'

The professional accountant should assume that all unpublished information about a prospective, current or previous client's or employer's affairs, however gained, is confidential. Information should then:

- Be kept confidential (confidentiality should be actively preserved)
- Not be disclosed, even inadvertently such as in a social environment
- Not be used to obtain personal advantage

Fundamental Principle 5 – 'Professional behaviour'

Behaving professionally means:

- Complying with relevant laws and regulations

- Avoiding any action that discredits the profession (the standard to be applied is that of a reasonable and informed third party with knowledge of all relevant information)

- Conducting oneself with

  - Courtesy and
  - Consideration

When marketing themselves and their work, professional accountants should:

- Be honest and truthful

- Avoid making exaggerated claims about:

  - What they can do
  - What qualifications and experience they possess

- Avoid making disparaging references to the work of others

6.2.2 Threats and safeguards

Threats to compliance with the fundamental principles, such as **self-interest** or **intimidation threats** to **objectivity** or **professional competence** and **due care**, are created where a professional accountant in business is pressured (either externally or by the possibility of personal gain) to become associated with misleading information or to become associated with misleading information through the actions of others.

Accordingly, professional accountants should take steps to ensure they are not associated with reports, returns, communications or other information where they believe that the information:

- Contains a materially false or misleading statement.

- Contains statements or information furnished recklessly.

- Omits or obscures information required to be included where such omission or obscurity would be misleading.

The significance of such threats depends on factors such as **the source of the pressure** and **the degree to which the information is, or may be, misleading**. The significance of the threat should be evaluated and safeguards applied where necessary to eliminate them or reduce them to an acceptable level. Such safeguards include consultation with superiors within the employing organisation (such as a line manager), the audit committee, or those charged with governance of the organisation, or the ICAEW.

Where it is not possible to reduce the threat(s) to an acceptable level, the professional accountant in business should **refuse to be or remain associated with any information they determine to be misleading**.

On occasion, a professional accountant in business may be **unknowingly associated with misleading information**. Upon becoming aware of this, the professional accountant in business should take steps to be disassociated from the information.

In determining whether there is a requirement to report, the professional accountant in business may consider obtaining **legal advice**. In addition, the professional accountant my consider whether to resign.

Summary

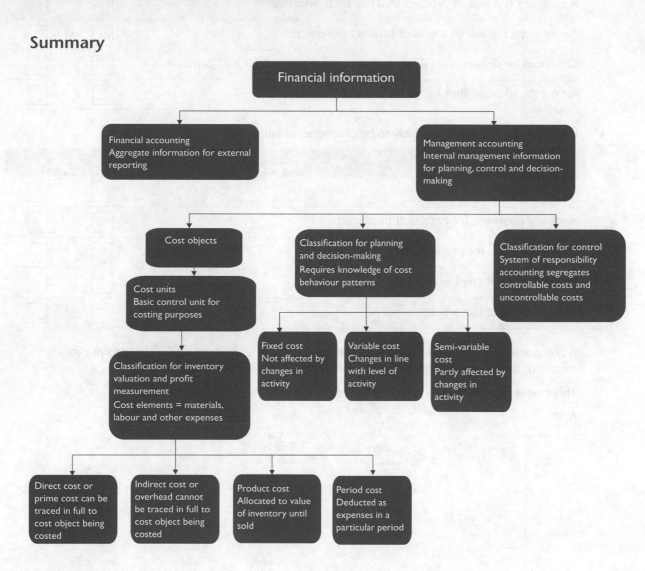

Self-test

Answer the following questions.

1   Which of the following statements about a direct cost are correct?

(a)   A direct cost can be traced in full to the product, service or department that is being costed.
(b)   A particular cost can be a direct cost or an indirect cost, depending on what is being costed.
(c)   A direct cost might also be referred to as an overhead cost.
(d)   Expenditure on direct costs will probably vary every period.

A   (a) and (b) only
B   (a) and (c) only
C   (a), (b) and (d) only
D   (a), (b), (c) and (d)

2   Which one of the following items might be a cost unit within the management accounting system of a university or college of further education?

A   Business studies department
B   A student
C   A college building
D   The university itself

3   Identify whether the statements shown below are true or false.

	True	False
A cost unit is a unit of product that has costs attached	☐	☐
A cost object is always a unit of product or service	☐	☐
Costs can be divided into three elements: materials, labour and expenses	☐	☐
An overhead is another name for an indirect cost	☐	☐

4   Which of the following are likely to be classed as variable costs?

	Yes	No
Telephone bill	☐	☐
A royalty payment for each unit produced	☐	☐
Direct materials for production	☐	☐
Annual salary of chief accountant	☐	☐
Annual salary of factory supervisor	☐	☐

5   A company hires its vehicles under an agreement where a constant rate is charged per mile travelled, up to a maximum monthly payment regardless of the miles travelled.

This cost is represented by which of the following graphs?

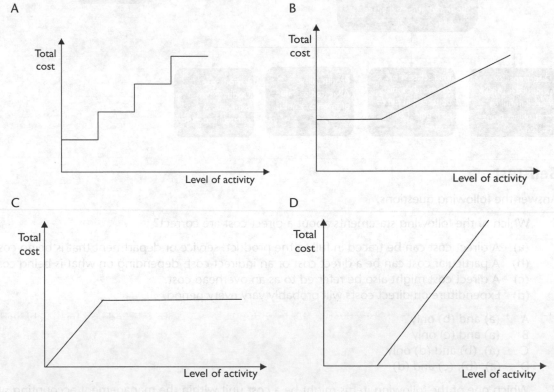

6   Cost units are:

A   Units of a product or service for which costs are ascertained
B   Amounts of expenditure attributable to a number of different products
C   Functions or locations for which costs are ascertained
D   Things for which we are trying to ascertain the cost

7 Which of the following items might be a suitable cost unit within the sales department of a manufacturing company?

	Suitable	Unsuitable
Sales commission	☐	☐
Order obtained	☐	☐
Unit of product sold	☐	☐

8 In a factory one supervisor is required for every five employees. Which one of the following graphs depicts the cost of supervisors?

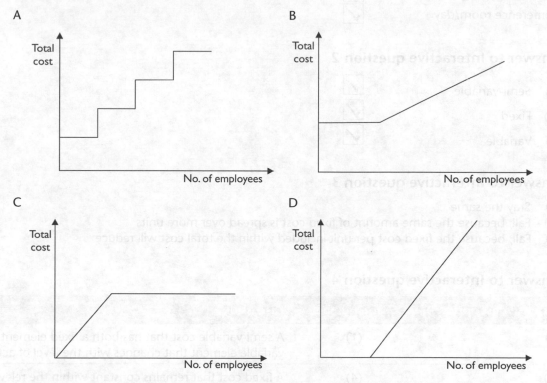

9 Which of the following might describe a cost unit?

A   A unit of production or service to which costs can be related
B   A cost incurred in selling a product or service
C   A cost that can be traced in full to the product, service or department that is being costed
D   A cost identified with the goods produced or purchased for resale

10 Prime cost is:

A   All cost incurred in manufacturing a product
B   The total of direct costs
C   The material cost of a product
D   The cost of operating a department

Now go back to the Learning Objectives in the Introduction. If you are satisfied you have achieved these objectives, please tick them off.

Answer to Interactive question 1

Suitable cost unit

Room/night	✓
Meal served	✓
Conference delegate	✓
Conference room/day	✓

Answer to Interactive question 2

(a)	Semi-variable	✓
(b)	Fixed	✓
(c)	Variable	✓

Answer to Interactive question 3

(a)   Stay the same
(b)   Fall; because the same amount of fixed cost is spread over more units
(c)   Fall; because the fixed cost per unit included within the total cost will reduce

Answer to Interactive question 4

Expense description	Graph number	Discussion
(a)	(1)	A semi-variable cost that has both a fixed element and a variable element that changes with the level of activity
(b)	(4)	A fixed cost that remains constant within the relevant range
(c)	(2)	A variable cost that varies in direct proportion to the level of activity
(d)	(3)	Graph passes through origin because at zero activity no cost is incurred. Variable cost pattern until maximum cost is reached. Thereafter cost is fixed
(e)	(1)	A semi-variable cost that has both a fixed element and a variable element that changes with the level of activity

ICAEW

Answers to Self-test

1   C   The correct answer is: (a), (b) and (d) only.

Statement (a) is correct. Direct costs are specific and traceable to the relevant product, service or department.

Statement (b) is correct. For example, a departmental manager's salary is a direct cost of the department but it is an indirect cost of the individual cost units passing through the department.

Statement (c) is incorrect. An indirect cost (not a direct cost) might also be referred to as an overhead cost.

Statement (d) is correct. It is likely that activity will change from period to period, in which case so will the expenditure on direct costs, as direct costs are traced directly to cost units.

2   B   A student is likely to be a cost unit (cost per student per course). The others are all cost objects but not the most basic unit of product or service for which costs are determined.

3   The correct answers are:

	True	False
A cost unit is a unit of product that has costs attached	✓	
A cost object is always a unit of product or service		✓
Costs can be divided into three elements: materials, labour and expenses	✓	
An overhead is another name for an indirect cost	✓	

A cost object is anything for which we are trying to ascertain the cost. It could be a unit of product or service but it could also be other items such as a department, a function or an item of equipment.

4

	Yes	No
Telephone bill		✓
A royalty payment for each unit produced	✓	
Direct materials for production	✓	
Annual salary of chief accountant		✓
Annual salary of factory supervisor		✓

The royalty payments described and the cost of direct materials for production are likely to increase in line with output levels and are therefore classed as variable costs.

A telephone bill is a typical example of a semi-variable cost, with a fixed line rental and a variable cost element that relates to the number of telephone calls made.

Salaries are a typical example of a fixed cost.

5   C   The correct graph is:

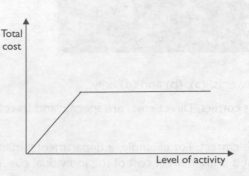

The cost described begins as a linear variable cost, increasing at a constant rate in line with activity. After a certain level of activity is reached, the total cost reaches a maximum as demonstrated by the horizontal line on the graph. The cost becomes fixed regardless of the level of activity.

6   A   Amounts of expenditure attributable to a number of products (option B) are classed as overheads.

Functions or locations for which costs are ascertained (option C) are cost objects.

Option D is the definition of a cost object.

7

	Suitable	Unsuitable
Sales commission		✓
Order obtained	✓	
Unit of product sold	✓	

Either calculating the cost of each order obtained or the cost of each unit of product sold would be suitable cost units within the sales department.

Sales commission is an expense of the business, and therefore not suitable to use as a cost unit.

8   A   The correct graph is:

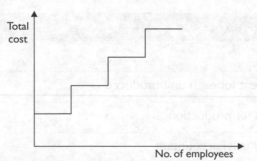

9   A   Cost units are the basic units for costing purposes. Different organisations would use different cost units, such as patient/day in a hospital or meals served in a restaurant.

A cost incurred in selling a product or service (option B) describes a period cost.

A cost that can be traced in full to the product, service or department that is being costed (option C) describes a direct cost.

A cost identified with the goods produced or purchased for resale (option D) describes a product cost.

10   B   Prime cost is the total of direct material, direct labour and direct expenses.

Option A describes total production cost, including a share of production overhead. Option C is only a part of prime cost. Option D is an overhead or indirect cost.

CHAPTER 2

Calculating unit costs (Part 1)

Introduction

Examination context

Topic List

1 Identifying direct and indirect costs for cost units

2 Inventory valuation

Summary and Self-test

Answers to Interactive questions

Answers to Self-test

Learning objectives

Tick off

- Classify costs as direct or indirect as regards cost units

- Calculate direct material and direct labour costs from information provided

The specific syllabus reference for this chapter is: 1c.

Syllabus links

A thorough understanding of the valuation of materials inventory will underpin your understanding of inventory valuation for the Accounting syllabus.

Examination context

The context of much of this chapter provides scope for a range of numerical questions. However, you should also be prepared to deal with narrative questions that examine your understanding of the implications of the techniques you are using.

Narrative questions on the pricing of materials issues and on the classification of costs have been popular in past examinations.

In the examination, candidates may be required to:

- Classify costs as direct or indirect

- Calculate the prime cost of a cost unit

- Calculate the price of materials and the value of inventory using ('first in, first out') FIFO, ('last in, first out') LIFO and average pricing methods

It is important to realise that in this chapter and the next, ideas from Chapter 1 are being applied in determining the cost of a unit of output. The cost object is, therefore, the unit of output and all terms such as direct and indirect are used in that context. It is also essential to appreciate that direct and variable costs and indirect and fixed costs are NOT the same thing. The narrative is as important as the calculations for FIFO, LIFO and weighted average inventory valuations.

1 Identifying direct and indirect costs for cost units

Section overview

- Direct costs are those that can be specifically identified with the cost unit being costed.
- Direct material cost is all material becoming part of the cost unit, unless used in negligible amounts.
- Direct labour cost is all wages paid to labour that can be identified with a specific cost unit.
- Direct expenses are expenses incurred on a specific cost unit, other than direct material and direct labour costs.
- Indirect costs are those that cannot be identified directly with the cost unit being costed.

For the purposes of this chapter and Chapter 3 the cost object is a cost unit (eg a unit of product, a job, a batch, a unit of service).

1.1 Direct material cost

Direct material is **all material becoming part of the cost unit** (unless used in negligible amounts and/or having negligible cost).

Direct material costs are charged to the cost unit as part of the **prime cost**. Examples of direct material are as follows.

- **Component parts** or other materials purchased for a particular product, service, job, order or process.
- **Primary packing materials** like cartons and boxes.

Materials used in negligible amounts and/or having negligible cost can be grouped under indirect materials as part of overhead.

1.2 Direct wages or direct labour costs

Direct wages are all **wages paid for labour** (either as basic hours or as overtime) that can be identified with the cost unit.

Direct wages costs are charged to the cost unit as part of the **prime cost**.

Examples of groups of labour receiving payment as direct wages are as follows.

- Workers engaged in **altering** the condition, conformation or composition of the product.
- Inspectors, analysts and testers **specifically required** for such production.

1.3 Direct expenses

Direct expenses are any expenses that are incurred on a specific cost unit **other than direct material cost and direct wages**.

Direct expenses are charged to the product as part of the **prime** cost. Examples of direct expenses are as follows.

- The cost of special designs, drawings or layouts for a particular job.
- The hire of tools or equipment for a particular job.

1.4 Indirect costs

Indirect costs or overheads are those costs that cannot be traced in full to a specific cost unit.

For example, a garage carries out a repair job on a customer's car.

- The direct material cost of the job will include the replacement parts used.

- The direct labour cost will be wages paid to the mechanics who carried out the work. The labour is treated as a direct cost in this case, even if the mechanics are paid a fixed amount each period. This is because it is possible to measure exactly how long each person worked on the repair, and their hourly rate of pay.

- The indirect costs of the repair job will include a share of the overhead costs incurred in the garage, such as the rent, the buildings insurance, the depreciation of the garage equipment and so on. These costs cannot be traced to any single job worked on during the period.

Try this interactive question to ensure you have understood the principle of how to distinguish a direct cost from an indirect cost.

Interactive question 1: Direct cost or indirect cost?   [Difficulty level: Intermediate]

Indicate whether each of the following costs would be classified as a direct cost or an indirect cost of a particular car repair in a garage. The repair was worked on in overtime hours due to an unusually large number of repairs being booked into the garage that day.

Cost incurred	Direct or indirect?
The salary of the garage's accountant	
The cost of heating the garage	
A can of engine oil used in the repair	
A smear of grease used in the repair	
An overtime premium paid to the mechanic carrying out the repair	
An idle time payment made to the mechanic while waiting for a delivery of parts for a number of jobs	
The wages of the supervisor overseeing the mechanic carrying out the repair	

See **Answer** at the end of this chapter.

1.5 Direct and indirect costs: some further points

There are a few possible misconceptions about direct and indirect costs that should be clarified at this stage.

- **Direct costs are not necessarily bigger in size than indirect costs**. In highly-automated service industries, direct materials and direct labour costs are likely to be very small, relative to overhead costs. The relative size of direct and indirect costs per unit of output varies according to the type of output, the industry, the technology, etc.

- **Indirect costs are not less important than direct costs.** Although they cannot be directly attributed to individual units of output or to individual jobs, they represent expenditure on resources that are essential for the units to be made or the jobs to be done. In the example of the garage repair job, the rent of the garage is an indirect cost, but the rental cost represents a share of the use of the garage space, without which the job could not have been done.

- **It is easy to confuse fixed and variable costs with indirect and direct costs.** A direct cost is often also a variable cost: for example, the cost of raw materials that goes into making a unit of product is both a direct cost and a variable cost. However, a direct cost may be a fixed cost rather than a variable cost. For example, the direct cost of the labour employed to do a certain type of work is a fixed cost to the business if the employees are paid a fixed amount of wages or salary regardless of the amount of work they do. Similarly, an indirect cost may a variable cost. For example, the cost of heating in a manufacturing plant may rise as more hours are worked. The cost of heating cannot be directly attributed to an individual job or unit of output. Nevertheless, it is a cost that rises with the level of activity, and is a variable cost. Variable indirect costs are more commonly referred to as **variable overheads**.

2 Inventory valuation

Section overview

- The pricing of issues of inventory items and the valuation of closing inventory have a direct effect on the calculation of profit. Several different methods can be used in practice.

- With FIFO all issues are priced at the cost of the earliest delivery remaining in inventory.

- With LIFO all issues are priced at the cost of the most recent delivery remaining in inventory.

- The cumulative weighted average pricing method calculates a weighted average price for all units in inventory whenever a new delivery of materials is received into store.

- The periodic weighted average pricing method calculates a single weighted average price at the end of the period. The average is based on the opening inventory plus all units received in the period.

- Each method of inventory valuation usually produces different figures for the value of closing inventories and the cost of material issues. Therefore, profit figures using the different inventory valuations are usually different.

2.1 Valuing inventory in financial accounts

You may be aware from your studies of Accounting that, for financial accounting purposes, inventories are valued at the **lower of cost and net realisable value**. In practice, inventories will probably be valued at cost in the stores records throughout the course of an accounting period. Only when the period ends will the value of the inventory in hand be reconsidered so that items with a net realisable value below their original cost will be revalued downwards, and the inventory records altered accordingly.

2.2 Charging units of inventory to cost of production or cost of sales

It is important to be able to distinguish between the way in which the physical items in inventory are actually issued and the way in which inventory is costed. In practice a storekeeper may issue goods in the following way.

- The oldest goods first
- The latest goods received first
- Randomly
- Those that are easiest to reach

By comparison, the cost of goods issued must be determined on a **consistently applied basis**, and must ignore the likelihood that the materials issued will be costed at a price different from the amount paid for them.

This may seem a little confusing at first, and it may be helpful to explain the point further by looking at an example.

2.3 Example: Inventory valuation

Suppose that there are three units of a particular material in inventory.

Units	Date received	Purchase cost
A	June 20X1	£100
B	July 20X1	£106
C	August 20X1	£109

In September, one unit is issued to production. As it happened, the physical unit actually issued was B. The accounting department must put a value or cost on the material issued, but the value would not be the cost of B, £106. The principles used to value the materials issued are not concerned with the actual unit issued, A, B, or C. Nevertheless, the accountant may choose to make one of the following assumptions.

- The unit issued is valued as though it were the earliest unit received into inventory, ie at the purchase cost of A, £100. This valuation principle is called **FIFO**, or **first in, first out**.

- The unit issued is valued as though it were the most recent unit received into inventory, ie at the purchase cost of C, £109. This method of valuation is **LIFO**, or **last in, first out**.

- The unit issued is valued at an **average** price of A, B and C. The three units cost a total of £315, an average of £105 each.

2.4 Pricing methods in inventory valuation

In the following sections we will consider each of the pricing methods detailed above, using the following transactions to illustrate the principles in each case.

TRANSACTIONS DURING MAY 20X6

	Quantity	Unit cost	Total cost	Market value per unit on date of transaction
	Units	£	£	£
Opening balance, 1 May	100	2.00	200	
Receipts, 3 May	400	2.10	840	2.11
Issues, 4 May	200			2.11
Receipts, 9 May	300	2.12	636	2.15
Issues, 11 May	400			2.20
Receipts, 18 May	100	2.40	240	2.40
Issues, 20 May	100			2.42
Closing balance, 31 May	200			2.45
			1,916	

2.5 FIFO (first in, first out)

Definition

FIFO (first in, first out): is defined by CIMA as a method 'used to price issues of goods or materials based on the cost of the oldest units held, irrespective of the sequence in which the actual issue of units held takes place.'

FIFO assumes that materials are issued out of inventory in the order in which they were delivered into inventory: issues are priced at the cost of the earliest delivery remaining in inventory.

Worked example: FIFO

Using **FIFO**, the cost of issues and the closing inventory value of the transactions in Section 2.4 would be as follows.

Date of issue	Quantity issued Units	Value	£	£
4 May	200	100 b/f at £2	200	
		100 at £2.10	210	
				410
11 May	400	300 at £2.10	630	
		100 at £2.12	212	
				842
20 May	100	100 at £2.12		212
Cost of issues				1,464
Closing inventory value	200	100 at £2.12	212	
		100 at £2.40	240	
				452
				1,916

Using a tabular format, as below, is a practical way of tracking items when carrying out a FIFO calculation:

	£2.00	£2.10	£2.12	£2.40	Total
b/f	100				100
Receipt 3 May		400			400
Issue 4 May	(100)	(100)			(200)
Receipt 9 May			300		300
Issue 11 May		(300)	(100)		(400)
Receipt 18 May				100	100
Issue 20 May			(100)		(100)
	–	–	100	100	200

Points to note

1   The cost of materials issued plus the value of closing inventory equals the cost of purchases plus the value of opening inventory (£1,916).

2   The market price of purchased materials is rising dramatically. In a period of inflation, there is a tendency with FIFO for materials to be issued at a cost lower than the current market value, although closing inventories tend to be valued at a cost approximating to current market value.

2.6   Advantages and disadvantages of the FIFO method

Advantages	Disadvantages
It is a logical pricing method, which probably represents what is physically happening: in practice the oldest inventory is likely to be used first.	FIFO can be cumbersome to operate because of the need to identify each batch of material separately.
It is easy to understand and explain to managers.	Managers may find it difficult to compare costs and make decisions when they are charged with varying prices for the same materials.
The inventory valuation can be near to a valuation based on replacement cost.	In a period of high inflation, inventory issue prices will lag behind current market value.

Interactive question 2: FIFO

[Difficulty level: Intermediate]

Complete the table below in as much detail as possible using the information from the last worked example.

Date	Receipts			Issues			Inventory		
	Quantity	Unit price £	Amount £	Quantity	Unit price £	Amount £	Quantity	Unit price £	Amount £

See **Answer** at the end of this chapter.

2.7 LIFO (last in, first out)

Definition

LIFO (last in, first out): is defined by CIMA as a method 'used to price issues of goods or materials based on the cost of the most recently received units.'

LIFO assumes that materials are issued out of inventory in the reverse order from that in which they were delivered: the most recent deliveries are issued before earlier ones, and issues are priced accordingly.

Worked example: LIFO

Using LIFO, the cost of issues and the closing inventory value of the transactions in Section 2.4 would be as follows.

Date of issue	Quantity issued Units	Valuation	£	£
4 May	200	200 at £2.10		420
11 May	400	300 at £2.12	636	
		100 at £2.10	210	
				846
20 May	100	100 at £2.40		240
Cost of issues				1,506
Closing inventory value	200	100 at £2.10	210	
		100 at £2.00	200	
				410
				1,916

A tabular format similar to that in Section 2.5 can also be used in Section 2.7.

Points to note

1   The cost of materials issued plus the value of closing inventory equals the cost of purchases plus the value of opening inventory (£1,916).

2   In a period of inflation there is a tendency with **LIFO** for the following to occur.

   –   Materials are issued at a price that approximates to current market value.
   –   Closing inventories become undervalued when compared to market value.

2.8   Advantages and disadvantages of the LIFO method

Advantages	Disadvantages
Inventories are issued at a price which is close to current market value.	The method can be cumbersome to operate because it sometimes results in several batches being only part-used in the inventory records before another batch is received.
Managers are continually aware of recent costs when making decisions, because the costs being charged to their department or products will be current costs.	LIFO is often the opposite of what is physically happening and can therefore be difficult to explain to managers.
	As with FIFO, decision making can be difficult because of the variations in prices.

2.9   Cumulative weighted average pricing

Definition

Average cost: is defined by CIMA as a method 'used to price issues of goods or materials at the weighted average cost of all units held.'

The cumulative weighted average pricing method calculates a **weighted average price** for all units in inventory. Issues are priced at this average cost, and the balance of inventory remaining would have the same unit valuation. The average price is determined by dividing the total cost by the total number of units.

A new weighted average price is calculated **whenever a new delivery of materials is received into store.** This is the key feature of cumulative weighted average pricing.

Worked example: Cumulative weighted average pricing

Using cumulative weighted average pricing, issue costs and closing inventory values of the transactions in Section 2.4 would be as follows.

Date	Received Units	Issued Units	Balance Units	Total inventory value £	Unit cost £	£
Opening inventory			100	200	2.00	
3 May	400			840	2.10	
			* 500	1,040	2.08	
4 May		200		(416)	2.08	416
			300	624	2.08	
9 May	300			636	2.12	
			* 600	1,260	2.10	
11 May		400		(840)	2.10	840
			200	420	2.10	
18 May	100			240	2.40	
			* 300	660	2.20	
20 May		100		(220)	2.20	220
Cost of issues						1,476
Closing inventory value			200	440	2.20	440
						1,916

* A new inventory value per unit is calculated whenever a new receipt of materials occurs.

Points to note

1   The cost of materials issued plus the value of closing inventory equals the cost of purchases plus the value of opening inventory (£1,916).

2   In a period of inflation, using the cumulative weighted average pricing system, the value of material issues will rise gradually, but will tend to lag a little behind the current market value at the date of issue. Closing inventory values will also be a little below current market value.

2.10   Advantages and disadvantages of cumulative weighted average pricing

Advantages	Disadvantages
Fluctuations in prices are smoothed out, making it easier to use the data for decision making.	The resulting issue price is rarely an actual price that has been paid, and can run to several decimal places.
It is easier to administer than FIFO and LIFO, because there is no need to identify each batch separately.	Prices tend to lag a little behind current market values when there is gradual inflation.

Interactive question 3: Inventory valuation methods   [Difficulty level: Intermediate]

Shown below is an extract from records for inventory item number 988988.

Date	Receipts Qty	Value £	Total £	Issues Qty	Value £	Total £	Balance Qty	Value £	Total £
5 June							30	2.50	75
8 June	20	3.00	60						
10 June				10		A			
14 June				20		B			
18 June	40	2.40	96						
20 June				6		C			D

(a) The values that would be entered on the stores record for A, B, C and D in a cumulative weighted average pricing system would be:

A £ ....

B £ ....

C £ ....

D £ ....

(b) The values that would be entered on the stores record for A, B, C and D in a LIFO system would be:

A £ ....

B £ ....

C £ ....

D £ ....

See **Answer** at the end of this chapter.

2.11 Periodic weighted average pricing

This average method differs from the cumulative weighted average method. Instead of calculating a new inventory value per unit whenever a receipt occurs, a single average is calculated at the end of the period based on all purchases for the period. **Unless stated to the contrary, assume the cumulative method is required in an exam question.**

Worked example: Periodic weighted average pricing

Using periodic weighted average pricing, the issue costs and closing inventory of the transactions in Section 2.4 would be as follows.

$$\text{Periodic weighted average price} = \frac{\text{Cost of opening inventory} + \text{Total cost of receipts in period}}{\text{Units in opening inventory} + \text{Total units received in period}}$$

$$= \frac{(\pounds 200 + \pounds 1,716)}{(100 + 800)}$$

$$= \pounds 2.129 \text{ per unit}$$

This average price is used to value all the units issued and the units in the closing inventory.

	£
Cost of issues = 700 units × £2.129	1,490
Closing inventory value = 200 units × £2.129	426
	1,916

Notice that once again the cost of materials issued plus the value of closing inventory equals the cost of purchases plus the value of opening inventory (£1,916).

2.12 Inventory valuation and profitability

Each method of inventory valuation usually produces different figures for the value of closing inventories and the cost of material issues. A summary of the valuations based on the transactions in Section 2.4 is as follows.

Valuation method	Closing inventory value £	Cost of issues £	Total £
FIFO (Section 2.5)	452	1,464	1,916
LIFO (Section 2.7)	410	1,506	1,916
Cumulative weighted average (Section 2.9)	440	1,476	1,916
Periodic weighted average (Section 2.11)	426	1,490	1,916

Since material costs affect the cost of production, and the cost of production works through eventually into the cost of sales (which is also affected by the value of closing inventories), it follows that **different methods of inventory valuation will provide different profit figures**.

The following example will help to illustrate the point.

Worked example: Inventory valuation and profitability

On 1 November 20X2, Delilah's Dresses Ltd held 3 pink satin dresses with orange sashes, designed by Freda Swoggs. These were valued at £120 each. During November 20X2, 12 more of the dresses were delivered as follows.

Date	Dresses received	Purchase cost per dress
10 November	4	£125
20 November	4	£140
25 November	4	£150

A number of the pink satin dresses with orange sashes were sold during November as follows.

Date	Dresses sold	Sales price per dress
14 November	5	£200
21 November	5	£200
28 November	1	£200

Requirements

Calculate the gross profit from selling the pink satin dresses with orange sashes in November 20X2, applying the following principles of inventory valuation.

(a) FIFO
(b) LIFO
(c) Cumulative weighted average pricing

Calculate gross profit using the formula: gross profit = (sales – (opening inventory + purchases – closing inventory)).

Solution

(a) **FIFO**

Date	Cost of sales	Total £	Closing inventory £
14 November	3 units × £120 + 2 units × £125		
		610	
21 November	2 units × £125 + 3 units × £140		
		670	
28 November	1 unit × £140	140	
Closing inventory	4 units × £150		600
		1,420	600

(b) **LIFO**

Date	Cost of sales	Total £	Closing inventory £
14 November	4 units × £125 + 1 unit × £120	620	
21 November	4 units × £140 + 1 unit × £120	680	
28 November	1 unit × £150	150	
Closing inventory	3 units × £150 + 1 unit × £120		570
		1,450	570

(c) **Cumulative weighted average pricing**

	Units	Unit cost £	Balance in inventory £	Cost of sales £	Closing inventory £
1 November	3	120.00	360		
10 November	4	125.00	500		
	7	122.86	860		
14 November	5	122.86	614	614	
	2		246		
20 November	4	140.00	560		
	6	134.33	806		
21 November	5	134.33	672	672	
	1		134		
25 November	4	150.00	600		
	5	146.80	734		
28 November	1	146.80	147	147	
30 November	4	146.80	587	1,433	587

Profitability

	FIFO £	LIFO £	Weighted average £
Opening inventory	360	360	360
Purchases	1,660	1,660	1,660
	2,020	2,020	2,020
Closing inventory	600	570	587
Cost of sales	1,420	1,450	1,433
Sales (11 × £200)	2,200	2,200	2,200
Gross profit	780	750	767

2.13 Profit differences

In this example, **different inventory valuation methods produced different costs of sale and hence different gross profits. As opening inventory values and purchase costs are the same for each method, the different costs of sale are due to different closing inventory valuations. The differences in gross profits therefore equal the differences in closing inventory valuations.**

The profit differences are only **temporary**. In the example, the opening inventory in December 20X2 will be £600, £570 or £587, depending on the inventory valuation method used. Different opening inventory values will affect the cost of sales and profits in December, so that in the long run, inequalities in costs of sales each month will even themselves out.

Summary and Self-test

Summary

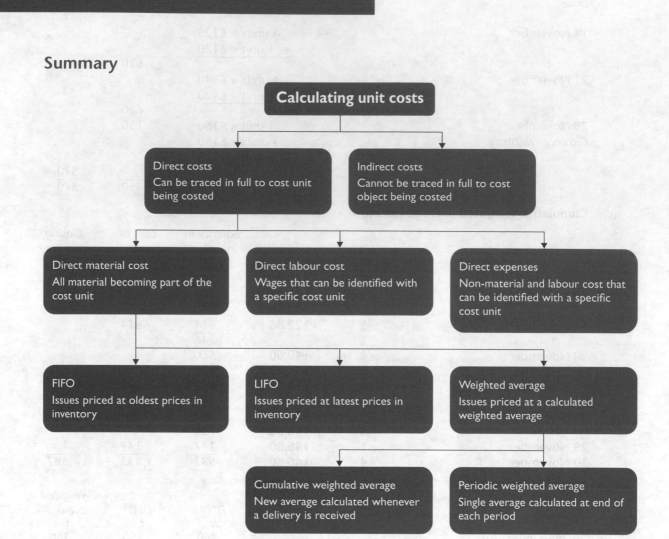

Self-test

Answer the following questions.

1   Which TWO of the following are cost objects?

    A   A packing machine
    B   The factory canteen
    C   Direct materials for production
    D   Annual salary of the chief accountant
    E   A telephone bill

2   Which TWO of the following are classified as indirect costs of individual units of output or of individual projects?

    A   The cost of overtime worked specifically to complete a one-off project
    B   The depreciation of a machine on an assembly line
    C   Primary packing materials, eg cartons and boxes
    D   The hire of maintenance tools or equipment for a factory

3　Which one of the following would be classified as an indirect cost of individual batches of output, units of service or of individual projects of the organisation concerned?

A　The cost of sugar used for a batch of cakes in a bakery

B　The lease rental cost of a leased car used by a site foreman travelling to a specific construction project

C　The accountant's salary in a factory

D　The cost of drinks served on an intercity train journey

4　When costing cost units, wage payments for idle time within a production department are classified as

A　Direct labour cost
B　Prime cost
C　Administration overhead
D　Factory overhead

5　A retailer currently uses the LIFO method to value its inventory of goods for sale.

If the retailer decides instead to use the FIFO method, in a **period of rising prices**

A　The closing inventory value will be lower and the gross profit will be lower
B　The closing inventory value will be lower and the gross profit will be higher
C　The closing inventory value will be higher and the gross profit will be lower
D　The closing inventory value will be higher and the gross profit will be higher

6　A wholesaler had an opening inventory of 750 units of geronimos valued at £80 each on 1 March.

The following receipts and sales were recorded during March.

4 March	Received 180 units at a cost of	£85 per unit
18 March	Received 90 units at a cost of	£90 per unit
24 March	Sold 852 units at a price of	£110 per unit

Using the weighted average cost method of valuation, what was the cost of geronimos sold on 24 March? (to the nearest £)

A　£35,320
B　£38,016
C　£38,448
D　£69,660

7　At the beginning of week 10 there were 400 units of component X held in the stores. 160 of these components had been purchased for £5.55 each in week 9 and 240 had been purchased for £5.91 each in week 8.

On day 3 of week 10 a further 120 components were received into stores at a purchase cost of £5.96 each.

The only issue of component X occurred on day 4 of week 10, when 150 units were issued to production.

Using the FIFO valuation method, what was the value of the closing inventory of component X at the end of week 10?

A　£1,980.45
B　£2,070.15
C　£2,135.10
D　£2,200.55

8   A wholesaler had an opening inventory of 330 units of product T valued at £168 each on 1 April.

The following receipts and sales were recorded during April.

4 April	Received 180 units at a cost of	£174 per unit
18 April	Received 90 units at a cost of	£186 per unit
24 April	Sold 432 units at a price of	£220 per unit

Using the LIFO valuation method, what was the gross profit earned from the units sold on 24 April?

A   £16,350
B   £18,120
C   £18,520
D   £19,764

9   Which of the following statements is/are correct?

	True	False
Using LIFO, managers are continually aware of recent costs when making decisions, because the costs being charged to their departments or products will be current costs	☐	☐
FIFO lets managers value issues at current prices in a period of high inflation	☐	☐
The use of the cumulative average pricing method of inventory valuation is easier to administer than FIFO and LIFO because there is no need to identify each batch separately	☐	☐

10   A business buys and sells boxes of item J. The transactions for the latest quarter are shown below.

Opening inventory   400 boxes valued at £1,000

	Purchases		Sales
	Boxes	Value £	Boxes
July	1,000	2,600	1,100
August	1,200	3,300	900
September	1,000	3,000	800

The business values its inventories using a periodic weighted average price calculated at the end of each quarter.

To the nearest £, the value of the inventory at the end of September is £...

Now go back to the Learning Objectives in the Introduction. If you are satisfied you have achieved these objectives, please tick them off.

Answers to Interactive questions

Answer to Interactive question 1

Cost incurred	Direct or indirect?
The salary of the garage's accountant	Indirect
The cost of heating the garage	Indirect
A can of engine oil used in the repair	Direct. This cost can be directly attributed to this particular repair.
A smear of grease used in the repair	Indirect. This cost is negligible and would not be recorded separately as a direct cost.
An overtime premium paid to the mechanic carrying out the repair	Indirect. The overtime is being worked due to a generally heavy work load. This particular repair has not caused the overtime premium to be incurred. The cost is indirect and must be shared over all the repair jobs carried out.
An idle time payment made to the mechanic while waiting for a delivery of parts for a number of jobs	Indirect. The cost cannot be identified with any particular repair job.
The wages of the supervisor overseeing the mechanic carrying out the repair	Indirect. The supervisor is overseeing all repair jobs being undertaken.

Answer to Interactive question 2

Date	Receipts			Issues			Inventory		
	Quantity	Unit price £	Amount £	Quantity	Unit price £	Amount £	Quantity	Unit price £	Amount £
1.5.X6							100	2.00	200.00
3.5.X6	400	2.10	840.00				100	2.00	200.00
							400	2.10	840.00
							500		1,040.00
4.5.X6				100	2.00	200.00			
				100	2.10	210.00	300	2.10	630.00
9.5.X6	300	2.12	636.00				300	2.10	630.00
							300	2.12	636.00
							600		1,266.00
11.5.X6				300	2.10	630.00			
				100	2.12	212.00	200	2.12	424.00
18.5.X6	100	2.40	240.00				200	2.12	424.00
							100	2.40	240.00
							300		664.00
20.5.X6				100	2.12	212.00	100	2.12	212.00
							100	2.40	240.00
31.5.X6							200		452.00

Answer to Interactive question 3

(a) A £27
     B £54
     C £15
     D £135

WORKINGS

				£
8 June	Inventory balance =	30	units × £2.50	75
		20	units × £3.00	60
		50		135
			Weighted average price	= 135/50
				= 2.70
10 June	Issues =	10	units × £2.70	£27
14 June	Issues =	20	units × £2.70	£54
18 June	Inventory balance = remaining	20	units × £2.70	54
	receipts	40	units × £2.40	96
		60		150
			Weighted average price	= 150/60
				= 2.50
20 June	Issues =	6	units × £2.50	£15
	Inventory balance =	54	units × £2.50	135

(b) A £30
     B £55
     C £14.40
     D £131.60

WORKINGS

				£
10 June		10	units × £3.00	30.00
4 June	Issues	10	units × £3.00	30.00
		10	units × £2.50	25.00
				55.00
20 June	Issues:	6	units × £2.40	14.40
	Balance:	34	units × £2.40	81.60
		20	units × £2.50	50.00
		54		131.60

1   A, B   It is possible to ascertain the cost of these two cost objects.

The other three items are costs that might be attributed to a particular cost object, but they are not cost objects in themselves.

2   B, D   The cost of overtime worked specifically to complete a one-off project (option A) is direct labour.

Primary packing materials, eg cartons and boxes, (option C) are direct materials.

3   C   The accountant's salary is an indirect cost because it cannot be traced to a specific cost unit. It would be classified as an administration overhead.

All of the other costs can be traced to a specific cost unit.

The cost of sugar would be a direct ingredients cost of a specific batch of cakes.

The lease rental cost would be a direct cost of a construction project.

The cost of drinks served would be a direct cost of a particular train journey.

4   D   Idle time is usually treated as an overhead; in this case it is within the production department and is therefore a factory overhead.

5   D   The FIFO method prices issues from inventory at the cost of the earliest delivery remaining in inventory.

The closing inventory will therefore be valued at the higher prices paid.

The charge to cost of sales will be lower than with LIFO, therefore the gross profit will be higher.

6   D

			£
Weighted average cost per unit:			
750	units × £80		60,000
180	units × £85		15,300
90	units × £90		8,100
1,020			83,400

Weighted average cost per unit	= £83,400/1,020
	= £81.76
Cost of units sold on 24 March	= £81.76 × 852 units
	= £69,660

7   C   Components issued on day 4 = 150 from week 8 receipts

Closing inventory week 10:

			£
Remaining	90	Components from week 8 × £5.91	531.90
	160	Components from week 9 × £5.55	888.00
	120	Components from week 10 × £5.96	715.20
	370		2,135.10

8 D The LIFO method uses the cost of the most recent batches first.

		£
Cost of units sold on 24 April:		
90	units × £186	16,740
180	units × £174	31,320
162	units × £168	27,216
432		75,276

	£
Sales revenue = 432 units × £220	95,040
Less cost of units sold	75,276
Gross profit	19,764

9

	True	False
Using LIFO, managers are continually aware of recent costs when making decisions, because the costs being charged to their departments or products will be current costs	✓	
FIFO lets managers value issues at current prices in a period of high inflation		✓
The use of the cumulative average pricing method of inventory valuation is easier to administer than FIFO and LIFO because there is no need to identify each batch separately	✓	

FIFO lets managers value issues at current prices in a period of high inflation is incorrect. Under FIFO, inventory issues are valued at the cost of the earliest delivery remaining in inventory. In times of inflation, this will mean that issue prices will be lower than current prices.

10 To the nearest £, the value of the inventory at the end of September is £2,200.

Total inventory available during quarter:

	Boxes	Value £
Opening inventory	400	1,000
Purchases: July	1,000	2,600
August	1,200	3,300
September	1,000	3,000
	3,600	9,900

Periodic weighted average price	= £9,900/3,600
	= £2.75 per box
Closing inventory	= 3,600 – (1,100 + 900 + 800)
	= 800 boxes
Value of closing inventory	= 800 × £2.75
	= £2,200

CHAPTER 3

Calculating unit costs (Part 2)

Introduction
Examination context
Topic List
1 Absorption costing
2 Activity based costing
3 Costing methods
4 Other approaches to cost management
Summary and Self-test
Answers to Interactive questions
Answers to Self-test

Introduction

Learning objectives

Tick off

- Calculate unit costs from information provided, using absorption costing

- Select the most appropriate method of costing for a given product or service

The specific syllabus references for this chapter are: 1c, d.

Syllabus links

A knowledge of the method of determining a full unit cost will underpin your understanding of inventory valuation for the Accounting syllabus.

Examination context

20% of the marks in the examination will be allocated in one scenario-based question. Specific topics from this chapter that may be examined in this form include allocation, apportionment, absorption of overheads and activity based costing.

You may also be examined on the contents of this chapter by multiple choice, multi-part multiple choice or multiple response questions.

Numerical questions on the calculation of overhead absorption rates and of over and under absorption of overheads have been popular in past papers.

You should also be prepared to tackle narrative questions on overhead absorption as well as on the selection of the most appropriate costing method in specific circumstances.

You will **not** be required to answer numerical questions about activity based costing but you should be able to demonstrate a general understanding of the underlying principles of this costing system.

In the examination, candidates may be required to:

- Calculate the full cost of a cost unit using absorption costing

- Demonstrate an understanding of the basic principles of activity based costing

- Identify the most appropriate costing method in specific circumstances

- Demonstrate an understanding of the general principles of target costing, life cycle costing and just in time

It is essential to appreciate the difference between the allocation and apportionment of overheads, which links back to the ideas about direct and indirect cost covered earlier.

A common difficulty is failing to allow for under/over absorption when predetermined overhead rates are used.

1 Absorption costing

Section overview

- In absorption costing the full cost of a cost unit is equal to its prime cost plus an absorbed share of overhead cost.

- The three stages in determining the share of overhead to be attributed to a cost unit are allocation, apportionment and absorption.

- Overheads are absorbed into product or service costs using a predetermined overhead absorption rate, usually set annually in the budget.

- The absorption rate is calculated by dividing the budgeted overhead by the budgeted level of activity. For production overheads, the level of activity is often measured in terms of direct labour hours or machine hours.

- Over or under absorption of overhead arises because the absorption rate is based on estimates.

1.1 Calculating the absorption cost of a cost unit

To calculate the full cost of an item using absorption costing (sometimes referred to as full costing) it is necessary first to establish its direct cost or prime cost and then to add a fair share of indirect costs or overhead.

The full or absorption cost per unit is therefore made up as follows.

	£
Direct materials	X
Direct labour	X
Direct expenses (if any)	X
Total direct cost (prime cost)	X
Share of indirect cost/overhead	X
Absorption (full) cost	X

There are three stages in determining the share of overhead to be attributed to a cost unit.

- Overhead allocation
- Overhead apportionment
- Overhead absorption

1.2 Overhead allocation

The first step in absorption costing is **allocation**. Allocation is the process by which whole cost items are charged direct to a cost centre. A cost centre acts as a **collecting place** for costs before they are analysed further.

Cost centres may be one of the following types.

- A **production department**, to which production overheads are charged.

- A **production service department**, to which production overheads are charged.

- An **administrative department**, to which administration overheads are charged.

- A **selling** or a **distribution department**, to which sales and distribution overheads are charged.

- An **overhead cost centre**, to which items of expense which are shared by a number of departments, such as rent and rates, heat and light and the canteen, are charged.

The following are examples of costs that would be charged direct to cost centres via the process of allocation.

- The cost of a warehouse security guard will be charged to the warehouse cost centre.
- Paper on which computer output is recorded will be charged to the computer department.

Worked example: Overhead allocation

Consider the following costs of a company.

	£
Wages of the supervisor of department A	200
Wages of the supervisor of department B	150
Indirect materials consumed in department A	50
Rent of the premises shared by departments A and B	300

The cost accounting system might include three cost centres.

Cost centre: 101   Department A

             102   Department B

             201   Rent

Overhead costs would be allocated directly to each cost centre, ie £200 + £50 to cost centre 101, £150 to cost centre 102 and £300 to cost centre 201. The rent of the factory will be subsequently shared between the two production departments, but for the purpose of day to day cost recording in this particular system, the rent will first of all be charged in full to a separate cost centre.

1.3   Overhead apportionment

The next step in absorption costing is overhead **apportionment**. This involves apportioning general overheads to cost centres (the first stage) and then reapportioning the costs of service cost centres to production departments (the second stage).

1.3.1   First stage: apportioning general overheads

Overhead apportionment follows on from overhead allocation. The first stage of overhead apportionment is to identify all overhead costs as production department, production service department, administration or selling and distribution overhead. This means that the costs for heat and light, rent and rates, the canteen and so on (that is, costs which have been allocated to general overhead cost centres) must be shared out between the other cost centres.

Overhead costs should be shared out on a fair basis. You will appreciate that because of the complexity of items of cost it is rarely possible to use only one method of apportioning costs to the various cost centres of an organisation. The bases of apportionment for the most usual cases are given below.

Overhead to which the basis applies	Basis
Rent, rates, heating and light, repairs and depreciation of buildings	Floor area occupied by each cost centre
Depreciation, insurance of equipment	Cost or book value of equipment
Personnel office, canteen, welfare, wages and cost offices, first aid	Number of employees, or labour hours worked in each cost centre
Heating, lighting (see above)	Volume of space occupied by each cost centre

Interactive question 1: Bases of apportionment   [Difficulty level: Easy]

The following **bases of apportionment** are used by a factory.

A   Volume of cost centre
B   Value of machinery in cost centre
C   Number of employees in cost centre
D   Floor area of cost centre

Complete the table below using one of A to D to show the bases on which the **production overheads listed in the table** should be **apportioned**.

Production overheads	Basis
Rent	
Heating costs	
Insurance of machinery	
Cleaning costs	
Canteen costs	

See **Answer** at the end of this chapter.

Worked example: Overhead apportionment

McQueen Co has incurred the following overhead costs.

	£'000
Depreciation of factory	100
Factory repairs and maintenance	60
Factory office costs (treat as production overhead)	150
Depreciation of equipment	80
Insurance of equipment	20
Heating	39
Lighting	10
Canteen	90
	549

Information relating to the production and service departments in the factory is as follows.

	Department			
	Production 1	Production 2	Service 100	Service 101
Floor space (square metres)	1,200	1,600	800	400
Volume (cubic metres)	3,000	6,000	2,400	1,600
Number of employees	30	30	15	15
Book value of equipment	£30,000	£20,000	£10,000	£20,000

The overhead costs are apportioned using the following general formula.

$$\frac{\text{Total overhead cost}}{\text{Total value of apportionment base}} \times \text{Value of apportionment base of cost centre}$$

For example, heating for department 1 = $\dfrac{£39,000}{13,000} \times 3,000 = £9,000$

		Total	To department			
Item of cost	Basis of apportionment	cost	1	2	100	101
		£	£	£	£	£
Factory depreciation	(floor area)	100	30.0	40	20.0	10.0
Factory repairs	(floor area)	60	18.0	24	12.0	6.0
Factory office costs	(number of employees)	150	50.0	50	25.0	25.0
Equipment depreciation	(book value)	80	30.0	20	10.0	20.0
Equipment insurance	(book value)	20	7.5	5	2.5	5.0
Heating	(volume)	39	9.0	18	7.2	4.8
Lighting	(floor area)	10	3.0	4	2.0	1.0
Canteen	(number of employees)	90	30.0	30	15.0	15.0
Total		549	177.5	191	93.7	86.8

Interactive question 2: Allocating and apportioning overheads [Difficulty level: Easy]

Rose Ceramics Ltd rents office premises and owns a factory and a warehouse. There are four cost centres in the factory, the offices are the fifth cost centre, and the warehouse forms a sixth.

On 25 January, several invoices were received for overheads. For each of these decide:

(a) Whether the cost would be allocated or apportioned
(b) The cost centre(s) to be charged
(c) A suitable basis if apportionment is required

Overhead	(a) Allocate or apportion?	(b) Cost centre(s) charged?	(c) Basis of apportionment
Factory light & heat			
Rent			
Factory rates			
Office stationery			
Cleaning of workers' overalls			
Roof repair to warehouse			

See **Answer** at the end of this chapter.

Interactive question 3: Apportioning overheads [Difficulty level: Easy]

Pippin Co has three production departments (forming, machining and assembly) and two service departments (maintenance and general).

The following is an analysis of budgeted overhead costs for the forthcoming twelve-month period.

	£	£
Rent and rates		8,000
Power		750
Light, heat		5,000
Repairs, maintenance:		
Forming	800	
Machining	1,800	
Assembly	300	
Maintenance	200	
General	100	
		3,200
Departmental expenses:		
Forming	1,500	
Machining	2,300	
Assembly	1,100	
Maintenance	900	
General	1,500	
		7,300
Depreciation:		
Plant		10,000
Fixtures and fittings		250
Insurance:		
Plant		2,000
Buildings		500
Indirect labour:		
Forming	3,000	
Machining	5,000	
Assembly	1,500	
Maintenance	4,000	
General	2,000	
		15,500
		52,500

These overheads are to be allocated and apportioned as fairly as possible to the five departments using the following information:

	Floor area m²	Plant value £	Fixtures & fittings £	Effective horse-power
Forming	2,000	25,000	1,000	40
Machining	4,000	60,000	500	90
Assembly	3,000	7,500	2,000	15
Maintenance	500	7,500	1,000	5
General	500	–	500	–
	10,000	100,000	5,000	150

Allocate and apportion the budgeted overheads to the five departments.

	Forming £	Machining £	Assembly £	Maint'nce £	General £
Rent, rates					
Power					
Light, heat					
Repairs, maintenance					
Departmental expenses					
Dep'n of plant					
Dep'n of F&F					
Insurance of plant					
Insurance of buildings					
Indirect labour					

See **Answer** at the end of this chapter.

1.3.2 Second stage: service cost centre cost apportionment

The second stage of overhead apportionment concerns the treatment of **service cost centres**. For example, a factory is divided into several production departments and also a number of service departments, but only the production departments are directly involved in the manufacture of the units. In order to be able to add production overheads to unit costs, it is necessary to have all the overheads charged to (or located in) the production departments. The next stage in absorption costing is, therefore, to apportion the costs of service cost centres to the production cost centres. Examples of possible apportionment bases are as follows.

Service cost centre	Examples of possible bases of apportionment
Stores	Number of materials requisitions
Maintenance	Hours of maintenance work done for each cost centre
Production planning	Direct labour hours worked in each production cost centre

Interactive question 4: Production and service cost centres [Difficulty level: Easy]

Which of the following are production cost centres and which are service cost centres?

Cost centre	Production cost centre (✓)	Service cost centre (✓)
Finished goods warehouse		
Canteen		
Machining department		
Offices		
Assembly department		

See **Answer** at the end of this chapter.

Worked example: Service centre cost apportionment

JPE Ltd is divided into five departments that are also cost centres. These are departments A, B and C (through which cost units physically pass), an administrative department and a canteen.

Some details of the business are as follows:

	A	B	C	Canteen	Admin
Floor area (sq metres)	5,000	5,000	4,000	4,000	2,000
Personnel (persons)	10	20	10	10	5
Remuneration per month					
Direct (£)	1,920	3,600	2,240	–	–
Indirect (£)	360	480	240	320	870
Direct materials consumed (£)	5,500	250	400	–	–
Machine hours per month	600	2400	200	–	–
Power costs per month (£)	50	500	20	80	–
General overheads per month (£)	1,000	2,000	1,200	650	1,230

The monthly takings of the canteen are £600. Food bills for the canteen totalled £470. None of the administrative staff use the canteen.

The monthly electricity charge for heat and light is £1,000. The monthly rent of the company's premises is £6,000.

The administration costs are made up mainly of personnel-related costs.

Requirement

Apportion all overheads to the production cost centres.

Solution

Step 1: Primary allocation and apportionment
Where possible, costs should be allocated directly to each cost centre. Where costs are shared, a fair basis of apportionment should be selected. Remember that the analysis is concerned only with overheads. Direct material and direct wages costs are not included.

Cost item	Basis of apportionment	A £	B £	C £	Canteen £	Admin £
Indirect labour	Allocation	360	480	240	320	870
Power	Allocation	50	500	20	80	0
General overhead	Allocation	1,000	2,000	1,200	650	1,230
Canteen takings	Allocation				(600)	
Food	Allocation				470	
Rent	Floor area	1,500	1,500	1,200	1,200	600
Electricity	Floor area	250	250	200	200	100
		3,160	4,730	2,860	2,320	2,800

Point to note

The apportionment of rental costs and electricity costs have been made on the basis of floor area, because this seems 'fair'. The choice of the fairest basis, however, in practice, is a matter for judgement.

Step 2: Re-apportion the service centre costs

The next step is to apportion the costs of the service cost centres to the production cost centres. The method illustrated here is as follows.

- The first apportionment is for the service cost centre with the largest costs. These costs are shared between all the other cost centres, including the other service cost centre, on a fair basis.

- The costs of the second service cost centre, which will now include some of the first service cost centre's costs, are apportioned between the production cost centres, on a fair basis. This is illustrated below.

Cost item	Basis of apportionment	A £	B £	C £	Canteen £	Admin £
Costs allocated and apportioned		3,160	4,730	2,860	2,320	2,800
Apportion admin	No. of employees excluding admin	560	1,120	560	560	(2,800)
		3,720	5,850	3,420	2,880	0
Apportion canteen	No. of employees in A, B and C	720	1,440	720	(2,880)	–
		4,440	7,290	4,140	0	0

Points to note

1 The costs of the administration department were taken first because these are the largest service centre costs. The basis of apportionment selected is number of employees, since administration costs are largely personnel-related.

2 The costs of the canteen have also been apportioned on the basis of number of employees, because canteen work is primarily employee-related.

3 Service centre costs must ultimately be apportioned to the production cost centres; otherwise there will be no mechanism for absorbing the costs into the cost of output units.

4 WORKINGS: **Apportionment of administration department costs**

$$\frac{£2,800}{(10+20+10+10)} = £56.00 \text{ per employee}$$

The apportionment of costs is therefore (10 × £56) = £560 to Department A, (20 × £56) = £1,120 to Department B, (10 × £56) = £560 to Department C, and (10 × £56) = £560 to the canteen.

5 WORKINGS: **Apportionment of canteen costs**

$$\frac{£2,880}{(10+20+10)} = £72.00 \text{ per employee}$$

The apportionment of costs is therefore (10 × £72) = £720 to Department A, (20 × £72) = £1,440 to Department B, and (10 × £72) = £720 to Department C.

Interactive question 5: Reapportioning overheads   [Difficulty level: Easy]

Shah Co has two production departments (machining and assembly) and two service departments (maintenance and canteen). The accountant has already completed the initial allocation and apportionment of budgeted overheads to the four departments and now wishes to reapportion the service department overheads to the production departments. She has provided the following information.

	Machining	Assembly	Maintenance	Canteen
Total overhead (£)	520,000	600,000	200,000	70,000
Number of employees	50	40	30	15

Maintenance works 40% of the time for Machining, 10% for Canteen and 50% for Assembly.

Reapportion the service department overheads to the production departments, rounding to the nearest £.

	Machining	Assembly	Maintenance	Canteen
Total overhead (£)	520,000	600,000	200,000	70,000
First reapportionment (£)				
Revised total overheads (£) (enter figures in all 4 boxes)				
Second reapportionment (£)				
Revised total overheads (£) (enter figures in all 4 boxes)				

See **Answer** at the end of this chapter.

1.4 Overhead absorption

Having allocated and/or apportioned all overheads, the next stage in absorption costing is to add them to, or **absorb them into**, the cost of production or sales.

- **Production overheads** are added to the prime cost (direct materials, labour and expenses), the total of the two being the factory cost, or full cost of production. Production overheads are therefore included in the value of inventories of finished goods.

- **Administration, selling and distribution overheads** are then included. The aggregate of the factory cost and these non-production overheads is the total cost of sales. These non-production overheads are therefore **not** included in the value of closing inventory.

1.4.1 Predetermined absorption rates

In absorption costing, it is usual to add overheads into product costs by applying a **predetermined overhead absorption rate**. The predetermined rate is usually set annually in advance, as part of the budgetary planning process.

Overheads are not absorbed on the basis of the actual overheads incurred but on the basis of estimated or budgeted figures (calculated prior to the beginning of the period). There are several reasons why the rate at which overheads are included in production costs (the **absorption rate**) is determined before the accounting period begins.

- Goods are produced and sold throughout the year, but many actual overheads are not known until the end of the year. It would be inconvenient to wait until the year end in order to decide what overhead costs should be included in production costs.

- An attempt to calculate overhead costs more regularly (such as each month) is possible, although estimated costs must be added for periodic expenditure such as rent and rates (usually incurred quarterly). The difficulty with this approach would be that actual overheads from month to month could fluctuate therefore overhead costs charged to production would be inconsistent. For example, a unit made in one week might be charged with £4 of overhead, in a subsequent week with £5, and in a third week with £4.50. Only units made in winter would be charged with the heating overhead. Such charges are considered misleading for costing purposes and administratively inconvenient.

- Similarly, production output might vary each month. For example, actual overhead costs might be £20,000 per month and output might vary from, say, 1,000 units to 20,000 units per month. The unit rate for overhead would be £20 and £1 per unit respectively, which would again lead to administration and control problems.

1.4.2 Calculating predetermined overhead absorption rates

The **absorption rate** is calculated by dividing the **budgeted** overhead by the **budgeted** level of activity. For production overheads the level of activity is often budgeted direct labour hours or budgeted machine hours.

Overhead absorption rates are therefore predetermined as follows.

- The overhead **likely to be incurred** during the coming period is estimated.

- The total hours, units, or direct costs on which the overhead absorption rates are to be based (the activity level) are estimated.

- The estimated overhead is divided by the budgeted activity level to arrive at an absorption rate for the forthcoming period.

1.4.3 Selecting the appropriate absorption base

Management should try to establish an absorption rate that provides a **reasonably 'accurate' estimate** of overhead costs for jobs, products or services.

There are a number of different **bases of absorption** (or 'overhead **recovery** rates') that can be used. Examples are as follows.

- A rate per machine hour
- A rate per direct labour hour
- A rate per unit
- A percentage of direct materials cost
- A percentage of direct labour cost
- A percentage of prime cost

The choice of an absorption basis is a matter of judgement and common sense. There are no strict rules or formulae involved, although factors that should be taken into account are set out below. What is required is an absorption basis that realistically reflects the characteristics of a given cost centre and avoids undue anomalies, for example:

- A **direct labour** hour basis is most appropriate in a **labour intensive** environment.

- A **machine hour** rate would be used in departments where production is controlled or dictated by **machines**. This basis is becoming more appropriate as factories become more heavily automated.

- A rate per unit is only effective if all units are identical in terms of the resources utilised in their manufacture in each cost centre.

Worked example: overhead absorption bases

The budgeted production overheads and other budget data of Calculator Co are as follows.

Budget	Production dept 1	Production dept 2
Production overhead cost	£36,000	£5,000
Direct materials cost	£32,000	
Direct labour cost	£40,000	
Machine hours	10,000	
Direct labour hours	18,000	
Units of production		1,000

The production overhead absorption rates using the various bases of apportionment would be as follows.

- **Department 1**

  - Percentage of direct materials cost = $\dfrac{£36,000}{£32,000} \times 100\% = 112.5\%$

  - Percentage of direct labour cost = $\dfrac{£36,000}{£40,000} \times 100\% = 90\%$

  - Percentage of prime cost = $\dfrac{£36,000}{£72,000} \times 100\% = 50\%$

  - Rate per machine hour = $\dfrac{£36,000}{10,000 \text{ hrs}} = £3.60$ per machine hour

  - Rate per direct labour hour = $\dfrac{£36,000}{18,000 \text{ hrs}} = £2$ per direct labour hour

- **Department 2**
  - The department 2 absorption rate will be based on units of output.

$$\frac{5,000}{1,000 \text{ units}} = £5 \text{ per unit produced}$$

The choice of the basis of absorption is significant in determining the cost of individual units, or jobs, produced. In this example, suppose that an individual product has a material cost of £80, a labour cost of £85, and requires 36 labour hours and 23 machine hours to complete. The production overhead cost of the product would vary, depending on the basis of absorption used by the company for overhead recovery.

- As a percentage of direct materials cost, the overhead cost would be 112.5% × £80   = £90.00
- As a percentage of direct labour cost, the overhead cost would be 90% × £85   = £76.50
- As a percentage of prime cost, the overhead cost would be 50% × £165   = £82.50
- Using a machine hour basis of absorption, the overhead cost would be 23 hrs × £3.60   = £82.80
- Using a labour hour basis, the overhead cost would be 36 hrs × £2   = £72.00

In theory, each basis of absorption would be possible, but the company should choose a basis for its own costs that seems to be 'fairest'. In our example, this choice will be significant in determining the cost of individual products, as the following summary shows, but the **total cost** of production overheads is the budgeted overhead expenditure, no matter what basis of absorption is selected. It is the relative share of overhead costs borne by individual products and jobs that is affected by the choice of overhead absorption basis.

A summary of the product costs is shown below.

	Basis of overhead recovery				
	Percentage of materials cost	Percentage of labour cost	Percentage of prime cost	Machining hours	Direct labour hours
	£	£	£	£	£
Direct material	80.00	80.00	80.00	80.00	80.00
Direct labour	85.00	85.00	85.00	85.00	85.00
Production overhead	90.00	76.50	82.50	82.80	72.00
Total production cost	255.00	241.50	247.50	247.80	237.00

Interactive question 6: Overhead absorption rates   [Difficulty level: Easy]

Use the following information to determine suitable overhead absorption rates for a company's three production cost centres.

	Forming	Machining	Assembly
Budgeted cost centre overheads	£13,705	£28,817	£9,978
Budgeted direct labour hours per annum	5,482	790	4,989
Budgeted machine hours per annum	1,350	5,240	147

(a) The forming department rate is   £ [   ] per direct labour hour/ machine hour
(delete as appropriate)

(b) The machining department rate is £ [   ] per direct labour hour/ machine hour
(delete as appropriate)

(c) The assembly department rate is   £ [   ] per direct labour hour/ machine hour
(delete as appropriate)

See **Answer** at the end of this chapter.

1.4.4 Important note for the exam

It is usual to use predetermined absorption rates as described in 1.4.1 to 1.4.3. However, using estimates for a predetermined rate may lead to an incorrect overhead charge (called over- or under-absorption in Section 1.6) which leads to an adjustment. In order to avoid this type of adjustment, you may see actual absorption rates used in certain situations in the scenario-based questions. This will make more sense when you start to practise some questions.

1.5 Blanket absorption rates and departmental absorption rates

A **blanket or single factory overhead absorption rate** is an absorption rate **used throughout a factory** and for all jobs and units of output irrespective of the department in which they were produced.

For example, if total overheads were £500,000 and there were 250,000 machine hours during the period, the **blanket overhead rate** would be £2 per machine hour and all units of output passing through the factory would be charged at that rate.

Such a rate is not appropriate, however, if there are a number of departments and units of output do not spend an equal amount of time in each department.

Worked example: Absorption rates

AB plc has two production departments, for which the following budgeted information is available.

	Department 1	Department 2	Total
Budgeted overheads	£360,000	£200,000	£560,000
Budgeted direct labour hours	200,000 hrs	40,000 hrs	240,000 hrs

If a single factory overhead absorption rate is applied, the rate of overhead recovery would be:

$$\frac{£560,000}{240,000 \text{ hours}} = £2.33 \text{ per direct labour hour}$$

If separate departmental rates are applied, these would be:

Department 1

$$\frac{£360,000}{200,000 \text{ hours}} = £1.80 \text{ per direct labour hour}$$

Department 2

$$\frac{£200,000}{40,000 \text{ hours}} = £5 \text{ per direct labour hour}$$

Department 2 has a higher overhead cost per hour worked than department 1.

Now let us consider two separate products.

- Product A has a prime cost of £100, takes 30 hours in department 2 and does not involve any work in department 1.
- Product B has a prime cost of £100, takes 28 hours in department 1 and 2 hours in department 2.

Requirements

What would be the production cost of each product, using the following rates of overhead recovery?

(a) A single factory rate of overhead recovery
(b) Separate departmental rates of overhead recovery

Solution

			Product A £		Product B £
(a)	**Single factory rate**				
	Prime cost		100.00		100.00
	Production overhead (30 × £2.33)		70.00		70.00
	Production cost		170.00		170.00
			£		£
(b)	**Separate departmental rates**				
	Prime cost		100.00		100.00
	Production overhead: Department 1	(0 × £1.80)	0.00	(28 × £1.80)	50.40
	Department 2	(30 × £5)	150.00	(2 × £5)	10.00
	Production cost		250.00		160.40

Using a single factory overhead absorption rate, both products would cost the same. However, since product A is produced entirely within department 2 where overhead costs are relatively higher, and product B is produced mostly within department 1, where overhead costs are relatively lower, it is arguable that product A should cost more than product B. This can be seen to be the case if separate departmental overhead recovery rates are used to reflect the work done on each job in each department separately.

Interactive question 7: Calculating the overhead to be absorbed

[Difficulty level: Intermediate]

In relation to calculating total absorption cost, label the following descriptions in the correct order as Steps 1 – 5.

Description	Step
A Apportion fixed costs over cost centres	
B Establish the overhead absorption rate	
C Choose fair methods of apportionment	
D Apply the overhead absorption rate to products	
E Reapportion service cost centre costs	

See **Answer** at the end of this chapter.

1.6 Over and under absorption of overheads

The overhead absorption rate is based on **estimates** (of both numerator and denominator) and it is quite likely that either one or both of the estimates will not agree with what *actually* occurs. Actual overheads incurred are unlikely to be equal to the overheads absorbed into the cost of production.

(a) **Over absorption** means that the overheads charged to the cost of production are greater than the overheads actually incurred.

(b) **Under absorption** means that insufficient overheads have been included in the cost of production.

Worked example: Over and under absorption of overheads

Suppose that the budgeted production overhead in a production department is £80,000 and the budgeted activity is 40,000 direct labour hours. The overhead recovery rate (using a direct labour hour basis) would be £2 per direct labour hour.

Actual production overheads in the period are, say, £84,000, and 45,000 direct labour hours are worked.

	£
Overhead incurred (actual)	84,000
Overhead absorbed (45,000 × £2)	90,000
Over absorption of overhead	6,000

In this example, the cost of produced units or jobs has been charged with £6,000 more than was actually spent. An adjustment to reconcile the overheads charged to the actual overhead is necessary and the over absorbed overhead will be written as a credit to the **income statement** at the end of the accounting period. By making this adjustment the total overhead in the income statement would be reduced to £84,000, matching the overhead cost actually incurred.

ICAEW

1.6.1 The reasons for under/over absorbed overhead

The overhead absorption rate is **predetermined from budget estimates** of overhead cost and the expected volume of activity. Under or over recovery of overhead will occur in the following circumstances.

- Actual overhead costs are different from budgeted overheads; or
- The actual activity level is different from the budgeted activity level.

It is mathematically possible, but unlikely, that if both variations occur together they could cancel each other out so that no over or under absorption occurs.

Interactive question 8: Under and over absorption of overheads

[Difficulty level: Intermediate]

Using your answer to Interactive question 4 and the following information, determine whether the overhead in each of the three production departments is under or over absorbed and by how much for the year.

	Forming	Machining	Assembly
Actual direct labour hours	5,370	950	5,400
Actual machine hours	1,300	6,370	100
Actual overhead	£13,900	£30,300	£8,500

(a) The overhead in the forming department is under/over* absorbed by   £ ☐

(b) The overhead in the machining department is under/over* absorbed by   £ ☐

(c) The overhead in the assembly department is under/over* absorbed by   £ ☐

* Delete as applicable

See **Answer** at the end of this chapter.

2 Activity based costing

Section overview

- Activity based costing (ABC) is a development of absorption costing.

- ABC involves the identification of the factors (cost drivers) that cause the costs of an organisation's major activities.

- Activity costs are assigned to products or services on the basis of the number of the activity's cost drivers that each product or service generates.

- The resulting product costs provide more accurate information for cost management and control.

2.1 The problem with traditional absorption costing

We have seen that the traditional absorption costing system relies on subjective judgement concerning the basis of apportionment of overheads to cost centres. To a greater or lesser extent, all methods of apportionment and absorption are arbitrary in nature. Where overheads form a relatively low proportion of the total costs of a business, the arbitrary nature of overhead apportionment and absorption may not be a serious issue. However, a significant feature of many modern businesses is the relatively **high level of overhead costs in relation to total costs**. In this situation, the traditional absorption costing system can create a problem for management seeking to accurately identify unit costs and exert control over these costs. This problem has particular significance given the highly competitive environment faced by many businesses.

Worked example: The problem with traditional absorption costing

A business sells 20,000 coffee mugs per year comprising large mugs (10,000), medium size mugs (8,000) and small mugs (2,000). The time spent by direct labour is the same for each mug and the time spent on the machines is also the same for each mug. This will mean that, using either the direct labour hour method or the machine hour method of apportionment, the overheads absorbed by each mug will be the same. Thus, assuming the total overheads are £15,000, each mug will bear £0.75 (ie £15,000/20,000) of the total overheads.

Overall, the large mugs will absorb 50 per cent of the total overheads (ie 10,000/20,000), the medium size mugs will absorb 40 per cent of the total overheads (ie 8,000/20,000) and the small mugs will absorb 10 per cent (ie 2,000/20,000). However, this may not be an equitable apportionment of overhead costs. For example, where there are high set up costs or there are demanding requirements concerning a particular product, the volume of output may be an unreliable guide to the time and effort expended by the service departments on each product. It may be that each type of mug produced places equal demands on the support departments such as administration, distribution, packaging, etc. If this situation occurs, it can be argued that the large mugs and medium size mugs, which are the higher volume items, will bear too high a proportion of the total overheads and the small mugs, which have a lower volume of output, will bear too low a proportion of the total overheads if the traditional approach is followed.

2.2 The activity based costing approach

Activity based costing (ABC) provides an **alternative to the traditional method of absorption costing**. The objective of this method is to establish a better means of relating overheads to output. It is claimed that the ABC method provides managers with a **better basis for both cost control and for the analysis of profitability**.

The major concepts underlying ABC can be demonstrated as follows.

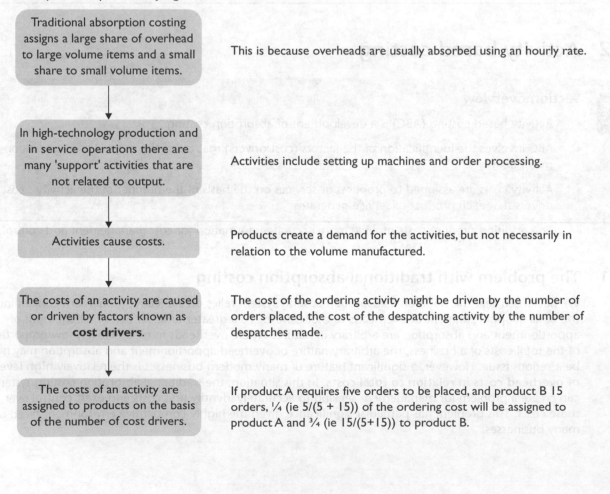

Traditional absorption costing assigns a large share of overhead to large volume items and a small share to small volume items.

This is because overheads are usually absorbed using an hourly rate.

In high-technology production and in service operations there are many 'support' activities that are not related to output.

Activities include setting up machines and order processing.

Activities cause costs.

Products create a demand for the activities, but not necessarily in relation to the volume manufactured.

The costs of an activity are caused or driven by factors known as **cost drivers**.

The cost of the ordering activity might be driven by the number of orders placed, the cost of the despatching activity by the number of despatches made.

The costs of an activity are assigned to products on the basis of the number of cost drivers.

If product A requires five orders to be placed, and product B 15 orders, ¼ (ie 5/(5 + 15)) of the ordering cost will be assigned to product A and ¾ (ie 15/(5+15)) to product B.

2.2.1 Cost drivers

For those costs that **vary with production levels in the short term**, ABC uses **volume-related cost drivers** such as labour hours or machine hours. The cost of oil used as a lubricant on machines would therefore be added to products on the basis of the number of machine hours, since oil would have to be used for each hour the machine ran.

For costs that **vary with some other activity and not volume of production**, ABC uses **transaction-related cost drivers** such as the number of production runs for the production scheduling activity.

2.2.2 Calculating product costs using ABC

Step 1
Identify an organisation's major activities.

Step 2
Identify the factors (cost drivers) which cause the costs of the activities.

Step 3
Collect the costs associated with each activity into **cost pools**.

Cost pools are equivalent to cost centres used with traditional absorption costing.

Step 4
Charge the costs of activities to products on the basis of their usage of the activities. A product's usage of an activity is measured by the quantity of the activity's cost driver it generates.

Suppose the cost pool for the ordering activity totalled £100,000 and that there were 10,000 orders (orders being the cost driver). Each product would therefore be charged with £10 for each order it required. A batch requiring five orders would therefore be charged with £50.

Although you will not be required to perform numerical calculations using ABC in your exam, the following example will help to clarify the differences between ABC and traditional absorption costing.

Worked example: Comparing ABC with traditional absorption costing

Suppose that Cooplan plc manufactures four products, W, X, Y and Z. Output and cost data for the period just ended are as follows.

	Output	No. of production runs in the period	Material cost per unit	Direct labour hours per unit	Machine hours per unit	Total machine or labour hours
	Units		£			
W	10	2	20	1	1	10
X	10	2	80	3	3	30
Y	100	5	20	1	1	100
Z	100	5	80	3	3	300
		14				

Direct labour cost per hour is £10. Overhead costs are as follows.

	£
Short-run variable costs	3,080
Set-up costs	10,920
Production and scheduling costs	9,100
Materials handling costs	7,700
	30,800

Traditional absorption costing

Using absorption costing and an absorption rate based on either direct labour hours or machine hours, the product costs would be as follows.

	W £	X £	Y £	Z £	Total £
Direct material	200	800	2,000	8,000	11,000
Direct labour	100	300	1,000	3,000	4,400
Overheads *	700	2,100	7,000	21,000	30,800
	1,000	3,200	10,000	32,000	46,200
Units produced	10	10	100	100	
Cost per unit	£100	£320	£100	£320	

* £30,800 ÷ 440 hours = £70 per direct labour or machine hour

Activity based costing

Using activity based costing and assuming that the number of production runs is the cost driver for set up costs, production and scheduling costs and materials handling costs and that machine hours are the cost driver for short run variable costs, unit costs would be as follows.

	W £	X £	Y £	Z £	Total £
Direct material	200	800	2,000	8,000	11,000
Direct labour	100	300	1,000	3,000	4,400
Short-run variable overheads (W1)	70	210	700	2,100	3,080
Set-up costs (W2)	1,560	1,560	3,900	3,900	10,920
Production and scheduling costs (W3)	1,300	1,300	3,250	3,250	9,100
Materials handling costs (W4)	1,100	1,100	2,750	2,750	7,700
	4,330	5,270	13,600	23,000	46,200
Units produced	10	10	100	100	
Cost per unit	£433	£527	£136	£230	

WORKINGS

(1) £3,080 ÷ 440 machine hours   = £7 per machine hour
(2) £10,920 ÷ 14 production runs   = £780 per run
(3) £9,100 ÷ 14 production runs   = £650 per run
(4) £7,700 ÷ 14 production runs   = £550 per run

Summary

Product	Absorption costing Unit cost £	ABC Unit cost £	Difference £
W	100	433	+ 333
X	320	527	+ 207
Y	100	136	+ 36
Z	320	230	– 90

The figures suggest that the traditional volume based absorption costing system is flawed.

- It under allocates overhead costs to low volume products (here, W and X) and over allocates overheads to higher volume products (here Z in particular).

- It under allocates overhead costs to less time consuming products (here W and Y with just one hour of work needed per unit) and over allocates overheads to more time consuming products (here X and particularly Z).

3 Costing methods

Section overview

- An organisation's costing method will depend on the nature of its operations.

- Specific order costing methods are appropriate when each cost unit is separately identifiable.

- Types of specific order costing method are job, batch and contract costing.

- Job and batch costing are appropriate when jobs are of relatively short duration. Each batch is a separate job consisting of a number of identical units.

- Contract costing is appropriate when cost units are of relatively long duration. Contracts are usually undertaken away from the organisation's own premises.

- The process costing method is appropriate when output consists of a continuous flow of identical units.

- In a process costing environment unit costs are determined on an averaging basis.

Regardless of the materials pricing method that is selected by management or whatever basis is used to absorb overheads into cost units, the overall costing method used by an organisation will ultimately depend on the nature of the organisation's operations.

3.1 Specific order costing

Some organisations produce 'one off' products or services to a customer's specific requirements, where each cost unit is separately identifiable from all others. The operations of these organisations can range from providing plumbing services, repairing vehicles or manufacturing a custom-made garden bench, to building a school or a hospital or a block of flats.

3.1.1 Job costing

Job costing is appropriate where **each separately identifiable cost unit or job is of relatively short duration,** such as the plumbing services and the garden bench in the examples above. Each job would be allocated a separate job number and costs would be accumulated against this number in order to determine the total cost of the job.

- Issues of direct material would be charged to each job using FIFO or LIFO, etc.

- Direct labour charges would be determined from detailed time records kept for each employee.

- Overhead costs would be absorbed into the total cost of each job using the predetermined overhead absorption rate for each cost centre through which the job passes.

> **Direct material issues**
>
> FIFO, LIFO etc

> **Direct labour costs**
>
> Based on time records

> **Job No.**
> **XXXX**

> **Production overhead costs**
>
> Absorbed from cost centre A,
> cost centre B, etc

3.1.2 Contract costing

Contract costing is appropriate where **each separately identifiable cost unit is of relatively long duration,** such as the building of the school or hospital in the examples above. Contracts are often undertaken away from the organisation's own premises.

Each contract would be allocated a separate number and costs would be accumulated against this number in order to determine the total cost of the contract.

- Many direct materials would be delivered straight to the contract but issues of direct material from stores would be charged to each contract using FIFO or LIFO, etc.

- Many direct employees would be permanently employed on the contract site but direct labour charges for those employees travelling between sites would be determined from detailed time records kept for each employee.

- Many overhead costs can be allocated directly to the contract but administrative overhead might be absorbed into contract costs using some form of absorption basis.

3.1.3 Batch costing

Batch costing is similar to job costing except that **each separately identifiable cost unit would be a batch of identical items.** For example, batch costing can be applied when production takes the form of separately identifiable batches of shoes or batches of printed advertising leaflets.

Each batch would be allocated a number to identify it and costs would be accumulated for the batch in the same way as for a job in job costing. The cost per unit manufactured in a batch is the total batch cost divided by the number of units in the batch.

3.2 Process (continuous operation) costing

Some organisations have a continuous flow of operations and produce a large number of identical products. Food processing is one example and oil refining is another.

Such operations often consist of a number of consecutive processes where the output of one process becomes the input of the subsequent process and so on until the finished output is produced.

For example, the processes involved in making bottled sauces might be as follows.

Each process usually acts as a cost centre and material, labour and overhead costs are collected to derive a total cost for each process for each period. **The cost per unit of output from each process is determined by dividing the total process cost by the number of units produced each period.** This unit cost then becomes an input cost for the subsequent process and so on until the final cost of a completed unit is accumulated.

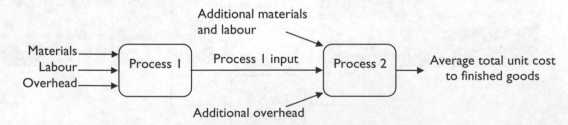

Process costing can also be applied in a service environment. For example, in an organisation that provides a shirt laundering service the processes involved might be as follows.

The cost per shirt laundered would be determined by the same averaging process as described earlier.

Interactive question 9: Costing methods   [Difficulty level: Intermediate]

Tick **one** costing method that would be appropriate in each of the following industries.

	Process	Job	Contract	Batch
Fitting kitchens	☐	☐	☐	☐
Manufacturing components	☐	☐	☐	☐
Manufacturing chemicals	☐	☐	☐	☐
Building offices	☐	☐	☐	☐

See **Answer** at the end of this chapter.

4   Other approaches to cost management

Section overview

- Life cycle costing tracks and accumulates the costs and revenues attributable to each product over its entire life cycle.

- Life cycle costs include those incurred in developing the product and bringing it to market, as well as the costs incurred after sales of the product have ceased.

- Target costing begins with a concept for a new product for which a required selling price is determined after consideration of the market conditions.

- The required profit margin is deducted from the selling price to determine the target cost for the product.

- The costs to be incurred over the product's entire life cycle are then examined to ensure that the target cost is achieved.

- Just in time (JIT) is an approach to operations planning and control based on the idea that goods and services should be produced only when they are needed.

4.1   Life cycle costing

A product incurs costs over the whole of its life cycle, from the design stage through development to market launch, production and sales, and its eventual withdrawal from the market.

Component elements of a product's costs over its life cycle include the following.

- **Research and development costs**: design, testing and so on.
- **Training costs**: including initial operator training.
- **Production costs**: materials, labour and so on.
- **Distribution costs**: transportation, handling, inventory cost.
- **Marketing costs**: advertising, customer service.
- **Retirement and disposal costs**: dismantling specialised equipment.

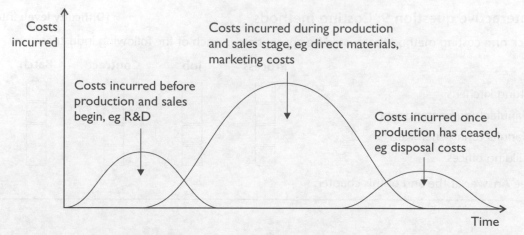

Figure 3.1: Costs incurred during the life cycle of a product or service

Traditional management accounting systems are based on the accounting year and tend to dissect the product's life cycle in a series of annual sections. This means that a product's profitability over its entire life is not assessed, but rather its profitability is assessed on a periodic basis.

In contrast, **life cycle costing tracks and accumulates actual costs and revenues attributable to each product over its entire life cycle**, hence the total profitability of any given product can be determined.

4.2 Target costing

We have seen how the full cost of a product can be determined using some form of absorption costing. This full cost is often used as the basis of the selling price decision: a desired profit mark-up is added to the full cost to determine the product's selling price.

Target costing works the other way round. It begins with a concept for a new product and, after considering the situation in the potential market for the product, a required selling price is determined.

From this price is deducted the desired profit margin, and the resulting acceptable cost becomes the target cost. **Thus the selling price determines the cost rather than the other way round.**

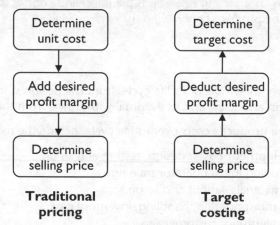

The costs to be incurred over the product's entire life cycle are then examined and engineered in order to ensure that the target cost is achieved.

Of particular importance is the initial design of the product. This is because **many of the costs to be incurred over the product's entire life cycle are built into the product at the design stage**.

4.3 Just in time

Just in time (JIT) is an approach to operations planning and control based on the idea that **goods and services should be produced only when they are needed**. They should not be produced too early, so that inventories build up, nor too late, so that the customer has to wait.

JIT consists of JIT purchasing and JIT production.

- JIT production is driven by demand for a product so that no items are produced until they are needed by a customer or by the next stage in a production process.

- JIT purchasing requires that material is delivered by the supplier just as it is needed in the production process.

JIT systems are often referred to as 'pull' systems, whereby demand from a customer pulls products through the production process. This is in contrast to traditional manufacturing systems, which are 'push' systems because a delivery from a supplier pushes products through production into inventory.

'Push' systems	**'Pull' systems**
Supplier → Production → Customer	Supplier ← Production ← Customer

4.3.1 Operational requirements for JIT

A number of operational requirements are vital to the success of a JIT system.

- **High quality**. Production must not be disrupted by quality failures.

- **Speed**. Throughput in the operation must be fast so that customer orders can be met by production rather than out of inventory.

- **Reliability**. Supplies and production must be reliable, to avoid hold-ups.

- **Flexibility**. To respond immediately to customer orders, production must be flexible and in small batch sizes.

- **Efficient production planning**. To ensure that goods are ready just when they are needed and that overproduction does not occur.

- **Reliable sales forecasting**. More accurate sales forecasts ensure that sales and production are better coordinated. This helps to avoid the build-up of inventories when forecasts are over-optimistic, or delays when production is not ready in time to meet sales requirements which exceed forecasts.

4.3.2 JIT and cost management

An efficient JIT system enables managers to control and reduce costs in a number of areas, including the following.

- **Warehousing costs**. Reduced storage costs result from holding lower inventories.

- **Improved capacity utilisation**. Efficient production planning enables capacity to be used in the most effective way with a faster throughput, thus reducing unit costs.

- **Reduction in waste**. The focus on high quality reduces the incidence of costs due to rejects.

- **Reduction in write-offs due to obsolescence**. Since goods are produced only as customers need them there is a reduction in obsolescence costs due to unexpected changes in customer requirements.

Summary

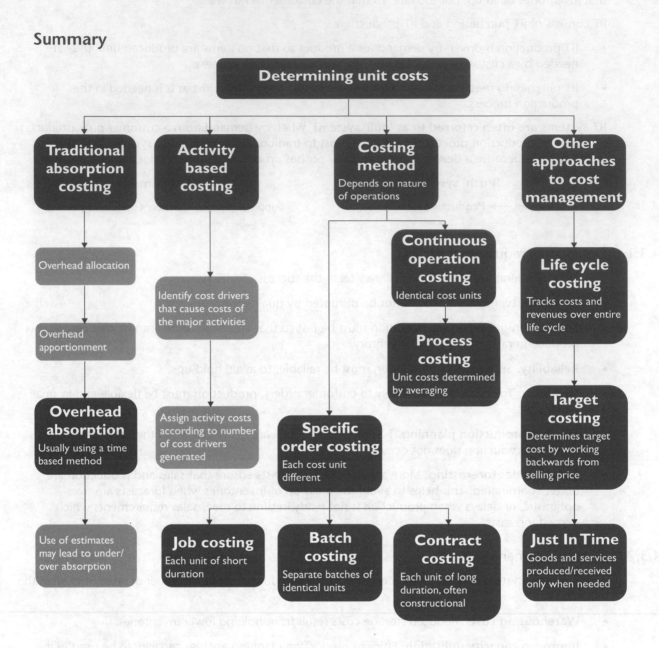

Self-test

Answer the following questions.

1 The direct materials involved in the manufacture of a Whoopie cost £2 per unit and the direct labour cost is £2.50 per unit. There are also direct expenses of £0.50 per Whoopie.

Fixed costs allocated to one Whoopie amount to £3.15.

Calculate the prime cost of a Whoopie.

The prime cost of a Whoopie is £ _____

2   A company has two production departments and two service departments with production overheads as shown in the following table.

	Production dept W	Production dept X	Service dept Y	Service dept Z
Production overheads (£'000)	500	600	600	800

Service department Y divides its time between the other departments in the ratio 3:2:1 (for W, X and Z respectively).

Department Z spends 40% of its time servicing department W and 60% of its time servicing department X. If all service department overheads are apportioned to production departments, the total fixed overhead cost of department W is: £ ⬚

3   An overhead absorption rate is used to:

A   Share out common costs to benefiting cost centres
B   Find the total overheads for a cost centre
C   Charge overheads to products
D   Control overheads

4   A company produces two products, Bubble and Squeak, in two production cost centres. The initial allocation and apportionment of budgeted production overheads has been completed. Extracts from the budget are as follows:

	Machining cost centre	Finishing cost centre
Production overheads	£38,000	£10,350
Machine hours per unit:		
product Bubble	6	2
product Squeak	4	1

Production overheads are absorbed on a machine hour basis. Budgeted production is 800 units of Bubble and 700 units of Squeak.

The budgeted production overhead cost per unit of Bubble is

A   £39.00
B   £45.00
C   £45.20
D   £54.00

5   ABC Co has been using an overhead absorption rate of £6.25 per labour hour in its packing department throughout the year.

During the year the overhead expenditure amounted to £257,500, and 44,848 labour hours were used.

Which of the following statements is correct?

A   Overheads were under absorbed by £27,600
B   Overheads were under absorbed by £22,800
C   Overheads were over absorbed by £27,600
D   Overheads were over absorbed by £22,800

6   Budgeted and actual data for the year ended 31 December 20X1 is shown in the following table.

	Budget	Actual
Production (units)	5,000	4,600
Fixed production overheads	£10,000	£10,000
Sales (units)	4,500	4,000

Fixed production overheads are absorbed on a per unit basis, based on a normal capacity of 5,000 units per annum.

Why did under absorption of fixed production overheads occur during the year ended 31 December 20X1?

A   The company sold fewer units than it produced
B   The company sold fewer units than budgeted
C   The company produced fewer units than budgeted
D   The company budgeted to sell fewer units than produced

7   A management consultancy absorbs overheads on chargeable consulting hours. Budgeted overheads were £615,000 and actual consulting hours were 32,150. Overheads were under-absorbed by £35,000.

If actual overheads were £694,075, what was the budgeted overhead absorption rate per hour?

A   £19.13
B   £20.50
C   £21.59
D   £22.68

8   Which TWO of the following statements about traditional absorption costing and ABC are correct?

A   Traditional absorption costing tends to assign too small a proportion of overheads to high volume products

B   ABC costing systems will provide accurate unit costs because cost drivers are used to trace overhead costs to products and services

C   An ABC system does not use volume-related cost drivers

D   Cost pools in an ABC system are equivalent to cost centres used in traditional absorption costing

E   A cost driver is the factor that influences the cost of an activity

9   Which TWO of the following statements are correct?

A   Process costing is the most appropriate costing method when a continuous flow of identical units is produced

B   Job costing and contract costing can only be applied where work is undertaken on the organisation's own premises

C   In process costing the cost per unit is derived using an averaging calculation

D   Process costing cannot be applied in a service environment

E   For batch costing to be applied each unit in the batch must be separately identifiable.

10   Which TWO of the following statements are correct?

A   Life cycle costing is the profiling of cost over a product's production life

B   The aim of target costing is to reduce life cycle costs of new products in order to achieve a cost that will produce the target profit

C   Once a product's target cost has been determined, the desired profit mark up is added to derive the product's selling price

D   JIT systems are referred to as 'push' systems because they push products through the production process as quickly as possible

E   JIT purchasing requires small, frequent deliveries from suppliers as near as possible to the time the raw materials and parts are needed

Now go back to the Learning Objectives in the Introduction. If you are satisfied you have achieved these objectives, please tick them off.

Answers to Interactive questions

Answer to Interactive question 1

Production overheads	Basis	Production overheads	Basis
Rent	D	Cleaning costs	D
Heating costs	A	Canteen costs	C
Insurance of machinery	B		

Answer to Interactive question 2

Overhead	(a) Allocate or apportion?	(b) Cost centre(s) charged?	(c) Basis of apportionment?
Factory light & heat	Apportion	The four factory cost centres	Floor area or volume occupied
Rent	Allocate	Office (this is the only cost centre rented)	
Factory rates	Apportion	The four factory cost centres	Floor area
Office stationery	Allocate	Offices	
Cleaning of workers' overalls	Apportion	The four factory cost centres and the warehouse	Number of workers using overalls
Roof repair to warehouse	Allocate	Warehouse	

Answer to Interactive question 3

	Basis	Forming £	Machining £	Assembly £	Maint'nce £	General £
Rent, rates	1	1,600	3,200	2,400	400	400
Power	2	200	450	75	25	0
Light, heat	1	1,000	2,000	1,500	250	250
Repairs, maintenance		800	1,800	300	200	100
Departmental expenses		1,500	2,300	1,100	900	1,500
Dep'n of plant	3	2,500	6,000	750	750	0
Dep'n of F&F	4	50	25	100	50	25
Insurance of plant	3	500	1,200	150	150	0
Insurance of buildings	1	100	200	150	25	25
Indirect labour		3,000	5,000	1,500	4,000	2,000

Basis of apportionment:

1   Floor area
2   Effective horsepower
3   Plant value
4   Fixtures and fittings value

Answer to Interactive question 4

Cost centre	Production cost centre	Service cost centre
Finished goods warehouse		✓
Canteen		✓
Machining department	✓	
Offices		✓
Assembly department	✓	

Only the machining department and assembly department are directly involved in the manufacture of units. The other cost centres support the production activity and are therefore service cost centres.

Answer to Interactive question 5

	Machining	Assembly	Maintenance	Stores	Workings
Total overhead (£)	520,000	600,000	200,000	70,000	
First reapportionment (£)	80,000	100,000	(200,000)	20,000	Maintenance is larger cost 4:5:1
Revised total overheads (£) (enter figures in all 4 boxes)	600,000	700,000	0	90,000	
Second reapportionment (£)	50,000	40,000	0	(90,000)	No of employees 5:4
Revised total overheads (£) (enter figures in all 4 boxes)	650,000	740,000	0	0	

Answer to Interactive question 6

The relative proportions of labour hours and machine hours in each cost centre can be used to identify whether the cost centre is labour intensive or machine intensive.

(a) Forming (labour intensive) $\dfrac{£13,705}{5,482}$ = £ 2.50 per direct labour hour

(b) Machining (machine intensive) $\dfrac{£28,817}{5,240}$ = £ 5.50 per machine hour

(c) Assembly (labour intensive) $\dfrac{£9,978}{4,989}$ = £ 2 per direct labour hour

Answer to Interactive question 7

	Description	Step
A	Apportion fixed costs over cost centres	2
B	Establish the overhead absorption rate	4
C	Choose fair methods of apportionment	1
D	Apply the overhead absorption rate to products	5
E	Reapportion service cost centre costs	3

Answer to Interactive question 8

(a) | Under | absorbed by £ | 475 |

(b) | Over | absorbed by £ | 4,735 |

(c) | Over | absorbed by £ | 2,300 |

WORKINGS

Forming

	£
Overhead absorbed (£2.50 × 5,370)	13,425
Overhead incurred	13,900
Under absorbed overhead	475

Machining

	£
Overhead absorbed (£5.50 × 6,370)	35,035
Overhead incurred	30,300
Over absorbed overhead	4,735

Assembly

	£
Overhead absorbed (£2 × 5,400)	10,800
Overhead incurred	8,500
Over absorbed overhead	2,300

Answer to Interactive question 9

	Process	Job	Contract	Batch
Fitting kitchens		✓(1)		
Manufacturing components				✓(2)
Manufacturing chemicals	✓(3)			
Building offices			✓(4)	

Points to note

1   Each fitted kitchen would be a separately identifiable cost unit of relatively short duration, hence job costing is most appropriate.

2   A number of identical components would be manufactured in each separately identifiable batch.

3   Chemical manufacture involves a continuous flow of processes.

4   Each office building would be a separately identifiable cost unit of relatively long duration. Therefore contract costing is most appropriate.

1 £5

	£ per unit
Whoopie prime cost	
Direct materials	2.00
Direct labour	2.50
Direct expenses	0.50
Prime cost	5.00

Remember that prime cost is the total of all direct costs. The fixed cost of £3.15 per unit is excluded from the prime cost calculation.

2 £1,160,000

	Production dept W £'000	Production dept X £'000	Service dept Y £'000	Service dept Z £'000
Production overheads	500	600	600	800
Apportion Y (3:2:1)	300	200	(600)	100
				900
Apportion Z (40:60)	360	540	–	(900)
	1,160			

3 C A is incorrect because this is overhead apportionment.

B is incorrect because total overheads are found for cost centres by analysing cost information.

D is incorrect because overheads are controlled using budgets and other management information.

4 A

	Machining		Finishing
Budgeted machine hours:			
Bubble (6 × 800)	4,800	(2 × 800)	1,600
Squeak (4 × 700)	2,800	(1 × 700)	700
	7,600		2,300
Production overhead absorption rate per machine hour (£38,000/7,600)	£5.00	(£10,350/2,300)	£4.50

Production overhead per unit of Bubble = (6 hours × £5.00) + (2 hours × £4.50)
= £39.00

5 D Actual overheads were £257,500. Absorbed overheads = £6.25 × 44,848 = £280,300

Actual overheads – Absorbed overheads = £257,500 – £280,300

= £22,800 over absorbed

Overheads were therefore over absorbed by £22,800.

6 C Options A and B are incorrect because it is the levels of production that bring about under/over absorption.

Option D is incorrect because the company was budgeting to produce the normal capacity on which the absorption rate is based. This would have led to zero under or over absorption, whatever the level of sales achieved.

7　B

	£
Actual overheads	694,075
Under absorbed overheads	35,000
Overheads absorbed by 32,150 hours	659,075

Overheads absorbed = Consulting hours × Budgeted absorption rate

£659,075 = 32,150 × Budgeted absorption rate

Budgeted absorption rate $= \dfrac{£659,075}{£32,150}$

$= £20.50$

8　D,E　Statement A is incorrect because traditional absorption costing tends to assign too large a proportion of overheads to high volume products, because it uses volume-related cost drivers.

Statement B is incorrect. ABC costing systems tend to provide more accurate unit costs than traditional absorption costing systems. However, some arbitrary apportionments and absorptions will still be necessary, therefore the unit costs are not accurate.

Statement C is incorrect. An ABC system uses volume-related cost drivers such as labour hours or machine hours for costs that vary with production levels in the short term, such as machine power costs.

Statement D is correct. Cost pools are used as collecting places to accumulate the costs associated with each activity.

Statement E is correct. The cost of an activity increases in line with the number of cost drivers.

9　A,C　Statement A is correct. Process costing is a form of continuous operation costing.

Statement B is incorrect. Both job costing and contract costing can be applied where work is undertaken on the customer's premises, for example, a decorating job (job costing) and building an extension on a school (contract costing).

Statement C is correct because process costs are divided by the number of units produced to derive an average unit cost for the period.

Statement D is incorrect because process costing can be applied in a service environment where there is a continuous flow of identical units.

Statement E is incorrect. Each batch must be separately identifiable but the units within each batch will be identical.

10　B,E　Statement A is incorrect because life cycle costing includes development costs and other cost incurred prior to production as well as any costs such as dismantling costs incurred after production has ceased.

Statement B is correct. The target cost is calculated by deducting the target profit from a predetermined selling price based on the market situation.

Statement C is incorrect. The target cost is derived by deducting the desired profit margin from a competitive market price.

Statement D is incorrect. JIT systems are 'pull' systems because demand from a customer pulls products through production.

Statement E is correct. JIT relies heavily on reliable, high quality suppliers.

CHAPTER 4

Marginal costing and absorption costing

Introduction
Examination context
Topic List
    1   Marginal cost and marginal costing
    2   Marginal costing and absorption costing compared
Summary and Self-test
Answers to Interactive questions
Answers to Self-test

Learning objectives

Tick off

- Understand the basic principles of marginal costing

- Calculate and reconcile profits under absorption costing or marginal costing

The specific syllabus references for this chapter are: 1c, 3f.

Syllabus links

A knowledge of marginal costing and absorption costing will underpin your understanding of inventory valuation for the Accounting syllabus.

Examination context

20% of the marks in the examination will be allocated in one scenario-based question. Absorption costing v marginal costing profits/losses and reconciling absorption and marginal costing profits/losses, which are covered in this chapter, may be examined in this form.

You may also be examined on the contents of this chapter by multiple choice, multi-part multiple choice or multiple response questions.

The calculation of the different profits reported under marginal costing and absorption costing is likely to be a popular examination topic. You are also likely to be asked to reconcile the difference between the profits reported under the two systems.

In the examination, candidates may be required to:

- Calculate the profit reported under marginal costing and under absorption costing using the same basic set of data

- Reconcile the difference between the profits reported under the two systems

- Derive the marginal costing profit from data provided that is prepared using absorption costing, and vice versa

1 Marginal cost and marginal costing

Section overview

- In a marginal costing system only variable production costs are included in the valuation of units.

- All fixed costs are treated as period costs and are charged in full against the sales revenue for the period.

- Contribution towards fixed costs and profit is calculated as sales revenue less variable cost of sales.

- Marginal costing profit for the period = contribution less fixed costs.

1.1 Marginal costing

Marginal costing is an alternative costing system to absorption costing. With marginal costing, only variable production costs are included in the valuation of units. **All fixed costs are treated as period costs** and are charged in full against the sales revenue for the period.

The marginal production cost per unit usually consists of the following:

- Variable materials
- Variable labour
- Variable production overheads

1.2 Contribution

Contribution is an important measure in marginal costing, and it is calculated as the difference between sales value and marginal cost.

The term 'contribution' is really short for 'contribution towards fixed overheads and profit'.

The contribution per unit can be calculated as follows.

	£ per unit	£ per unit
Selling price		x
Variable materials	x	
Variable labour	x	
Variable production overheads	x	
Marginal production cost	x	
Variable selling, distribution and administrative cost	x	
Total marginal cost		(x)
Contribution		x

Interactive question 1: Contribution   [Difficulty level: Easy]

A particular electrical good is sold for £1,009.99. The variable material cost per unit is £320, the variable labour cost per unit is £192 and the variable production overhead cost per unit is £132. Fixed overheads per annum are £100,000 and the budgeted production level is 1,000 units.

The contribution per unit of the electrical good is £ [   ]

See **Answer** at the end of this chapter.

Worked example: Marginal costing

Water Ltd makes a product, the Splash, which has a variable production cost of £6 per unit and a sales price of £10 per unit. At the beginning of September 20X0, there was no opening inventory and production during the month was 20,000 units. Fixed costs for the month were £45,000 (production, administration, sales and distribution). There were no variable marketing costs.

Requirements

Calculate the contribution and profit for September 20X0, using marginal costing principles, if sales were as follows.

(a) 10,000 Splashes
(b) 15,000 Splashes
(c) 20,000 Splashes

The first stage in the profit calculation must be to identify the variable costs, and then the contribution. Fixed costs are deducted from the total contribution to derive the profit. All closing inventories are valued at marginal or variable production cost (£6 per unit).

	10,000 Splashes £	10,000 Splashes £	15,000 Splashes £	15,000 Splashes £	20,000 Splashes £	20,000 Splashes £
Sales (at £10)		100,000		150,000		200,000
Opening inventory	0		0		0	
Variable production cost	120,000		120,000		120,000	
	120,000		120,000		120,000	
Less value of closing inventory (at marginal cost)	60,000		30,000		–	
Variable cost of sales		60,000		90,000		120,000
Contribution		40,000		60,000		80,000
Less fixed costs		(45,000)		(45,000)		(45,000)
Profit/(loss)		(5,000)		15,000		35,000
Profit/(loss) per unit		£(0.50)		£1		£1.75
Contribution per unit		£4		£4		£4

1.3 Conclusions

The conclusions that may be drawn from this example are as follows.

(a) The **profit per unit varies** at differing levels of sales, because the average fixed overhead cost per unit changes with the volume of sales.

(b) The **contribution per unit is constant** at all levels of output and sales. Total contribution, which is the contribution per unit multiplied by the number of units sold, increases in direct proportion to the volume of sales.

(c) Since the **contribution per unit does not change**, the most effective way of calculating the expected profit at any level of output and sales would be as follows.

    (i)   First calculate the total contribution.
    (ii) Then deduct fixed costs as a period charge in order to find the profit.

This calculation method is much quicker and is therefore useful for certain types of multiple choice questions in the exam. The contribution and profit figures would be calculated as follows, arriving at the same answers as above.

	10,000 Splashes £	15,000 Splashes £	20,000 Splashes £
Total contribution at £4 per unit	40,000	60,000	80,000
Less fixed costs	(45,000)	(45,000)	(45,000)
Profit/(loss)	(5,000)	15,000	35,000

However, in the scenario-based questions you will be required to calculate the sales figures and cost figures separately so this method is not appropriate for the scenario-based questions.

Interactive question 2: Marginal costing principles [Difficulty level: Intermediate]

Plumber plc makes two products, the Loo and the Wash. Information relating to each of these products for April 20X1 is as follows.

	Loo	Wash
Opening inventory	nil	nil
Production (units)	15,000	6,000
Sales (units)	10,000	5,000

	£	£
Sales price per unit	20	30
Unit costs		
Variable materials	8	14
Variable labour	4	2
Variable production overhead	2	1
Variable sales overhead	2	3

Fixed costs for the month	£
Production costs	40,000
Administration costs	15,000
Sales and distribution costs	25,000

Requirements

Using marginal costing principles and the approach in Section 1.3, calculate the profit in April 20X1.

Then calculate the profit again using the format shown below.

	Loo		Wash		Total	
	£	£	£	£	£	£
Sales						
Variable production costs						
Opening inventory						
Closing inventory						
Production cost of sales						
Variable selling overhead						
Contribution						
Fixed production costs						
Profit/(loss)						

See **Answer** at the end of this chapter.

2 Marginal costing and absorption costing compared

Section overview

- In a marginal costing system inventories are valued at marginal or variable production cost; all fixed overhead is charged against sales for the period in which it is incurred.

- In an absorption costing system an amount of absorbed fixed production overhead is included in the inventory valuation.

- Reported profit figures using marginal and absorption costing will differ if there is any change in the level of inventories during the period.

- If the fixed production overhead absorption rate per unit is the same each period, the difference in reported profit is calculated as the change in inventory units x fixed production overhead absorption rate per unit.

- If the fixed production overhead absorption rate is not the same each period, the difference in reported profit is equal to the change in the fixed production overhead in the inventory.

- In the long run the total reported profit will be the same whether marginal costing or absorption costing is used.

- Each of the costing systems has a number of advantages.

2.1 Summarising the differences between the two costing methods

The differences between the two costing systems can be summarised as follows:

- **In marginal costing**

  - Closing inventories are valued at **marginal or variable production cost**.
  - Fixed costs are charged in full against the profit of the period in which they are incurred.
  - No fixed costs are included in the inventory valuation.

- **In absorption costing** (sometimes referred to as **full costing**)

  - Inventories are valued at full **production cost**, and include a share of fixed production costs.

  - This means that the cost of sales in a period will include some fixed overhead incurred in a previous period (in opening inventory values) and will exclude some fixed overhead incurred in the current period which is carried forward in the closing inventory value. This will be a charge to a subsequent accounting period.

With these differences in mind, work through the following example.

Worked example: Marginal and absorption costing compared

TLF plc manufactures a single product, the Claud. The following figures relate to the Claud for a one-year period.

Sales and production (units)	800

	£
Sales	16,000
Production costs	
Variable	6,400
Fixed	1,600
Sales and distribution costs	
Variable	3,200
Fixed	2,400

The normal level of activity for the year is 800 units. Fixed costs are incurred evenly throughout the year, and actual fixed costs are the same as budgeted. A predetermined overhead absorption rate is used for the year.

There were no inventories of Claud at the beginning of the year.

In the first quarter, 220 units were produced and 160 units sold.

Requirements

For the first quarter:

(a) Calculate the fixed production costs absorbed by Clauds if absorption costing is used.
(b) Calculate inventory values per unit using both absorption costing and marginal costing.
(c) Calculate the under/over absorption of overheads.
(d) Calculate the profit using absorption costing.
(e) Calculate the profit using marginal costing.
(f) Explain why there is a difference between the answers to (d) and (e).

The requirements provide useful steps for analysing the example.

(a) $\dfrac{\text{Budgeted fixed production costs}}{\text{Budgeted output (normal level of activity)}} = \dfrac{£1,600}{800 \text{ units}}$

Absorption rate = £2 per unit produced.

During the quarter, the fixed production overhead absorbed would be 220 units × £2 = £440.

(b) **Inventory values per unit**

	Absorption costing £ per unit	Marginal costing £ per unit
Variable production cost (£6,400/800)	8	8
Fixed production cost (£1,600/800)	2	–
Inventory value per unit	10	8

(c)

	£	
Actual fixed production overhead	400	(1/4 of £1,600)
Absorbed fixed production overhead	440	
Over absorption of fixed production overhead	40	

(d) **Profit for the quarter, absorption costing**

In a scenario-based question the layout would be similar to the following:

	£	£
Sales (160 × £20)		3,200
Production costs		
Variable (220 × £8)	1,760	
Fixed (absorbed overhead (220 × £2))	440	
Total (220 × £10)	2,200	
Less closing inventories (60 × £10)	600	
Production cost of sales	1,600	
Adjustment for over-absorbed overhead	40	
Total production costs		1,560
Gross profit		1,640
Less sales and distribution costs		
Variable (160 × £4)	640	
Fixed (1/4 of £2,400)	600	
		1,240
Net profit		400

Using the 'short-cut' calculation method (suitable for multiple choice questions) this answer can be derived as follows.

	£ per unit	£
Sales price	20	
Less: Full absorption cost	(10)	
Variable sales and distribution cost	(4)	
	6	
× sales volume 160 units		960
Less fixed sales and distribution costs		(600)
		360
Adjust for over absorbed overhead		40
Net profit		400

(e) **Profit for the quarter, marginal costing**

In a scenario-based question the layout would be similar to the following:

	£	£
Sales		3,200
Variable production costs	1,760	
Less closing inventories (60 × £8)	480	
Variable production cost of sales	1,280	
Variable sales and distribution costs	640	
Total variable costs of sales		1,920
Total contribution		1,280
Less: Fixed production costs	400	
Fixed sales and distribution costs	600	
		1,000
Net profit		280

Using the 'short-cut' calculation method (suitable for multiple choice questions) this answer can be derived as follows.

	£ per unit	£
Sales price	20	
Less: Variable production cost	(8)	
Variable sales and distribution cost	(4)	
Contribution per unit	8	
× sales volume 160 units = contribution		1,280
Less: Fixed production costs		(400)
Fixed sales and distribution costs		(600)
Net profit		280

(f) The difference in profit is due to the different valuations of closing inventory. In absorption costing, the 60 units of closing inventory include absorbed fixed overheads of £120 (60 × £2), which are therefore costs carried over to the next quarter and not charged against the profit of the first quarter. In marginal costing, all fixed costs incurred in the period are charged against profit.

	£
Absorption costing profit	400
Fixed production costs carried forward in inventory values (60 units × £2)*	120
Marginal costing profit	280

* Change in inventory units × fixed production cost per unit

2.2 Conclusions

We can draw a number of conclusions from this example.

(a) **Marginal costing** and **absorption costing** are different techniques for assessing profit in a period.

(b) If there are **changes in inventories during a period, marginal costing and absorption costing give different results for profit obtained**.

Assuming that the variable cost per unit and the fixed cost per unit are constant:

(i) **If inventory levels increase, absorption costing will report a higher profit** because some of the fixed production overhead incurred during the period will be carried forward in closing inventory. This reduces cost of sales and carries forward cost to be set against sales revenue in the following period.

(ii) **If inventory levels decrease, absorption costing will report a lower profit** because as well as the fixed overhead incurred, fixed production overhead which had been brought forward in opening inventory is released and is included in cost of sales.

(c) If the opening and closing inventory levels are the same, marginal costing and absorption costing will give the same profit figure if unit costs remain constant.

(d) In the long run, total profit for a company will be the same whether marginal costing or absorption costing is used as all inventory is sold. Different accounting conventions merely affect the profit of individual accounting periods.

Interactive question 3: Reconciling the difference in reported profits
[Difficulty level: Intermediate]

The overhead absorption rate for product X is £10 per machine hour. Each unit of product X requires five machine hours.

Production of product X last period was 4,800 units and the sales volume achieved was 4,750 units.

(a) The absorption costing profit would be (tick one box):

Greater than ☐

The same as ☐

Less than ☐

the marginal costing profit.

(b) The differences between the reported profits would be £ ☐

See **Answer** at the end of this chapter.

Worked example: Comparison of total profits

To illustrate the point in conclusion 2.2(d) above, let us suppose that a company makes and sells a single product. At the beginning of period 1, there are no opening inventories of the product, for which the variable production cost is £4 per unit and the sales price £6 per unit. Fixed costs are £2,000 per period, of which £1,500 are fixed production costs.

	Period 1	Period 2
Sales	1,200 units	1,800 units
Production	1,500 units	1,500 units

Requirements

What profit would be reported in each period and in total using the following costing systems?

(a) Absorption costing. Assume normal output is 1,500 units per period.
(b) Marginal costing.

(a) **Absorption costing**: the absorption rate for fixed production overhead is

$$\frac{£1,500}{1,500 \text{ units}} = £1 \text{ per unit}$$

	Period 1		Period 2		Total	
	£	£	£	£	£	£
Sales		7,200		10,800		18,000
Production costs						
Variable	6,000		6,000		12,000	
Fixed absorbed	1,500		1,500		3,000	
	7,500		7,500		15,000	
Add opening inventory b/f	–		1,500		–	
	7,500		9,000		15,000	
Less closing inventory c/f	1,500		–		–	
Production cost of sales	6,000		9,000		15,000	
(Under)/over absorbed overhead	–		–		–	
Total production costs		6,000		9,000		15,000
Gross profit		1,200		1,800		3,000
Other costs		500		500		1,000
Net profit		700		1,300		2,000

Using the 'short-cut' method of calculation the profit figures can be calculated as follows.

	£ per unit	Period 1 £	Period 2 £
Sales price	6		
Full absorption cost:			
Variable production cost	(4)		
Absorbed fixed production cost	(1)		
	1		
× sales volume		1,200	1,800
Other costs		500	500
Net profit		700	1,300

(b) **Marginal costing**

	Period 1		Period 2		Total	
	£	£	£	£	£	£
Sales		7,200		10,800		18,000
Variable production cost	6,000		6,000		12,000	
Add opening inventory b/f	–		1,200		–	
	6,000		7,200		12,000	
Less closing inventory c/f	1,200		–		–	
Variable production cost of sales		4,800		7,200		12,000
Contribution		2,400		3,600		6,000
Fixed costs		2,000		2,000		4,000
Profit		400		1,600		2,000

Using the 'short-cut' method of calculation the profit figures can be calculated as follows.

	£ per unit	Period 1 £	Period 2 £
Sales price	6		
Less variable production costs	(4)		
Contribution per unit	2		
× sales volume = total contribution		2,400	3,600
Less fixed costs		2,000	2,000
Profit		400	1,600

Points to note

The total profit over the two periods is the same for both costing systems, but the profit in each period is different.

It is important to notice that although production and sales volumes in each period are different (and therefore the profit for each period using absorption costing is different from the profit reported by marginal costing), over the full period, total production equals sales volume, the total cost of sales is the same, and therefore the total profit is the same using either system of accounting.

Interactive question 4: Marginal and absorption costing

[Difficulty level: Exam standard]

X plc commenced business on 1 March making one product only. Unit cost information for the product is as follows.

	£
Variable labour	5
Variable material	8
Variable production overhead	2
Fixed production overhead	5
Standard production cost	20

The fixed production overhead figure has been calculated on the basis of a budgeted normal output of 36,000 units per annum.

You are to assume that all the budgeted fixed expenses are incurred evenly over the year. March and April are to be taken as equal period months.

Selling, distribution and administration expenses are as follows.

Fixed   £120,000 per annum
Variable   15% of the sales value

The selling price per unit is £35 and the number of units produced and sold was as follows.

	March Units	April Units
Production	2,000	3,200
Sales	1,500	3,000

(a) Calculate the total value of the closing inventory for each month under marginal costing.

March £ _____

April £ _____

(b) Calculate the total value of the closing inventory for each month under absorption costing.

March £ _____

April £ _____

(c) Calculate the budgeted annual fixed production overhead. £ _____

C
H
A
P
T
E
R

4

(d) Calculate the profit or loss for March using both absorption costing and marginal costing.

March

	Absorption		Marginal	
	£	£	£	£
Sales				
Variable production costs				
Fixed production cost absorbed				
Opening inventory				
Closing inventory				
Production cost of sales				
Under/over absorption				
Variable selling, distrib'n and admin				
Fixed selling, distrib'n and admin				
Fixed production costs				
Profit/(loss)				

(e) Calculate the profit or loss for April using both absorption costing and marginal costing

April

	Absorption		Marginal	
	£	£	£	£
Sales				
Variable production costs				
Fixed production cost absorbed				
Opening inventory				
Closing inventory				
Production cost of sales				
Under/over absorption				
Variable selling, distrib'n and admin				
Fixed selling, distrib'n and admin				
Fixed production costs				
Profit/(loss)				

See **Answer** at the end of this chapter.

2.3 Marginal costing and absorption costing compared

(a) **Advantages of absorption costing**

  (i) Fixed production costs are **incurred in order to make output**; it is therefore 'fair' to charge all output with a share of these costs.

  (ii) Closing inventory values, by including a share of fixed production overhead, will be valued on the **principle required by accounting standards for the financial accounting valuation of inventories** for external reporting purposes.

  (iii) A problem with calculating the contribution of various products made by a company is that it may not be clear whether the contribution earned by each product is enough to cover fixed costs, whereas by charging fixed overhead to a product it is **possible to ascertain whether or not it is profitable.**

(b) **Advantages of marginal costing**

  (i) It is simple to operate.

  (ii) There are **no apportionments of fixed costs**, which are frequently done on an arbitrary basis. Many costs, such as the managing director's salary, are indivisible by nature.

  (iii) Fixed costs will be **the same regardless of the volume of output**, because they relate to a period of time and are period costs. It makes sense, therefore, to charge them in full as a cost to the period.

  (iv) The cost to produce an extra unit is the variable production cost. It is realistic to value closing inventory items at this **directly attributable cost**.

  (v) **Under or over absorption of overheads is avoided.**

  (vi) Marginal costing information can be more useful for decision making since it **focuses on the variable costs** that are most likely to be altered as the result of a decision.

Summary

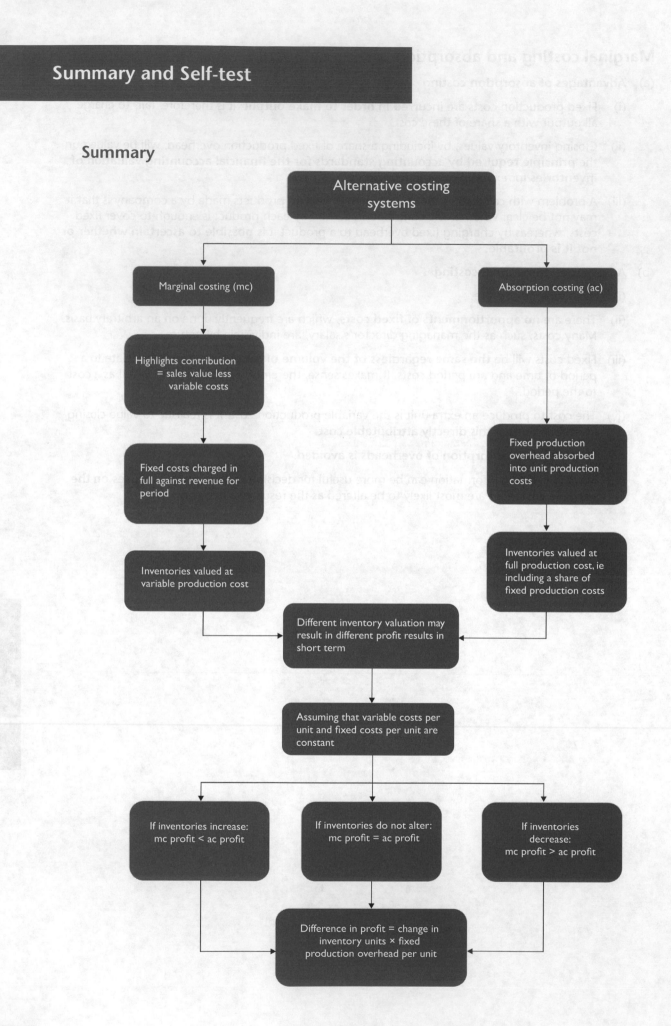

Alternative costing systems

Marginal costing (mc)

Absorption costing (ac)

Highlights contribution = sales value less variable costs

Fixed production overhead absorbed into unit production costs

Fixed costs charged in full against revenue for period

Inventories valued at variable production cost

Inventories valued at full production cost, ie including a share of fixed production costs

Different inventory valuation may result in different profit results in short term

Assuming that variable costs per unit and fixed costs per unit are constant

If inventories increase: mc profit < ac profit

If inventories do not alter: mc profit = ac profit

If inventories decrease: mc profit > ac profit

Difference in profit = change in inventory units × fixed production overhead per unit

ICAEW

Self-test

Answer the following questions.

1   The following cost card relates to one unit of Product EZ.

	£
Variable materials	20
Variable labour	40
Production overheads	
Variable	10
Fixed	5
Sales and distribution overheads	
Variable	5
Fixed	10
Total cost	90

The marginal production cost of one unit of Product EZ is £ ⬚

2   A new product has a variable material cost of £5.50 per unit, a variable labour cost of £2 per unit and a fixed overhead absorption rate of £3.50 per unit.

Production during the first month was 23,000 units and sales were 21,000 units.

Calculate to the nearest £ the inventory valuation under both marginal costing and absorption costing.

Marginal costing: £ ⬚ (to the nearest £)   Absorption costing: £ ⬚ (to the nearest £)

3   A company manufactures Luxury and Standard items. The following information relates to period 1.

	Luxury	Standard
Variable materials	£16 per unit	£12 per unit
Variable labour	£21 per unit	£9 per unit
Variable production overhead	£10 per unit	£8 per unit
Budgeted production	3,500 units	3,300 units
Actual production	3,500 units	3,300 units
Closing inventory	290 units	570 units

Variable labour is paid £6 per hour.

Fixed costs totalled £120,400 and are recovered on the basis of variable labour hours.

Calculate to the nearest £ the inventory valuation under both marginal and absorption costing.

	Luxury	Standard
Marginal costing:	£ ⬚	£ ⬚
Absorption costing:	£ ⬚	£ ⬚

4   A company has just completed its first year of trading. The budgeted production volume of 26,000 units was achieved and the sales volume was 24,500 units at £40 each.

The following actual cost information is available.

	£
Variable cost per unit	
Manufacturing	18.50
Selling and administration	9.20
Fixed costs (as budget)	
Manufacturing	91,000
Selling and administration	49,000

Calculate the net profit figures using both absorption and marginal costing.

Absorption net profit £ ⬚   Marginal net profit £ ⬚

5   When opening inventories were 8,500 litres and closing inventories 6,750 litres, a firm had a profit of £62,100 using marginal costing.

Assuming that the fixed overhead absorption rate was £3 per litre, what would be the profit using absorption costing?

A   41,850   C   67,350
B   56,850   D   82,350

6   Which of the following are arguments in favour of marginal costing?

☐ Closing inventory is valued in accordance with financial reporting standards.

☐ It is simple to operate.

☐ There is no under or over absorption of overheads.

☐ Fixed costs are the same regardless of activity levels.

☐ The information from this costing system may be more useful for decision making.

7   Which TWO of the following statements are correct assuming that unit costs are constant?

☐ A product showing a positive contribution under marginal costing will always show a profit under absorption costing.

☐ If inventory levels increase, marginal costing will report a lower profit than absorption costing.

☐ If inventory levels decrease, marginal costing will report a lower profit than absorption costing.

☐ If inventory levels increase, marginal costing will report a higher profit than absorption costing.

☐ If opening and closing inventory levels are the same, marginal costing and absorption costing will report the same profit figure.

8   Last period a company reported absorption costing profits of £36,000. Actual fixed production overheads were £42,000 and the actual production volume of 6,000 units resulted in over absorbed fixed production overhead of £6,000.

A sales volume of 7,100 units was achieved during the period.

The marginal costing profit for the period would have been £ ⬚ .

9   Last period 17,500 units were produced at a total cost of £16 each. Three quarters of the costs were variable and one quarter fixed. 15,000 units were sold at £25 each. There were no opening inventories.

By how much will the profit calculated using absorption costing principles differ from the profit if marginal costing principles had been used?

A   The absorption costing profit would be £10,000 less
B   The absorption costing profit would be £10,000 greater
C   The absorption costing profit would be £30,000 greater
D   The absorption costing profit would be £40,000 greater

10   In a period, a company had opening inventory of 31,000 units and closing inventory of 34,000 units. Profits based on marginal costing were £850,500 and on absorption costing were £955,500.

If the budgeted total fixed costs for the company were £1,837,500 what was the budgeted level of activity in units?

A   32,500   C   65,000
B   52,500   D   105,000

Now go back to the Learning Objectives in the Introduction. If you are satisfied you have achieved these objectives, please tick them off.

Answer to Interactive question 1

The contribution per unit is £ | 365.99 | .

WORKING

	£	£
Selling price per unit		1,009.99
Marginal cost per unit		
Variable material	320	
Variable labour	192	
Variable production overhead	132	
		644.00
Contribution per unit		365.99

Absorbed fixed overheads are not included in the calculation of marginal cost per unit or contribution per unit.

Answer to Interactive question 2

	£
Contribution from Loos (unit contribution = £20 – £16 = £4 × 10,000 units)	40,000
Contribution from Washes (unit contribution = £30 – £20 = £10 × 5,000 units)	50,000
Total contribution	90,000
Fixed costs for the period	80,000
Profit	10,000

	Loo		Wash		Total
	£	£	£	£	£
Sales		200,000		150,000	
Variable production costs	210,000		102,000		
Opening inventory	0		0		
Closing inventory	(70,000)		(17,000)		
Production cost of sales		(140,000)		(85,000)	
Variable selling overhead		(20,000)		(15,000)	
Contribution		40,000		50,000	90,000
Fixed production costs					(80,000)
Profit/(loss)					10,000

C
H
A
P
T
E
R

4

ICAEW

Answer to Interactive question 3

(a) The absorption costing profit would be greater than the marginal costing profit.

This is because production exceeded sales, therefore the inventory level increased. Some of the fixed production overhead incurred during the period would be carried forward in the inventory value with absorption costing, thus reducing the charge to cost of sales.

(b) The difference between the reported profits would be £2,500.

This is calculated as follows.

Difference in profit = Change in inventory levels × Fixed overhead absorption rate per unit
= 50 units × (£10 × 5 hours)
= £2,500

Answer to Interactive question 4

(a) March £7,500   (500 units × £15)

   April £10,500   (700 units × £15)

(b) March £10,000   (500 units × £20)

   April £14,000   (700 units × £20)

(c) Overhead absorption rate = $\dfrac{\text{Budgeted overheads}}{\text{Budgeted output}}$

   $\therefore £5 = \dfrac{\text{Budgeted overheads}}{36,000 \text{ units}}$

   $\therefore$ Budgeted overheads = £180,000

(d) March

	Absorption		Marginal	
	£	£	£	£
Sales		52,500		52,500
Variable production costs	30,000		30,000	
Fixed production cost absorbed	10,000		0	
Opening inventory	0		0	
Closing inventory	(10,000)		(7,500)	
Production cost of sales		(30,000)		(22,500)
Under/over absorption		(5,000)		0
Variable selling, distrib'n and admin		(7,875)		(7,875)
Fixed selling, distrib'n and admin		(10,000)		(10,000)
Fixed production costs		0		(15,000)
Profit/(loss)		(375)		(2,875)

WORKING

Sales revenue = 1,500 × £35 = £52,500

Variable production costs = 2,000 × (£5 + £8 + £2) = £30,000

Fixed production cost absorbed = 2,000 × £5 = £10,000

Closing inventory = see (a) and (b)

Under absorption:

		£
Overhead absorbed	(2,000 × £5)	10,000
Overhead incurred	(£5 × 36,000 × 1/12)	15,000
Under/(over) absorbed		5,000

Variable selling, distribution and admin = £52,500 × 15% = £7,875

Fixed selling, distribution and admin = £120,000 ÷ 12 months = £10,000

Fixed production cost = (36,000 × £5) ÷ 12 = £15,000

(e) April

	Absorption £	Absorption £	Marginal £	Marginal £
Sales		105,000		105,000
Variable production costs	48,000		48,000	
Fixed production cost absorbed	16,000		0	
Opening inventory	10,000		7,500	
Closing inventory	(14,000)		(10,500)	
Production cost of sales		(60,000)		(45,000)
Under/over absorption		1,000		0
Variable selling, distrib'n and admin		(15,750)		(15,750)
Fixed selling, distrib'n and admin		(10,000)		(10,000)
Fixed production costs		0		(15,000)
Profit/(loss)		20,250		19,250

WORKING

Sales revenue = 3,000 × £35 = £105,000

Variable production costs = 3,200 × (£5 + £8 + £2) = £48,000

Fixed production cost absorbed = 2,000 × £5 = £10,000

Opening inventory = March closing inventory - see (a) and (b)

Closing inventory – see (a) and (b)

Over absorption:

		£
Overhead absorbed	(3,200 × £5)	16,000
Overhead incurred	(£5 × 36,000 × 1/12)	15,000
Under/(over) absorbed		(1,000)

Variable selling, distribution and admin = £105,000 × 15% = £15,750

Fixed selling, distribution and admin = £120,000 ÷ 12 months = £10,000

Fixed production cost = (36,000 × £5) ÷ 12 = £15,000

1   The correct answer is: £70.

Marginal production cost is the total of all variable production costs.

Marginal production cost of product EZ

	£ per unit
Variable materials	20
Variable labour	40
Variable production overheads	10
	70

2   The correct answers are: marginal costing: £15,000 and absorption costing: £22,000.

Marginal cost of product	=	Variable material cost + Variable labour cost
	=	£5.50 + £2
	=	£7.50 per unit

In marginal costing, closing inventories are valued at marginal production cost, which includes the variable material cost of £5.50 and the variable labour cost of £2 for 2,000 units.

Therefore inventory valuation	=	£7.50 × 2,000
	=	£15,000

Absorption cost of product	=	Marginal cost + Fixed production overheads
	=	£7.50 + £3.50
	=	£11 per unit

In absorption costing, closing inventories are valued at £11 each (this includes a share of fixed production overheads).

Therefore inventory valuation	=	£11 × 2,000
	=	£22,000

3

	Luxury	Standard
Marginal costing	£13,630	£16,530
Absorption costing	£20,735	£22,515

Marginal costing

In marginal costing, closing inventories are valued at marginal production cost (variable materials, variable labour and variable production overhead).

Luxury = £16 + £21 + £10 = £47 per unit.

There are 290 of them, so closing inventory value = 290 × £47 = £13,630.

Standard = £12 + £9 + £8 = £29 per unit.

There are 570 of them, so closing inventory value = 570 × £29 = £16,530.

Absorption costing basis

Absorption costing includes fixed production overheads in inventory values rather than charging them against profit.

Based on the labour costs, the number of hours to produce each item is Luxury 3.5 (£21 ÷ £6), Standard 1.5 (£9 ÷ £6).

Luxury = The overhead absorption rate is £120,400 / ((3,500 × 3.5) + (3,300 × 1.5)) = £7 per direct labour hour.

Absorption costing inventory values of luxury items are therefore £7 × 3.5 hours × 290 units greater than marginal costing inventory values, ie £13,630 + £7,105 = £20,735.

Standard = The overhead absorption rate is £7 per direct labour hour. Absorption costing inventory values are therefore £7 × 1.5 hours × 570 units greater than marginal costing inventory values, ie £16,530 + £5,985 = £22,515.

4   Absorption net profit £ $\boxed{166,600}$ Marginal net profit £ $\boxed{161,350}$

WORKING

Absorption net profit

Fixed manufacturing cost per unit = $\dfrac{£91,000}{26,000}$ = £3.50

Budgeted production = actual production, therefore no under or over absorption of overhead occurred.

	£	£
Sales revenue 24,500 × £40		980,000
Manufacturing cost of sales 24,500 × £(18.50 + 3.50)		(539,000)
Gross profit		441,000
Less selling and administration costs		
Variable 24,500 × £9.20	225,400	
Fixed	49,000	
		(274,400)
Absorption costing net profit		166,600

Using the 'short-cut' method:

	£ per unit
Sales price	40.00
Less: Variable manufacturing cost per unit	(18.50)
Variable selling and administration cost per unit	(9.20)
Fixed manufacturing cost per unit	(3.50)
	8.80

	£
× sales volume 24,500 units	215,600
Less fixed selling and administration costs	49,000
Absorption costing net profit	166,600

Inventories increased during the period, therefore the marginal costing net profit will be lower.

	£
Absorption costing net profit	166,600
Difference in profits (change in inventory 1,500 units × £3.50)	(5,250)
Marginal costing net profit	161,350

	£
Check using the 'short-cut' method:	
Marginal costing contribution = 24,500 × £(40 – 18.50 – 9.20)	301,350
Less fixed costs (£91,000 + £49,000)	(140,000)
Marginal costing profit	161,350

5   B

Difference in profit = (8,500 – 6,750) × £3 = £5,250

Absorption costing profit = £62,100 – £5,250 = £56,850

Since inventory levels reduced, the absorption costing profit will be lower than the marginal costing profit. You can therefore eliminate options C and D.

6   The following statements are arguments in favour of marginal costing

☑ It is simple to operate.

☑ There is no under or over absorption of overheads.

☑ Fixed costs are the same regardless of activity levels.

☑ The information from this costing system may be more useful for decision making.

The first statement is incorrect. A marginal costing system does not value inventory in accordance with financial reporting standards because it does not include absorbed fixed production overheads. The information from an absorption costing system is therefore more useful for external reporting purposes.

7   The correct statements are:

☑ If inventory levels increase, marginal costing will report a lower profit than absorption costing.

☑ If opening and closing inventory levels are the same, marginal costing and absorption costing will report the same profit figure.

The first statement is incorrect because a positive contribution will not always show a profit under either costing system. The level of reported profit will depend on the magnitude of fixed overheads.

The remaining statements can be assessed using the following rules:

- If inventory levels increase, absorption costing profit is higher than marginal costing profit (because of the fixed overhead carried forward in inventory).

- If inventory levels decrease, absorption costing profit is lower than marginal costing profit (because of the fixed overhead 'released' from inventory).

- If inventory levels remain the same then both costing systems will report the same profit figure.

8   The marginal costing profit for the period would have been £44,800.

WORKING

	£
Actual fixed production overhead	42,000
Over absorbed overhead	6,000
Absorbed fixed production overhead	48,000

$$\text{Therefore absorption rate per unit} = \frac{£48,000}{6,000} = £8 \text{ per unit}$$

Inventory decrease = 7,100 units – 6,000 units = 1,100 units

	£
Absorption costing profit	36,000
Profit difference (1,100 units × £8)	8,800
Marginal costing profit	44,800

9   B

Fixed costs per unit	= £16/4 = £4
Units in closing inventory	= 17,500 – 15,000 = 2,500 units
Profit difference	= Inventory increase in units × Fixed overhead per unit
	= 2,500 × £4 = £10,000

Inventories increased, therefore fixed overhead would have been carried forward in inventory using absorption costing and the profit would be higher than with marginal costing.

10   B

Inventory levels increased by 3,000 units and absorption costing profit is £105,000 higher (£955,500 – £850,500).

Therefore fixed production cost included in inventory increase = £105,000/3,000 = £35 per unit of inventory.

$$\frac{\text{Budgeted fixed costs}}{\text{Fixed cost per unit}} = \frac{£1,837,500}{35} = 52,500 \text{ units}$$

CHAPTER 5

Pricing calculations

Introduction
Examination context
Topic List
1   Full cost-plus pricing
2   Marginal cost-plus pricing
3   Mark-ups and margins
4   Transfer pricing
Summary and Self-test
Answers to Interactive questions
Answers to Self-test

Learning objectives

- Calculate the sales price for a given product or service using cost based pricing

- Calculate transfer prices for specified sales to internal customers which take account of appropriate costs

The specific syllabus references for this chapter are: 1e, f.

Syllabus links

An understanding of the use of cost information as a basis for pricing decisions will underpin your studies of strategic choice within the Business Strategy syllabus.

Examination context

20% of the marks in the examination will be allocated in one scenario-based question. Specific topics from this chapter that may be examined in this form include mark-ups and margins.

You may also be examined on the contents of this chapter by multiple choice, multi-part multiple choice or multiple response questions.

Pricing decisions could feature as a narrative question or as a calculation question.

The content of this chapter is deceptively straight forward. A thorough knowledge of this, and earlier topics such as fixed and variable costs, is required to answer questions in this area.

In the examination, candidates may be required to:

- Calculate a selling price using full cost-plus pricing

- Calculate a selling price using marginal cost-plus pricing

- Demonstrate an understanding of the difference between mark-up and margin and of the relationship between them

- Derive the mark up percentage that will achieve a desired return on the investment in a product

- Calculate a transfer price that will achieve profit maximisation and encourage an alignment of the goals of groups or individuals with the goals of the organisation as a whole

1 Full cost-plus pricing

Section overview

- In full cost-plus pricing the sales price is determined by calculating the full cost of the product or service and then adding a percentage mark-up for profit.

- The full cost may be a fully absorbed production cost only, or it may include some absorbed selling, distribution and administration overheads. In the former case the mark-up on costs must be greater in order to recover the other costs.

- The most important criticism of full cost-plus pricing is that it fails to recognise that since sales demand may be determined by the sales price, there will be a profit-maximising combination of price and demand.

1.1 Cost-plus pricing

In practice cost is one of the most important influences on price. While in economic theory it is possible to set a sales price that will maximise profit, in reality there is a **lack of precise information** about cost behaviour patterns and the effect of price on sales demand.

This will lead some organisations to base their selling price decision on simple cost-plus rules, whereby costs are estimated and then a percentage mark-up is added in order to set the price.

1.2 Setting full cost-plus prices

The full cost may be a fully absorbed production cost only, or it may include some absorbed selling, distribution and administration overhead.

Therefore there are two options for calculating a full cost-plus price.

Option 1

Unit sales price = Total production cost per unit + Percentage mark-up

Option 2

Unit sales price = Total production cost per unit + Other costs* per unit + Percentage mark-up

*Other costs include selling, distribution and administration costs

Clearly, to achieve the **same** sales price, the mark-up on cost must be greater under Option 1 than under Option 2 in order to recover the other costs.

Worked example: Calculating a cost-plus selling price

XY Ltd has begun to produce product S, for which the following cost estimates have been prepared.

	£ per unit
Variable materials	14.00
Variable labour at £12 per hour	54.00
Variable production overheads at £3 per hour	13.50
Variable production cost per unit	81.50

Fixed production overheads are budgeted to be £69,000 each period. The overhead absorption rate will be based on 17,250 budgeted direct labour hours each period.

The company wishes to add 20 per cent to the full production cost in order to determine the selling price per unit for product S.

C H A P T E R

5

Step 1

Calculate the fixed production overhead absorption rate.

Overhead absorption rate $= \dfrac{£69,000}{17,250}$

$= £4$ per direct labour hour

Step 2

Calculate the full production cost per unit.

Direct labour hours per unit = £54/£12 = 4.5 hours

	£ per unit
Variable production cost per unit	81.50
Fixed production overhead absorbed (4.5 hours × £4)	18.00
Full production cost per unit	99.50

Step 3

Add the required mark-up to determine the selling price.

	£ per unit
Full production cost per unit	99.50
Mark-up 20%	19.90
Full cost-plus selling price	119.40

Interactive question 1: Adjusting the mark-up percentage   [Difficulty level: Intermediate]

The full cost of providing a service is £40 per hour and its selling price is currently determined as full cost plus 60%. In each of the following separate situations, calculate the required profit mark-up percentage.

Situation	Write your answer here %
1 A competitor launches a similar service for £60 per hour. In order to sell the service at the same price as the competitor the percentage mark-up must be reduced to:	
2 The full cost of providing the service increases to £50 per hour. The required mark-up percentage to achieve the same absolute value of mark-up per hour of service provided is:	

See **Answer** at the end of this chapter.

1.3   Determining the mark-up percentage

A business may have an idea of the percentage profit mark-up it would like to earn, and so may decide on an average profit mark-up as a general guide for pricing decisions. This would be particularly useful for businesses that carry out a large amount of contract or jobbing work, for which individual job or contract prices must be quoted regularly to prospective customers.

However, **the percentage profit mark-up does not have to be rigid and fixed.** It can be varied to suit the circumstances. In particular, the percentage mark-up can be varied to suit anticipated supply and demand conditions in the market.

1.4 Determining the mark-up to achieve a required return on investment

A business might calculate the mark-up percentage for a product in order to achieve a required return on the investment in the product.

Worked example: Pricing to generate a return on investment

ZZ Ltd requires an annual return of 30% on the investment in all of its products. In the forthcoming year £800,000 will be invested in non-current assets and working capital to produce and sell 50,000 units of product Z. The full cost per unit of product Z is £100.

The annual return required on the investment in product Z   = £800,000 × 30%

                                    = £240,000

Total cost to be incurred on product Z = 50,000 units × £100 = £5,000,000

Mark-up as a percentage of full cost = (£240,000/£5,000,000) × 100% = 4.8%

The selling price can now be calculated as follows.

	£ per unit
Full cost	100.00
Mark-up 4.8%	4.80
Selling price of product Z	104.80

1.5 Allowing for inflation when setting selling prices

We have seen that the mark-up added to total cost must be sufficient to earn the required profit, or in the case of adding a mark-up to total production cost, the mark-up must be sufficient to recover all non-production costs in addition to earning the required profit.

Therefore managers must **estimate costs as accurately as possible** and must decide whether to include allowances for anticipated inflation. Even if some sort of allowance is added for inflation the **seller bears the risk of inflation when a selling price is determined prior to delivery of the goods or services**.

However, if the buyer agrees to prices based on actual cost incurred plus a profit mark-up then all of the cost increases caused by inflation can be passed to the buyer. Thus all of the inflation risk is borne by the buyer. The following points about this pricing policy should be noted.

- The buyer is likely to require **some form of assurance that costs are adequately controlled**. Otherwise the supplier's cost inefficiencies will be passed directly to the buyer and there is no incentive for the supplier to control costs. The principle of '**Open Book Accounting**' can be introduced, where the buyer is given open access to the cost information contained in the accounts of the seller.

- Moreover the supplier actually has an **incentive to overspend**, since all costs will be passed to the buyer and a profit mark-up will also be earned on all expenditure by the supplier.

- If a credit period is offered to the buyer then **the supplier will bear the inflation risk from the date that the final price is agreed until payment is received from the customer**. However in low inflation economies this additional inflation risk is likely to be acceptable to a supplier.

1.6 Advantages and disadvantages of full cost-plus pricing

The advantages of full cost-plus pricing are as follows.

- The price is **quick and easy to calculate**.
- **Pricing decisions can be delegated** to more junior employees. This is particularly important with jobbing work where many prices must be established and quoted each day.
- A price in excess of full cost should ensure that **an organisation working at normal capacity will cover all its costs**.

- **Price increases can be justified** as costs rise.

However full cost-plus pricing does have a number of disadvantages.

- It fails to recognise that since **demand may be determining price**, there will be a **profit-maximising** combination of price and demand.

- It **reduces incentives to control costs**.

- It requires **arbitrary absorption of overheads** into product costs.

- If full cost-plus pricing is applied strictly the organisation may be caught in a vicious circle like the one shown in Figure 5.1.

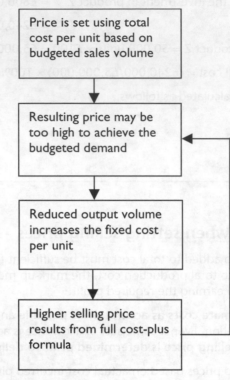

Figure 5.1: Application of cost-plus pricing

2 Marginal cost-plus pricing

Section overview

- Marginal cost-plus pricing involves adding a profit mark-up to the marginal or variable cost of production or sales.

- The chief advantage of marginal cost-plus pricing is that it avoids the arbitrary apportionment and absorption of fixed costs.

2.1 Setting marginal cost-plus prices

Marginal cost-plus pricing is a method of determining sales prices whereby a profit mark-up is added to either the marginal cost of production or the marginal cost of sales.

In practice, marginal cost-plus pricing is used in businesses where there is a readily identifiable basic variable cost. The most obvious example is retail organisations, where the price of goods in shops is often determined by adding a mark-up to the purchase price of the item.

Worked example: Calculating a marginal cost-plus price

Product Y incurs direct variable production costs of £7 per unit. Fixed production costs amount to £17,900 each period.

Variable selling and distribution costs are £3.80 per unit and fixed selling, distribution and administration costs amount to £24,800 each period.

Selling prices are determined on a marginal cost-plus basis, using a mark-up of 30% of the marginal cost of sales.

Calculate the selling price per unit of product Y and the profit that will result from sales of 26,800 units each period.

Step 1
Calculate the total marginal or variable cost of sales per unit.

	£ per unit
Variable production cost	7.00
Variable selling and distribution cost	3.80
Total marginal cost	10.80

Step 2
Add the required mark-up to determine the selling price.

	£ per unit
Total marginal cost	10.80
Mark-up 30%	3.24
Marginal cost-plus selling price	14.04

Step 3
Determine the total contribution and deduct the fixed costs to derive the period profit.

The mark-up per unit is the same as the contribution earned per unit. It contributes towards the fixed costs and profit for the period.

	£	£
Total mark-up/contribution (26,800 × £3.24)		86,832
Less fixed costs:		
Production	17,900	
Selling, distribution and administration	24,800	
		42,700
Profit		44,132

2.2 Advantages and disadvantages of marginal cost-plus pricing

The advantages of marginal cost-plus pricing are as follows.

- It is a **simple method to use**.

- It **avoids the arbitrary apportionment and absorption of fixed costs** that is necessary with absorption costing.

- It is **more useful than total cost-plus pricing for short-term management decision making**. This is because it draws management's attention to contribution and the effect on profit of higher or lower sales volumes. The level of contribution will vary in direct proportion to the sales volume.

The disadvantages of marginal cost-plus pricing are as follows.

- The **full costs might not be recovered in the long term**.

- Although the size of the mark-up can be varied in accordance with demand conditions, the pricing method **does not ensure that sufficient attention is paid to demand conditions, competitors' prices or profit maximisation**.

3 Mark-ups and margins

Section overview

- The mark-up is the profit expressed as a percentage of the marginal cost, total production cost or total cost.

- The margin is the profit expressed as a percentage of the sales price.

3.1 The difference between mark-up and margin

When sales prices are being determined on a cost-plus basis it is extremely important to be clear about whether the profit to be added to unit costs is calculated as a percentage of costs or as a percentage of selling price.

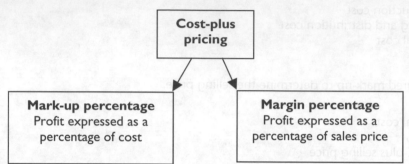

Figure 5.2: Mark-up percentage v margin percentage

Worked example: The difference between mark-up and margin

Product Q incurs a total cost of £80 per unit and its selling price is set at £100 per unit.

The mark-up applied to product Q	= (£20/£80) × 100% = 25% of total cost
The margin earned by product Q	= (£20/£100) × 100% = 20% of sales price

Interactive question 2: Mark-ups and margins   [Difficulty level: Intermediate]

Question	Write your answer here
1 If the full cost is £14 per unit, calculate the price to achieve a margin of 20% of the selling price.	
2 The selling price is £27 per unit, determined on the basis of full cost-plus. If the full cost is £18 per unit, calculate the mark-up percentage.	
3 A selling price of £165 per unit earns a mark-up of 106.25% of the full cost. What is the full cost per unit?	
4 A product's selling price is determined by adding 33.33% to its full cost. What percentage margin on sales price does this represent?	

See **Answer** at the end of this chapter.

ICAEW

4 Transfer pricing

Section overview

- A transfer price is the amount charged by one part of an organisation for the provision of goods or services to another part of the same organisation.

- A transfer pricing system has a number of aims, which may conflict with each other.

- Inappropriate transfer prices may lead to sub-optimal decisions and a lack of alignment of corporate goals (called goal congruence).

- In a perfectly competitive market the optimum transfer price is the market price. This should be reduced for savings in costs that are not incurred on internal transfers, such as distribution costs, advertising and marketing costs, and bad debts.

- A problem with cost-plus pricing is that the receiving division will perceive the transfer price to be a wholly variable cost, whereas it includes some costs which are fixed from the point of view of the company as a whole. This could lead to sub-optimal decision making.

- With two part transfer prices, all transfers are charged at a predetermined standard variable cost. A periodic charge for fixed costs would also be made by the supplying division to the receiving division.

- In a dual pricing system the receiving division is charged with the standard variable cost of all transfers. The supplying division is credited with the market value or a cost-plus price in order to provide a profit incentive to make the transfer.

4.1 What is a transfer price?

Transfer pricing is used when divisions of an organisation need to charge other divisions of the same organisation for goods or services that they provide to them. For example, subsidiary A might manufacture a component that is used as part of a product made by subsidiary B of the same company. The component can also be bought on or sold to the external market. Therefore there will be two sources of revenue for subsidiary A.

- External sales revenue from sales made to other organisations.
- Internal sales revenue from the transfer prices charged for components supplied to subsidiary B.

4.2 Aims of a transfer pricing system

- To enable the **realistic measurement of divisional profit**.

- To provide the supplier with a realistic profit and the receiver with a realistic cost.

- To give **autonomy** to managers.

- To **encourage goal congruence**, whereby individual managers' own goals are the same as the goals of the company as a whole.

- To ensure **profit maximisation** for the company as a whole.

It may be difficult to reconcile all of these aims.

CHAPTER

5

4.3 Practical methods of transfer pricing

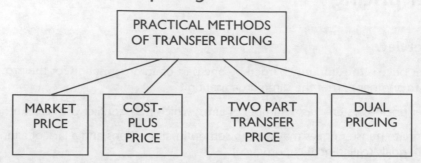

Figure 5.3: Practical methods of transfer pricing

4.3.1 Market price

If a perfectly competitive market exists for a product, then the **external market price is the optimum transfer price if the supplying division is operating at full capacity**.

The market price should be adjusted for savings in certain costs that may not be incurred on internal transfers, such as:

- Packaging costs
- Advertising costs
- Distribution costs
- Bad debts

Care must be taken to ensure that the division's product is the same as that offered by the external market (for example in terms of quality, delivery terms etc).

Using market price can, however, lead to problems. Interactive question 3 illustrates this.

Interactive question 3: Using market value as the transfer price

[Difficulty level: Intermediate]

	Division A £ per unit	Division B £ per unit
Variable cost	10	15
Transfer price at market value	–	20
Fixed costs	5	10
Profit	5	25
Transfer price/selling price	20	70

Division A can sell externally at £20 per unit or transfer internally to Division B at £20 per unit.

Division B receives an offer from a customer of £30 per unit for its final product.

Requirements

(a) Would Division B accept the offer of £30 per unit given the existing transfer price?

Yes ☐   No ☐

(b) Is this the correct decision from the company's point of view if:

(i) Division A has surplus capacity?

Yes ☐   No ☐

(ii) Division A is operating at full capacity?

Yes ☐   No ☐

See **Answer** at the end of this chapter.

4.3.2 A cost-plus approach to transfer pricing

This transfer pricing method works in the same way as cost-plus pricing, discussed earlier in this chapter. The supplying division determines the transfer price by adding a profit mark-up to the cost of the product or service. Some form of cost-based transfer pricing method will usually be necessary where there is no external market for the product or service. A number of issues arise with this transfer pricing method.

- **A pre-determined standard cost should be used rather than actual cost**. A standard cost is a predetermined unit cost which is calculated by taking account of the expected price and usage of resources to produce one unit of product or service. If standard costs are not used then all efficiencies and inefficiencies are transferred from one division to another and divisional profit measurement is distorted.

- **To ensure that overheads are recovered the supplying division will wish to base the transfer price on total cost**. However, the supplying division's fixed costs will then be perceived as variable costs from the point of view of the receiving division. This could lead to sub-optimal decisions.

Worked example: Sub-optimal decision making

A company has two divisions, S and R. Both divisions manufacture multiple products. Division S transfers its output of component C to division R at full cost plus 10%. Division R then incurs further costs to convert component C into finished product P for sale on the external market at £40 per unit.

Costs incurred are as follows.

	Division S £ per unit	Division R £ per unit
Variable cost	20	15
Fixed cost absorbed	10	
Full cost	30	

Requirements

Would the transfers be recommended from the point of view of:

(a) The company as a whole?
(b) The manager of division R?

Solution

(a) The transfers would be recommended from the point of view of the company as a whole.

The variable cost incurred by the company as a whole for each unit of product P is £35.

	£ per unit
Variable cost – Division S	20
– Division R	15
	35

The fixed costs are irrelevant to this analysis because they would be incurred even if the transfers are not made.

Therefore from the point of view of the company as a whole the transfers are worthwhile because product P earns a contribution of £5 per unit (£40 – £35).

(b) The transfers would not be recommended from the point of view of the manager of division R.

Transfer price per unit of component C = £30 + 10% = £33

The manager of division R would view the transfer price of component C as a variable cost, since it is an additional cost incurred by division R for every unit of product P manufactured.

Therefore, from the point of view of the manager of division R the variable cost of each unit of product P is £48.

	£ per unit
Variable cost – Component C (perceived variable cost)	33
– Additional cost incurred	15
	48

Division R would not recommend the transfer of component C and the manufacture of product P since the division would record a negative contribution of £8 for each unit manufactured.

	£ per unit of P
External market price	40
Division R perceived variable cost	(48)
Contribution	(8)

In this example the use of a full cost-plus transfer price has led to sub-optimal decision making. There is a lack of goal congruence because the manager of division R, in pursuing the division's own goals, was not at the same time automatically pursuing the goals of the company as a whole.

In the situation depicted in Interactive question 3 (b)(i) there was also a lack of goal congruence. The divisional manager's own goals were not congruent with those of the company as a whole. The transfer pricing system was leading the manager of division B to make a sub-optimal decision from the point of view of the company as a whole when division A had spare capacity.

4.3.3 Two part transfer price

To avoid the sub-optimal decisions that may occur when the fixed costs of one division are perceived as variable costs by another division, a two part transfer price might be used.

Transfers are charged at a predetermined standard variable cost. A periodic charge for fixed costs would also be made by the supplying division to the receiving division.

This helps to ensure goal congruence, since the receiving division would be fully aware of the cost behaviour patterns of the company as a whole.

4.3.4 Dual pricing

In dual pricing the supplying division is credited with a different price from that which is charged to the receiving division.

This transfer pricing method charges the receiving division for all transfers at variable or marginal cost. This may lead to improved decision making.

The supplying division is credited with the market value or with a cost-plus transfer price in order to provide a profit incentive to make the transfer.

The dual pricing method can be effective in avoiding sub-optimal decisions but it can be administratively cumbersome.

Summary

Pricing calculations

```
                    Pricing calculations
        ┌───────────────────┼─────────────────────────┐
  Full cost-          Marginal cost-            Transfer pricing
  plus pricing        plus pricing              for internal sales
        │                                 ┌────────┬────────┬────────┐
  Based on total                      Market    Cost-    Two      Dual
  cost or on                          price     plus     part     pricing
  total production                              price    price
  cost                                    │                │
        │                              Optimal price    Fixed and
        │                              in perfectly     variable
        │                              competitive      charges
        │                              market           separated
  ┌──────────────┐   ┌──────────────┐
  Mark-up            Margin              May lead to
  percentage         percentage          sub-optimal
  Profit expressed   Profit expressed    decisions
  as a percentage    as a percentage
  of cost            of sales price
        │                                                 Different
  Mark-up may                                             price used
  be derived to                                           for receiving
  earn a required                                         and supplying
  return on                                               division
  investment
```

Self-test

Answer the following questions.

1 The following variable costs are incurred producing each unit of product F.

	£ per unit
Variable material	8.00
Variable labour at £14 per hour	42.00

Variable production overheads are incurred at the rate of £4 per hour. Fixed production overheads of £60,000 are absorbed on the basis of 25,000 budgeted direct labour hours. Other overheads are recovered at five percent of total production cost.

If selling prices are set to recover the full cost plus 50% the selling price per unit of product F is:

A £72.66
B £99.62
C £103.80
D £108.99

2 The marginal cost per unit of a product is 70% of its full cost. Selling prices are set on a full cost-plus basis using a mark-up of 40 percent of full cost.

Which percentage mark-up on marginal cost would produce the same selling price as the full cost-plus basis described?

A 70%
B 90%
C 100%
D 200%

3 Jay operates a car valeting service and charges £16 per car. He incurs a total cost of £10 per car valeted.

Calculate the mark-up and margin earned per car valeted.

Mark-up   % [   ]

Margin   % [   ]

4 Which of the following statements is correct?

A A full cost-plus sales price will always be higher than a marginal cost-plus sales price

B If the selling price is agreed at the point of sale then the seller bears the inflation risk during any credit period offered to the buyer

C A selling price in excess of the full cost per unit will always result in an overall profit for the organisation

D A cost-plus selling price takes account of the effect of price on the quantity demanded

5 A company requires a 20% annual return on the investment in product F.

The budgeted investment in non-current assets and working capital for product F for the next year is £90,000. The full cost per unit of product F is £5.00 and budgeted production and sales for next year is 36,000 units.

The profit margin as a percentage of the sales price of product F is:

A 9.1%
B 10.0%
C 20.0%
D 50.0%

6   When goods are transferred from division A to division B a charge is made to division B at standard variable cost. Each quarter division B is also charged with a lump-sum as a share of A's fixed costs. This type of transfer pricing system is a:

    A   Marginal cost-plus system
    B   Dual pricing system
    C   Two part transfer pricing system
    D   Standard cost transfer pricing system

7   Which TWO of the following are advantages of marginal cost-plus pricing?

    A   It is simple to use
    B   The percentage mark-up can be varied
    C   It pays attention to profit maximisation
    D   It ignores fixed overheads in the pricing decision

8   Division U makes components which it sells to external customers at a price of £24 per unit, earning a mark-up of 20% of total cost. Variable costs account for 40% of Division U's total cost.

Division U also transfers components at market value to Division V within the same company. Division V incurs additional total costs of £8 per unit to convert and pack the component for international sales. Variable costs account for 70% of Division V's total cost.

Both divisions currently have surplus capacity.

Division V has an opportunity to sell a batch of components to a customer for £15 per unit.

Which of the following statements is correct with regard to this potential order?

    A   The order is not acceptable from the company's point of view and the manager of division V will make a sub-optimal decision

    B   The order is not acceptable from the company's point of view and the manager of division V will not make a sub-optimal decision

    C   The order is acceptable from the company's point of view and the manager of division V will make a sub-optimal decision

    D   The order is acceptable from the company's point of view and the manager of division V will not make a sub-optimal decision

9   Division M manufactures product R incurring a total cost of £30 per unit. Fixed costs represent 40% of the total unit cost.

Product R is sold to external customers in a perfectly competitive market at a price of £50 per unit. Division M also transfers product R to division N. If transfers are made internally then division M does not incur variable distribution costs, which amount to 10% of the variable costs incurred on external sales.

The total demand for product R exceeds the capacity of division M.

From the point of view of the company as a whole, enter the optimum price per unit at which division M should transfer product R to division N.

Transfer price per unit = £ ☐

10   The following data relate to the Columba group, a company with several divisions. Division D produces a single product, which it sells to Division R and also to organisations outside the Columba group.

	Division D sales to Division R £	Division D external sales £
Sales revenue at £70 per unit		700,000
Sales revenue at £60 per unit	300,000	
Variable costs at £36 per unit	(180,000)	(360,000)
Contribution	120,000	340,000
Fixed costs	(100,000)	(240,000)
Profit	20,000	100,000

The Columba group profit is £550,000.

A supplier offers to supply 3,000 units at £50 each to Division R.

Divisional managers of Columba are given freedom of choice for selling and buying decisions, and their performance is judged solely according to divisional profitability.

Calculate the profit for Division D and for Columba if Division D does not match the lower price offered by the external supplier and cannot increase its external sales, and Division R chooses to purchase from the external supplier.

Now go back to the Learning Objectives in the Introduction. If you are satisfied you have achieved these objectives, please tick them off.

Answers to Interactive questions

Answer to Interactive question 1

Situation	Write your answer here %
1 A competitor launches a similar service for £60 per hour. In order to sell the service at the same price as the competitor the percentage mark-up must be reduced to:	50%
2 The full cost of providing the service increases to £50 per hour. The required mark-up percentage to achieve the same absolute value of mark-up per hour of service provided is:	48%

WORKINGS

Situation 1

Absolute mark-up per hour of service sold = £(60 – 40) = £20

Mark-up percentage = (20/40) × 100% = 50%

Situation 2

Current absolute value of mark-up per hour of service sold = 60% × £40 = £24

Mark-up percentage required = (£24/£50) × 100% = 48%

Answer to Interactive question 2

Question	Write your answer here
1 If the full cost is £14 per unit, calculate the price to achieve a margin of 20% of the selling price.	£17.50
2 The selling price is £27 per unit, determined on the basis of full cost-plus. If the full cost is £18 per unit, calculate the mark-up percentage.	50%
3 A selling price of £165 per unit earns a mark-up of 106.25% of the full cost. What is the full cost per unit?	£80
4 A product's selling price is determined by adding 33.33% to its full cost. What percentage margin on sales price does this represent?	25%

WORKINGS

(1) Cost and selling price structure:

	%
Cost	80
Profit	20
Price	100

∴ Price = 100/80 × £14 = £17.50 per unit

(2) Profit per unit = £27 – £18 = £9

Mark-up percentage = £9/£18 = 50% of full cost

(3) Cost and selling price structure:

	%
Cost	100.00
Profit	106.25
Price	206.25

∴ Full cost = (100.00/206.25) × £165 = £80 per unit

(4) Cost and selling price structure:

	%
Cost	100.00
Profit	33.33
Price	133.33

Percentage margin on sales price = (33.33/133.33) × 100% = 25%

Answer to Interactive question 3

(a) No

Division B would reject the offer as there is a negative contribution of –£5 (£30 – £20 transfer price – £15 variable cost).

(b) (i) No

If division A has surplus capacity then no full-price external sales would be forgone as a result of transferring an additional unit to division B. Since the fixed costs are an arbitrary apportionment of costs that would be incurred anyway, the only marginal cost to be incurred within division A to provide another unit to B is £10 per unit.

From the point of view of the company as a whole, all the apportioned fixed costs can be ignored because they will be incurred anyway. The sale of a unit from B to a customer for £30 would earn a contribution of £5 as follows.

£30 – £10 variable cost in A – £15 variable cost in B = £5

Therefore division B's decision to reject the offer of £30 per unit would not be the correct decision from the company's point of view if division A has surplus capacity.

(ii) Yes

If division A is operating at full capacity then the transfer of an additional unit to division B would mean that a full price external sale at £20 per unit is displaced, thus forgoing contribution of:

£10 (£20 – £10 variable cost)

Therefore from the point of view of the company as a whole, the sale of a unit from B to a customer for £30 would generate a negative contribution of – £5 as follows.

	£ per unit
Selling price	30
Variable cost in division A	(10)
Forgone contribution in division A	(10)
Variable cost in division B	(15)
Contribution	(5)

Therefore division B's decision to reject the offer of £30 per unit would be the correct decision from the company's point of view if division A is operating at full capacity. In this situation there would be goal congruence and the manager of division B would not make a sub-optimal decision.

1   D

WORKINGS

Labour hours per unit = £42/£14 = 3 hours

Fixed production overhead absorption rate   = £60,000/25,000

                                             = £2.40 per hour

	£ per unit
Variable material	8.00
Variable labour	42.00
Variable production overhead (3 hrs at £4)	12.00
Fixed production overhead (3 hrs at £2.40)	7.20
Total production cost	69.20
Other overhead at 5%	3.46
Full cost	72.66
Mark-up at 50%	36.33
Selling price	108.99

2   C

WORKINGS

	%
Marginal cost	70
Absorbed fixed cost	30
Full cost	100
Mark-up	40
Selling price	140

Required mark up on marginal cost $= \dfrac{(30 + 40)}{70} \times 100\%$

$= 100\%$

3   Mark-up   = 60.0%

    Margin   = 37.5%

WORKINGS

Mark-up % $= \dfrac{£(16-10)}{£10} \times 100\%$

$= 60.0\%$

Margin % $= \dfrac{£(16-10)}{£16} \times 100\%$

$= 37.5\%$

4   B

A is incorrect because both prices will depend on the mark-up percentage that is added to cost. If a very large mark-up percentage is added to marginal cost then a higher selling price may result than with a full-cost plus sales price.

C is incorrect because the full cost includes fixed costs per unit which have been derived based on estimated or budgeted sales volumes. If the budgeted volumes are not achieved then the actual fixed cost per unit will be higher than estimated and the selling price might be lower than the actual cost per unit.

D is incorrect because one of the major criticisms of cost-plus pricing is that it fails to recognise that sales demand may be determined by the sales price.

5 A

WORKINGS

Required annual return from product F	= £90,000 × 20%
	= £18,000
Total cost incurred = 36,000 × £5	= £180,000
∴ Required percentage mark-up on cost	= (£18,000/£180,000) × 100%
	= 10%
Product F selling price	= £5 + 10%
	= £5.50
Profit margin as a percentage of sales price	= (£0.50/£5.50) × 100%
	= 9.1%

6 C A marginal cost-plus system would involve adding a percentage to marginal cost in order to provide the selling division with a contribution towards its fixed costs and profit.

A dual pricing system operates by charging the buying division for transfers at marginal cost and crediting the selling division with either the market value or with a cost-plus transfer price.

The description of a standard cost transfer pricing system is imprecise because it does not specify whether marginal or full cost is used.

7 A,B The method is simple to use and the mark-up can be adjusted to reflect demand conditions.

Option C is not an advantage. Although the size of the mark-up can be varied in accordance with demand conditions, it is not a method of pricing which ensures that sufficient attention is paid to demand conditions, competitors' prices and profit maximisation.

Option D is not an advantage. Although there is no arbitrary apportionment and absorption of fixed overheads, these costs are not ignored. They are taken into account in ensuring that the mark-up is large enough to make a profit after covering fixed costs.

8 C Since both divisions have surplus capacity no full-price sales will be forgone as a result of accepting this order. The fixed costs will not alter, therefore provided the order covers the variable costs and earns a contribution it will be acceptable.

Division U total cost = 100/120 × £24 = £20 per unit
Division U variable cost = 40% × £20 = £8

From the point of view of the company as a whole:

	£ per unit	£ per unit
Sales price per component		15.00
Variable cost incurred:		
Division U	8.00	
Division V (£8 × 70%)	5.60	
		13.60
Contribution		1.40

The order earns a contribution therefore it is acceptable from the company's point of view.

From the point of view of Division V:

	£ per unit	£ per unit
Sales price per component		15.00
Variable cost incurred:		
Transfer price	24.00	
Own variable cost	5.60	
		(29.60)
Negative contribution		(14.60)

The manager of Division V will perceive the transfer price to be a variable cost which is incurred for each component sold. Therefore, this order will not be accepted. The decision will be sub-optimal because the profit of the company as a whole will not be maximised.

9   Transfer price per unit = £48.20

The total demand for product R exceeds the capacity of division M therefore internal transfers will displace external sales. The optimum transfer price can be calculated as follows.

Optimum transfer price = External market price – Cost savings with internal transfer

Cost savings with internal transfer = 10% × Variable costs

Fixed costs represent 40% of the total unit cost therefore variable costs are equal to 60% of the total unit cost.

Cost savings with internal transfer	= 10% × (£30 × 60%)
	= £1.80
∴ Optimum transfer price	= £50 – £1.80
	= £48.20

10 The correct answer is profit for Division D = £48,000; profit for Columba Group = £508,000

Division R will buy the 3,000 units externally at a price of £50 per unit, leaving it with only 2,000 units to buy from Division D at £60 per unit.

Profits of Division D

	£'000
Contribution from external sales	340
Contribution from sales to Division R	48
	388
Fixed costs	340
Profit	48

The group as a whole will be paying £(50 – 36) = £14 per unit extra for each unit that Division R purchases externally, thus reducing Columba's profits by 3,000 × £14 = £42,000.

Columba's profit will therefore reduce to £550,000 – £42,000 = £508,000.

CHAPTER 6

Budgeting

Introduction

Examination context

Topic List

1 Why do organisations prepare budgets?

2 A framework for budgeting

3 Steps in the preparation of a budget

4 The master budget

5 Preparing forecasts

6 Alternative approaches to budgeting

Summary and Self-test

Answers to Interactive questions

Answers to Self-test

Learning objectives

- Apply forecasting techniques to assist management in performance measurement and planning

- Prepare budgets, or extracts therefrom, from information supplied

- Select the most appropriate of the following budgeting approaches and methods, taking into account their advantages and disadvantages for planning, control and motivation:

    - Bottom-up and top-down approaches to generating and managing budgets

    - Activity-based, responsibility-based and product-based structures

    - Zero-based and incremental budgeting

The specific syllabus references for this chapter are: 2a, b, c.

Syllabus links

You will need an understanding of how the annual budgeting exercise acts as a step towards the achievement of an organisation's longer-term plans when you study the Business Strategy syllabus.

Examination context

Numerical questions will be limited in scope (eg individual budgets). Narrative questions need to be read very carefully, particularly those that ask whether statements are true or false.

In the examination, candidates may be required to:

- Demonstrate an understanding of the

    - Objectives of a budgetary planning and control system
    - Difference between a budget and a forecast
    - Administrative process of budget preparation

- Prepare functional budgets and the income statement and balance sheet elements of a master budget from data supplied

- Calculate the effect on budget outcomes of changes in specified variables

- Demonstrate an understanding of a range of budgeting approaches and methods

1 Why do organisations prepare budgets?

Section overview

- An organisation's budgets fulfil many roles.

- A forecast is a prediction of what is likely to happen, whereas a budget is a plan of what the organisation intends should happen.

- To be useful for planning and control purposes a budget must be quantified, but not necessarily only in financial terms.

1.1 Reasons for preparing budgets

An organisation's budget fulfils many roles. Here are some of the reasons why budgets are used.

Function	Detail
Compel planning	Budgeting forces management to look ahead, to set out detailed plans for achieving the targets for each department, each operation and (ideally) each manager and to anticipate problems.
Communicate ideas and plans	A formal system is necessary to ensure that each person affected by the plans is aware of what he or she is supposed to be doing. Communication might be one-way, with managers giving orders to subordinates, or there might be two-way communication.
Coordinate activities	The activities of different departments need to be coordinated to ensure everyone in an organisation is working towards the same goals. This means, for example, that the purchasing department should base its budget on production requirements and that the production budget should in turn be based on sales expectations.
Means of allocating resources	It can be used to decide how many resources are needed (cash, labour and so on) and how many should be given to each area of the organisation's activities. Resource allocation is particularly important when some resources are in short supply. Budgets often set ceilings or limits on how much administrative departments and other service departments are allowed to spend in the period. Public expenditure budgets, for example, set spending limits for each government department or other public body.
Authorisation	A formal budget delegates authority to budget holders to take action and, within specified control limits, to incur expenditure on the organisation's behalf.
Provide a framework for responsibility accounting	Budgets require that managers are made responsible for the achievement of budget targets for the operations under their personal control.
Establish a system of control	Control over actual performance is provided by the comparison of actual results against the budget plan. Departures from budget can then be investigated and the reasons can be divided into controllable and uncontrollable factors.
Provide a means of performance evaluation	Budgets provide targets that can be compared with actual outcomes in order to assess employee performance. They also provide a means to establish a personal incentive and bonus scheme.
Motivate employees to improve their performance	The interest and commitment of employees can be retained if there is a system that lets them know how well or badly they are performing. The budget can act as a target for achievement, and the identification of controllable reasons for departures from budget with managers responsible provides an incentive for improving future performance.

1.2 Budgets compared with forecasts

A forecast is a prediction of what is likely to happen in the future, given a certain set of circumstances. This is different from a budget, which is a quantified plan of what the organisation intends should happen in the future.

The budget is based on the forecast, therefore the two are connected, but they are not the same thing. Measures might be taken to ensure that budgeted targets are achieved, thus a budget forces management into decision-making and taking action. For example, a gap between forecast sales revenue and the sales budget could force sales promotions or an increase in advertising.

1.3 Quantified budgets

To fulfil the range of purposes for which it is prepared, **a budget must be quantified**. For example, the following two statements would not be particularly useful for planning and control purposes.

> 'We plan to utilise fully all the available hours of semi-skilled labour next period.'
>
> 'We plan to minimise expenditure on advertising next period.'

Without quantification these are merely general statements of purpose. The following quantified budgets are more useful for planning and control.

> 'We plan to utilise 24,800 hours of semi-skilled labour next period.'
>
> 'We plan to spend £107,000 on advertising next period.'

These budgets provide **definite plans**, as well as **yardsticks for control purposes**. Notice that the labour hours budget is not expressed in financial terms. It still fulfils the role of a budget because it is quantified. Therefore a budget does not necessarily need to be expressed in financial terms. Of course the semi-skilled labour hours budgeted can be converted into a budget expressed in financial terms by applying a rate of pay per hour to the budgeted number of labour hours.

An important feature of any quantified budget is the fact that it is **time bound**. Just to say, 'We plan to spend £107,000 on advertising' without specifying a period over which this amount is to be spent would render the 'budget' useless.

2 A framework for budgeting

Section overview

- The budget committee is the coordinating body in the preparation and administration of budgets.

- The budget period is the period covered by the budget, which is usually one year. The budget is divided into a number of control periods, typically calendar months.

- The budget manual is a collection of instructions relating to the preparation and use of budgetary data.

2.1 Budget committee

The budget committee is the coordinating body in the preparation and administration of budgets. The budget committee is usually headed up by the managing director (as chairman) who is assisted by a **budget officer**, who is usually the finance director or another accountant. Every part of the organisation should be represented on the committee, so there should be a representative from sales, production, marketing and so on.

Functions of the budget committee include the following.

- **Coordination and allocation of responsibility** for the preparation of budgets
- Issuing of the **budget manual**
- Timetabling
- **Provision of information** to assist in the preparation of budgets

- **Communication** of final budgets to the appropriate managers
- **Monitoring the budgeting process** by comparing actual and budgeted results

Often the budget committee is the senior management team of an organisation or the board of directors itself.

2.2 The budget period

The budget period is the period covered by the budget, which is usually one year. However, budgets can be prepared and used for longer periods, for example capital expenditure budgets. Budgets can also be prepared for shorter periods, for example in an environment where technology or other factors are rapidly changing with the result that annual budgets quickly become out of date.

In the common situation where a budget is prepared for a year it will usually be divided into monthly **control periods** so that regular comparisons can be made of the actual and budgeted results.

Some organisations divide the annual budget into 13 periods of four weeks. Others have 12 budget periods but they are not calendar months, but periods of 4, 4 and 5 weeks for each quarter of the year.

2.3 The budget manual

The **budget manual** is a collection of instructions governing the responsibilities of persons and the procedures, forms and records relating to the preparation and use of budgetary data.

A budget manual may contain the following.

(a) An explanation of the **objectives** of the budgetary process

- The purpose of budgetary planning and control
- The objectives of the various stages of the budgetary process
- The importance of budgets in the long term planning of the business

(b) **Organisational structures**

- An organisation chart
- A list of individuals holding budget responsibilities

(c) An outline of the **principal budgets** and the **relationship between them**

(d) **Administrative details** of budget preparation

- Membership and terms of reference of the budget committee
- The sequence in which budgets are to be prepared
- A timetable

(e) **Procedural matters**

- Specimen forms and instructions for their completion
- Specimen reports
- Account codes (or a chart of accounts)
- The name of the budget officer to whom enquiries must be sent

3 Steps in the preparation of a budget

Section overview

- The principal budget factor is that factor which limits an organisation's activities. The budget for the principal budget factor must be prepared first.

- If sales volume is the limiting factor then the sales budget should be prepared first.

- The production budget will then be prepared by adjusting the sales budget for planned changes in finished goods inventory.

- The next stage will be the preparation of budgets for production resources such as direct materials usage and direct labour.

- The direct materials purchases budget is prepared by adjusting the direct materials usage budget for planned changes in raw materials inventory.

- Overhead cost budgets will be prepared, taking account of the level of activity to be achieved and the support needed to be given to the 'direct' operations. A budgeted income statement can then be produced.

- A number of budgets such as the capital expenditure budget, the working capital budget and the cash budget must be prepared in order to provide the necessary information for the budgeted balance sheet.

- Standard costs provide the basic unit rates to be used in the preparation of a number of functional budgets.

The procedures for preparing a budget will differ from organisation to organisation but the steps described below will be indicative of those followed by many organisations. The preparation of a budget may take weeks or months and the **budget committee** may meet several times before the **master budget** (budgeted income statement, budgeted balance sheet and budgeted cash flow) is finally agreed. **Functional budgets** (sales budgets, production budgets, direct labour budgets and so on), which are amalgamated into the master budget, may need to be amended many times as a consequence of discussions between departments, changes in market conditions and so on during the course of budget preparation.

Ideally, a master budget should be finished prior to the start of the period to which it relates.

3.1 Identifying the principal budget factor

The budget for the principal budget factor must be prepared first. The principal budget factor is that factor which limits an organisation's activities. This factor is usually **sales demand**. A company is usually restricted from making and selling more of its products because there would be no sales demand for the increased output at a price that would be acceptable/profitable to the company. The principal budget factor may alternatively be machine capacity, distribution and selling resources, the availability of key raw materials or the availability of cash. Once this factor is defined then the remainder of the budgets can be prepared. For example, if sales are the principal budget factor then the production manager can only prepare the production budget after the sales budget is complete.

3.2 The order of budget preparation

Assuming that sales has been identified as the principal budget factor, the stages involved in the preparation of a budget for a manufacturing business can be summarised as follows.

(a) The **sales budget** is prepared in terms of units of product, unit selling price and total sales value. The **finished goods inventory budget** can be prepared at the same time. This budget decides the planned increase or decrease in finished goods inventory levels.

(b) With the information from the sales and inventory budgets, the **production budget** can be prepared. This is, in effect, the sales budget in units plus (or minus) the increase (or decrease) in finished goods inventory. The production budget will be stated in terms of units.

(c) This leads on logically to budgeting the **resources for production**. This involves preparing a **materials usage budget, machine usage budget and a labour budget**.

(d) In addition to the materials usage budget, a **materials inventory budget** will be prepared, to decide the planned increase or decrease in the level of inventory held. Once the raw materials usage requirements and the raw materials inventory budget are known, the purchasing department can prepare a **raw materials purchases budget** in quantities and value for each type of material purchased. Similarly warehousing and distribution budgets can be prepared.

(e) During the preparation of the sales and production budgets, the managers of the cost centres of the organisation will prepare draft budgets for their department **overhead costs**. Such overheads will include maintenance, stores, administration, selling and research and development.

(f) From the above information a **budgeted income statement** can be produced.

(g) In addition, several other budgets must be prepared in order to arrive at the **budgeted balance sheet**. These are the **capital expenditure budget** (for non-current assets), the **working capital budgets** (for budgeted increases or decreases in the level of receivables and accounts payable as well as inventories), and a **cash budget**.

The following diagram shows the major budgets and their inter-relationships.

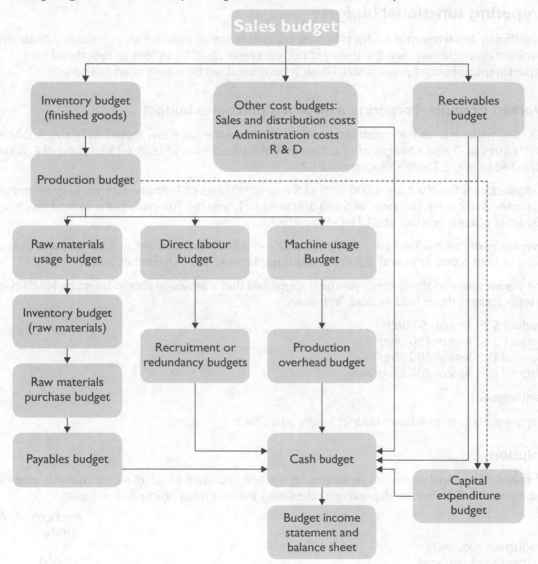

A similar flow chart could be prepared for a service based business.

Interactive question 1: The order of budget preparation   [Difficulty level: Intermediate]

For the following pairs of budgets use the table to identify, under normal circumstances, whether the first budget should be produced before or after the second or whether it does not matter. Tick **one** box for each row. Assume that sales demand is the principal budget factor.

	Before	After	Doesn't matter
Sales revenue; sales quantities	☐	☐	☐
Finished goods inventories; production volume	☐	☐	☐
Materials usage; labour hours	☐	☐	☐
Materials usage; materials purchases	☐	☐	☐

See **Answer** at the end of this chapter.

3.3   Preparing functional budgets

Functional/departmental budgets include budgets for sales, production, purchases, labour and administration. Having seen the theory of budget preparation, let us look at **functional** (or **departmental**) budget preparation, which is best explained by means of an example.

Worked example: Preparing a materials purchases budget

ECO Co manufactures two products, S and T, which use the same raw materials, D and E. One unit of S uses 3 litres of D and 4 kilograms of E. One unit of T uses 5 litres of D and 2 kilograms of E. A litre of D is expected to cost £3 and a kilogram of E £7.

Budgeted sales for 20X2 are 8,000 units of S and 6,000 units of T; finished goods in inventory at 1 January 20X2 are 1,500 units of S and 300 units of T, and the company plans to hold inventories of 600 units of each product at 31 December 20X2.

Inventories of raw material are 6,000 litres of D and 2,800 kilograms of E at 1 January and the company plans to hold 5,000 litres and 3,500 kilograms respectively at 31 December 20X2.

The warehouse and stores managers have suggested that a provision should be made for damages and deterioration of items held in store, as follows.

Product S :   loss of 50 units
Product T :   loss of 100 units
Material D :   loss of 500 litres
Material E :   loss of 200 kilograms

Requirement

Prepare a material purchases budget for the year 20X2.

Solution

To calculate material purchases requirements it is first necessary to calculate the material usage requirements. That in turn depends on calculating the budgeted production volumes.

	Product S Units	Product T Units
Production required		
To meet sales demand	8,000	6,000
To provide for inventory loss	50	100
For closing inventory	600	600
	8,650	6,700
Less inventory already in hand	(1,500)	(300)
Budgeted production volume	7,150	6,400

Material purchases budget

	Material D Litres	Material E Kgs
Usage requirements		
To produce 7,150 units of S	21,450	28,600
To produce 6,400 units of T	32,000	12,800
To provide for inventory loss	500	200
For closing inventory	5,000	3,500
	58,950	45,100
Less inventory already in hand	(6,000)	(2,800)
Budgeted material purchases	52,950	42,300
Unit cost	£3	£7
Cost of material purchases	£158,850	£296,100
Total cost of material purchases		£454,950

The basic principles for the preparation of each functional budget are similar to those above. Work carefully through the following question, which covers the preparation of a number of different types of functional budget.

Interactive question 2: Preparing functional budgets [Difficulty level: Intermediate]

XYZ company produces three products, X, Y and Z. For the coming accounting period budgets are to be prepared based on the following information.

Budgeted sales

Product X   2,000 at £100 each
Product Y   4,000 at £130 each
Product Z   3,000 at £150 each

Budgeted usage of raw material

	RM11	RM22	RM33
Product X	5	2	–
Product Y	3	2	2
Product Z	2	1	3
Cost per unit of material	£5	£3	£4

Finished inventory budget

	Product X	Product Y	Product Z
Opening	500	800	700
Closing	600	1,000	800

Raw materials inventory budget

	RM11	RM22	RM33
Opening	21,000	10,000	16,000
Closing	18,000	9,000	12,000

	Product X	Product Y	Product Z
Expected hours per unit	4	6	8
Expected hourly rate (labour)	£9	£9	£9

Fill in the blanks.

(a) Sales budget

	Product X	Product Y	Product Z	Total
Sales quantity				
Sales value	£	£	£	£

(b) Production budget

	Product X Units	Product Y Units	Product Z Units
Budgeted production	☐	☐	☐

(c) Material usage budget

	RM11 Units	RM22 Units	RM33 Units
Budgeted material usage	☐	☐	☐

(d) Material purchases budget

	RM11	RM22	RM33
Budgeted material purchases	£ ☐	£ ☐	£ ☐

(e) Labour budget

Budgeted total wages	£ ☐

See **Answer** at the end of this chapter.

3.4 The link between budgeting and standard costing

In the practical exercises in Section 3.3 involving the preparation of budgets you used data about the expected price and usage of the resources required to manufacture one unit of product in the budget. For example, to prepare the labour cost budget you were provided with information about the expected labour hours for each unit of product to be manufactured, as well as the expected rate to be paid for each hour of labour.

This information about the expected price and usage of resources is provided by a **standard costing system**. A standard cost is a **predetermined unit cost** that details the price and quantity of resources (material, labour and so on) required for each unit of product or service. This unit cost is multiplied by the budgeted activity level to determine the budgeted total cost for each of the relevant cost elements.

Thus standard costs provide the basic unit rates to be used in the preparation of a number of functional budgets. The detailed standard cost also **enables control to be exercised over actual performance**. The departures from budgets, or variances, can be analysed in detail using the standard cost information about the price and quantity of resources that should have been used for each unit of production or service.

In Chapter 8 you will study the use of budgets for control purposes, and in Chapter 9 the analysis of standard costing variances will be explored in detail.

4 The master budget

Section overview

- The master budget consists of the budgeted income statement, the budgeted balance sheet and the cash budget.

- The master budget provides a consolidation of all the subsidiary budgets and is likely to be of most interest to senior managers and directors.

- A sensitivity analysis might be carried out on the master budget to show the effect on the budgeted outcome of changes in the budgeted assumptions.

4.1 The content of the master budget

The master budget provides a **consolidation of all the subsidiary budgets** and normally comprises a budgeted income statement, a budgeted balance sheet and a cash budget.

Cash budgeting will be discussed in detail in Chapter 7. In this chapter we will focus on the budgeted income statement and budgeted balance sheet.

Worked example: Preparing a budgeted income statement and balance sheet

Use the following information to prepare a budgeted income statement for the six months ended 30 June and a budgeted balance sheet at that date.

A new business is to be started and details of budgeted transactions are as follows.

- Non-current assets will be purchased for £12,000. Depreciation will be charged on a straight line basis, assuming that the assets will have a useful life of five years after which they will have no residual value.

- Month-end inventories will be maintained at a level sufficient to meet the forecast sales for the following month.

- Forecast monthly sales are £4,000 for January to March, £5,000 for April to June and £6,000 per month for July onwards.

- The gross profit margin is budgeted to be 20% of sales value.

- Two months' credit will be allowed to customers and one month's credit will be received from suppliers of inventory.

- Operating expenses (excluding depreciation) are budgeted to be £350 each month.

- The budgeted closing cash balance as at 30 June is £16,700.

Solution

Budgeted income statement for six months ended 30 June

	£	£
Revenue ((£4,000 × 3) + (£5,000 × 3))		27,000
Cost of sales (£27,000 × 80/100)		21,600
Gross profit		5,400
Operating expenses (£350 × 6)	2,100	
Depreciation ((£12,000/5) × 6/12)	1,200	
		3,300
Budgeted profit		2,100

Budgeted balance sheet as at 30 June

	£	£
Non-current assets (£12,000 – £1,200 depreciation)		10,800
Current assets		
Inventories (July cost of sales = £6,000 × 80/100)	4,800	
Receivables (May and June sales)	10,000	
Cash	16,700	
	31,500	
Current liabilities		
Trade payables (June purchases = July cost of sales)	4,800	
Net current assets		26,700
		37,500
Owner's capital		37,500

4.2 Performing a sensitivity analysis

Since the master budget provides a summary of all the subsidiary budgets it is likely to be of most interest to senior managers and directors who may not need to be concerned with the detail of budgets outside their own areas of responsibility.

Of particular interest to senior managers will be the **sensitivity of the budget outcomes to changes in the budget assumptions**. For example, they might like to know the answers to questions such as the following.

- What will be the budgeted profit if sales revenue is five per cent higher or lower than the budget?

- What will be the total budgeted costs if direct material costs are ten per cent higher or lower than the budget?

A sensitivity analysis (sometimes called a **'what if?' analysis**) might be performed to show the effect of changes such as these, and to assess the impact on critical areas such as cash resources.

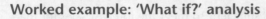

Worked example: 'What if?' analysis

R Ltd manufactures and sells a single product. The budgeted income statement contained in the master budget for the forthcoming year is as follows.

	£	£
Sales revenue (20,000 units)		640,000
Variable materials cost	190,000	
Variable labour cost	172,000	
Variable overhead	13,000	
Fixed overhead	155,000	
		530,000
Budgeted net profit		110,000

The directors wish to know what the budgeted profit will be if a higher quality material is used. This will increase material costs per unit by ten per cent but sales volume will be increased by five per cent. There will be no change in the unit selling price.

Assumptions

The budgeted sales volume will increase to 21,000 units and, in the absence of information to the contrary, we will assume there will be no changes in the total fixed overhead cost incurred and no changes in the variable labour and overhead costs per unit.

The revised budgeted income statement will look like this.

	£	£
Sales revenue (£640,000/20,000) × 21,000		672,000
Variable materials cost (£190,000/20,000) × 1.1 × 21,000	219,450	
Variable labour cost (£172,000/20,000) × 21,000	180,600	
Variable overhead (£13,000/20,000) × 21,000	13,650	
Fixed overhead	155,000	
		568,700
Budgeted net profit		103,300

The proposed changes are not worthwhile since the contribution from the increase in sales volume is not sufficient to compensate for the increase in material costs.

5 Preparing forecasts

Section overview

- Techniques that use past data to forecast future events assume that the past will provide a good indication of what will happen in the future.

- The high-low method is a technique for analysing the fixed and variable elements of a semi-variable cost and thus predicting the cost to be incurred at any activity level within the relevant range.

- A major disadvantage of the high-low method is that it takes account of only two sets of data.

- Linear regression analysis establishes a straight line equation to represent cost or revenue and activity data. It takes account of all sets of data that are available.

- Correlation is the degree to which one variable is related to another.

- The coefficient of correlation, r, can take any value between -1 (perfect negative correlation) and +1 (perfect positive correlation). If r = 0 then the variables are uncorrelated.

- The coefficient of determination, r², is a measure of the proportion of the change in one variable that can be explained by variations in the value of the other variable.

5.1 Forecasting using historical data

Numerous techniques have been developed for using past costs as the basis for forecasting future values. These techniques range from simple arithmetic to advanced computer-based statistical systems. With all these techniques the important presumption is made that **the past will provide guidance to the future**.

The forecasting methods that we will review in this section of the chapter are based on the assumption that a linear relationship links levels of cost and levels of activity.

5.2 Linear relationships

A linear relationship can be expressed in the form of an equation that has the general form $y = a + bx$, where

y is the dependent variable, depending for its value on the value of x

x is the independent variable, whose value helps to determine the corresponding value of y

a is a constant, a fixed amount

b is a constant, being the coefficient of x (that is, the number by which the value of x should be multiplied to derive the value of y)

For example if there is a linear relationship between total costs and the level of activity, y = total costs, x = level of activity, a = fixed cost and b = variable cost per unit.

5.3 The high-low method

The high-low method is a technique for analysing the fixed and variable cost elements of a semi-variable cost and thus predicting the cost to be incurred at any activity level within the relevant range.

The steps taken to prepare a forecast using the high-low method are as follows.

Step 1
Records of costs in previous periods are reviewed and the costs of the following two periods are selected.

- The period with the **highest** volume of activity ⎫ ie the high/low values of the independent
- The period with the **lowest** volume of activity ⎭ variable

The difference between the total cost of these two periods will be the **total variable cost** of the difference in activity levels (since the same fixed cost is included in each total cost).

Step 2
The variable cost per unit may be calculated from this as (Difference in total costs ÷ Difference in activity levels).

Step 3
The fixed cost may then be determined by substitution.

Step 4
The linear equation y = a + bx can be used to predict the cost for a given activity level.

Worked example: The high/low method

The costs of operating the maintenance department of a computer manufacturer, Bread and Butter Ltd, for the last four months have been as follows.

Month	Cost £	Production volume Units
1	110,000	7,000
2	115,000	8,000
3	111,000	7,700
4	97,000	6,000

Requirement

Calculate the costs that should be expected in month 5 when output is expected to be 7,500 units. Ignore inflation.

Solution

Step 1

		Units		£
High output		8,000	total cost	115,000
Low output		6,000	total cost	97,000
Total variable cost		2,000		18,000

Step 2
Variable cost per unit   £18,000/2,000 = £9

Step 3
Substituting in either the high or low volume cost:

		High £		Low £
Total cost		115,000		97,000
Variable costs	(8,000 × £9)	72,000	(6,000 × £9)	54,000
Fixed costs		43,000		43,000

Step 4
Estimated maintenance costs when output is 7,500 units:

	£
Fixed costs	43,000
Variable costs (7,500 × £9)	67,500
Total costs	110,500

Interactive question 3: High/low method [Difficulty level: Easy]

The Valuation Department of a large firm of surveyors wishes to develop a method of predicting its total costs in a period. The following past costs have been recorded at two activity levels.

	Number of valuations (V)	Total cost (TC)
Period 1	420	£82,200
Period 2	515	£90,275

Write the appropriate figures in the boxes below to derive an equation that can be used to represent the total cost model for a period.

TC = £ [   ] + £ [   ] V

See **Answer** at the end of this chapter.

A major disadvantage of the high-low method is that it **takes account of only two sets of data**, which may not be representative of all the data available. In particular, one of them could be a rogue set of data.

For example, the pattern of data might be as follows.

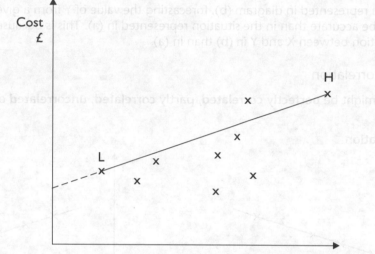

The straight-line equation derived using the high-low method, as shown in the diagram above using points H and L, would be inaccurate. It does not take into account all of the recorded combinations and fails to allow for the fact that the majority of points lie below the line joining the highest and lowest activity.

5.4 Linear regression analysis

Linear regression analysis is a statistical technique for establishing a straight line equation to represent a set of data. Linear regression analysis is **superior to the high-low method** because it **takes account of all sets of recorded data**, rather than only the highest and lowest activity.

However, even though the linear regression technique is more accurate than the high-low method, it is important to remember that its use in forecasting is still based on the presumption that past events are a good guide to what will happen in the future.

A further issue with the use of both the high-low method and linear regression analysis is that **the quality or reliability of the linear equation derived will depend upon the correlation between the variables**.

5.5 Correlation

Correlation is the degree to which one variable is related to another, ie the degree of interdependence between the variables.

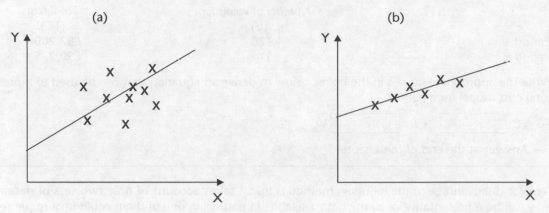

(a)   (b)

In the scatter diagrams above, you should agree that the straight line equation is more likely to reflect the 'real' relationship between X and Y in (b) than in (a). In (b), the pairs of data are all close to the line of best fit, whereas in (a), there is much more scatter around the line.

In the situation represented in diagram (b), forecasting the value of Y from a given value for X would be more likely to be accurate than in the situation represented in (a). This is because there would be greater correlation between X and Y in (b) than in (a).

5.5.1 Degrees of correlation

Two variables might be **perfectly correlated**, **partly correlated**, **uncorrelated** or subject to **non-linear correlation**.

Perfect correlation

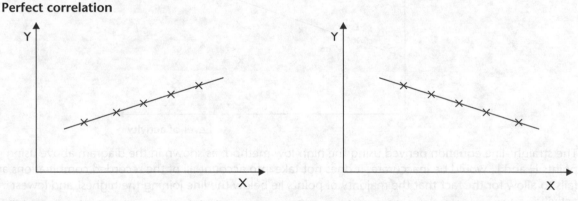

All the pairs of values lie on a straight line. An **exact linear relationship** exists between the two variables.

Partial correlation

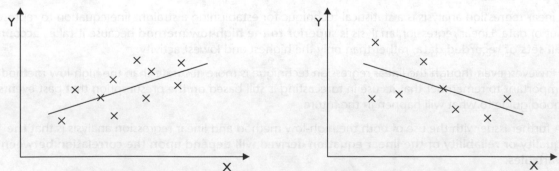

In the left-hand diagram, although there is no exact relationship, **low values of X tend to be associated with low values of Y, and high values of X with high values of Y.**

In the right-hand diagram, there is no exact relationship, but **low values of X tend to be associated with high values of Y and vice versa.**

No correlation

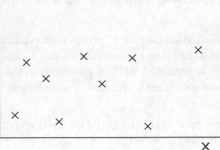

The values of these two variables are not correlated with each other.

Non-linear or curvilinear correlation

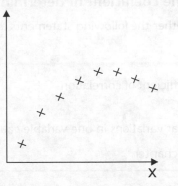

There is a relationship between X and Y since the points are on an obvious curve but it is not a linear relationship.

5.5.2 Positive and negative correlation

Correlation, whether perfect or partial, can be **positive** or **negative**.

- **Positive correlation** is the type of correlation where low values of one variable are associated with low values of the other, and high values of one variable are associated with high values of the other.

- **Negative correlation** is the type of correlation where low values of one variable are associated with high values of the other, and high values of one variable with low values of the other.

5.6 Measures of correlation

5.6.1 The coefficient of correlation, r

The degree of correlation between two variables can be measured using the coefficient of correlation, r.

r has a value between −1 (**perfect negative correlation**) and +1 (**perfect positive correlation**). If r = 0 then the variables are **uncorrelated**.

5.6.2 The coefficient of determination, r^2

The coefficient of determination, r^2, is a measure of the proportion of the change in one variable that can be explained by variations in the value of the other variable.

Worked example: The coefficient of determination

The coefficient of correlation, r, between vehicle maintenance costs and vehicle running hours has been calculated to be 0.96.

This indicates that there is a fairly high degree of positive correlation between x (vehicle running hours) and y (vehicle maintenance cost) because r is quite close to +1. The coefficient of determination, r^2, is equal to $(0.96)^2 = 0.9216$. This means that 92% of variations in the value of y (cost) can be explained by a linear relationship with x (running hours). This leaves only 8% of variations in y to be predicted from other factors.

Therefore it is likely that vehicle running hours could be used with a high degree of confidence to predict vehicle running costs during a period.

Interactive question 4: The coefficient of determination   [Difficulty level: Easy]

Tick the boxes to indicate whether the following statements about the coefficient of determination are true or false.

		True	False
(a)	It is the square of the coefficient of correlation	☐	☐
(b)	It can never quite equal 1	☐	☐
(c)	If it is high, this proves that variations in one variable cause variations in the other	☐	☐

See **Answer** at the end of this chapter.

6 Alternative approaches to budgeting

Section overview

- An organisation's budgeting style can be participative (bottom-up) or imposed (top-down).

- Participative budgeting tends to have the most favourable motivational impact but it does have its disadvantages.

- Budget slack is the intentional overstating of costs or understating of revenues in a budget, in order to set an 'easy' budget target.

- Incremental budgeting involves basing the next year's budget on the current year's results, with adjustments for known changes and inflation.

- Zero based budgeting requires all budgets to be prepared from the very beginning or zero.

- Rolling budgets, also known as continuous budgets, are continuously updated by adding a further month or quarter to the end of the budget as each month or quarter comes to a close.

- The structure of budgets may be designed around one of a number of frameworks, including product based budgets, responsibility based budgets and activity based budgets.

6.1 Participation in the budgeting process

It has been argued that participation in the budgeting process will improve motivation and so will improve the quality of budget decisions and the efforts of individuals to achieve their budget targets.

There are basically two ways in which a budget can be set: from the top down (imposed budget) or from the bottom up (participatory budget).

6.1.1 Imposed or top-down style of budgeting

In this approach to budgeting, **top management prepare a budget with little or no input from operating personnel**, which is then imposed upon the employees who have to work to the budgeted figures.

The times when imposed budgets are effective

* In newly-formed organisations
* In very small businesses
* During periods of economic hardship
* When operational managers lack budgeting skills
* When the organisation's different units require precise coordination

There are, of course, advantages and disadvantages to this style of setting budgets.

(a) **Advantages**

* Strategic plans are likely to be incorporated into planned activities.
* They enhance the coordination between the plans and objectives of divisions.
* They use senior management's awareness of total resource availability.
* They decrease the input from inexperienced or uninformed lower-level employees.
* They decrease the period of time taken to draw up the budgets.

(b) **Disadvantages**

* Dissatisfaction, defensiveness and low morale amongst employees. It is hard for people to be motivated to achieve targets set by somebody else, particularly if managers consider the budget targets to be unrealistic.

* The feeling of team spirit may disappear.

* The acceptance of organisational goals and objectives could be limited.

* The budget may be viewed as a punitive device.

* Managers who are performing operations on a day to day basis are likely to have a better understanding of what is achievable.

* Unachievable budgets could result if consideration is not given to local operating and political environments. This applies particularly to overseas divisions.

* Lower-level management initiative may be stifled.

6.1.2 Participative or bottom-up style of budgeting

In this approach to budgeting, **budgets are developed by lower-level managers who then submit the budgets to their superiors**. The budgets are based on the lower-level managers' perceptions of what is achievable and the associated necessary resources.

Advantages of participative budgets

* They are based on information from the employees most familiar with the department.

* Knowledge spread among several levels of management is pulled together (ie information asymmetry is reduced).

* Morale and motivation is improved.

* They increase operational managers' commitment to organisational objectives.

* In general they are more realistic.

* Co-ordination between units is improved.

* Specific resource requirements are included.

* Senior managers' overview is mixed with operational level details.

* Individual managers' aspiration levels are more likely to be taken into account.

Disadvantages of participative budgets

- They consume more time.

- Changes implemented by senior management may cause dissatisfaction.

- Budgets may be unachievable or much too soft if managers are not qualified to participate.

- They may cause managers to introduce budget slack (overstating costs or understating revenues) and budget bias.

- They can support 'empire building' by subordinates.

- An earlier start to the budgeting process could be required.

6.2 Incremental budgeting

The traditional approach to budgeting is to base the forthcoming year's budget on the current year's results modified for changes in activity levels, for example by adding an extra amount for estimated growth or inflation next year. This approach is known as incremental budgeting since it is **concerned mainly with the increments in costs and revenues which will occur in the coming period**.

Incremental budgeting is a reasonable approach if the current operations are as effective, efficient and economic as they can be.

In general, however, it is an inefficient form of budgeting. It encourages slack, which is unnecessary expenditure built into the budgets. **Past inefficiencies are perpetuated** because cost levels are rarely subjected to close scrutiny.

6.3 Zero based budgeting

Zero based budgeting (ZBB) is an approach to budgeting that attempts to ensure that inefficiencies are not concealed.

The principle behind ZBB is that, instead of using the current year's results as a starting point, **each budget should be prepared from the very beginning or zero**. Every item of expenditure must be justified separately to be included in the budget for the forthcoming period.

Increments of expenditure are compared with the expected benefits received, to ensure that resources are allocated as efficiently as possible.

ZBB can be particularly useful when applied to discretionary costs such as marketing and training costs. This type of cost is not vital to the continued existence of an organisation in the way that, say, raw materials are to a manufacturing business.

A major disadvantage of ZBB is that it is a **time-consuming task** that involves a great deal of work.

6.4 Rolling budgets

Rolling budgets are sometimes called **continuous budgets**. They are particularly useful when an organisation is facing a **period of uncertainty** so that it is difficult to prepare accurate plans and budgets. For example, it may be difficult to estimate the level of inflation for the forthcoming period.

Rolling budgets are an attempt to prepare **targets and plans** that are **more realistic** and **certain**, particularly with a regard to price levels, by shortening the period between preparing budgets.

Instead of preparing a **periodic budget annually** for the full budget period, budgets would be prepared, say, every one, two or three months (four, six, or even twelve budgets each year). Each of these budgets would plan for the next twelve months so that the current budget is extended by an extra period as the current period ends: hence the name rolling budgets. **Cash budgets**, which are the subject of the next chapter, are usually prepared on a rolling basis.

Suppose, for example, that a rolling budget is prepared every three months. The first three months of the budget period would be planned in great detail, and the remaining nine months in lesser detail, because of the greater uncertainty about the longer term future.

(a) The first continuous budget would show January to March Year 1 in detail, and April to December Year 1 in less detail.

(b) At the end of March, the first three months of the budget would be removed and a further three months would be added at the end for January to March Year 2.

(c) The remaining nine months for April to December Year 1 would be updated in the light of current conditions, adding more detail to the earliest three months, April to June Year 1.

The detail in the first three months would be principally important for the following.

- **Planning** working capital and short-term resources (cash, materials, labour and so on).

- **Control**: the budget for each control period should provide a more reliable yardstick for comparison with actual results.

The **advantages** of rolling budgets are as follows.

(a) They **reduce the element of uncertainty in budgeting**. If a high rate of inflation or major changes in market conditions or any other change that cannot be quantified with accuracy is likely, rolling budgets concentrate detailed planning and control on short-term prospects where the degree of uncertainty is much smaller.

(b) They **force managers to reassess the budget regularly**, and to produce budgets that are up to date in the light of current events and expectations.

(c) **Planning and control will be based on a recent plan** instead of an annual budget that might have been prepared many months ago and is no longer realistic.

(d) **There is always a budget that extends for several months ahead**. For example, if rolling budgets are prepared quarterly there will always be a budget extending for the next 9 to 12 months. If rolling budgets are prepared monthly there will always be a budget for the next 11 to 12 months. This is not the case when annual budgets are used.

The **disadvantages** of rolling budgets can be a deterrent to using them.

(a) A system of rolling budgets calls for the routine preparation of a new budget at regular intervals during the course of the one financial year. This involves more **time, effort and money** in budget preparation.

(b) Frequent budgeting might have an **off putting effect on managers** who doubt the value of preparing one budget after another at regular intervals, even when there are major differences between the figures in one budget and the next.

6.5 Alternative budget structures

The structure of budgets may be designed around one of a number of frameworks, including the following.

6.5.1 Product based budgets

Product based budgets are drawn up by preparing separate budgets for each product. For example a separate production budget would be established for product A, for product B and for product C as well as a separate marketing cost budget, a separate distribution cost budget, a separate sales revenue budget and so on.

This structure is **appropriate when the cost and revenue responsibilities differ for each product, or when a single manager is responsible for all aspects of one product**.

The individual product budgets might also be aggregated across products, for example where a distribution manager has overall responsibility for all product distribution costs.

The separate product budgets and the possibility for aggregation across products enables senior managers to look both down and across the whole organisation in terms of budgets.

6.5.2 Responsibility based budgets

Responsibility based budget systems **segregate budgeted revenues and costs into areas of personal responsibility** in order to monitor and assess the performance of each part of an organisation.

Budgetary control is based around a system of budget centres. Each budget centre will have its own budget, and an individual manager (a budget holder) will be responsible for managing the budget centre and ensuring that the budget is met.

Responsibility based budgets can have a positive motivational impact, as long as the budget holder is not held responsible for costs and revenues over which they have no control.

6.5.3 Activity based budgets

Activity based budgets are **based on a framework of activities**, and cost drivers are used as a basis for preparing budgets.

The budget for each activity is derived from the quantity of the activity's cost driver × the appropriate cost driver rate.

Worked example: Activity based budget

An organisation expects to place 500 orders with suppliers during the forthcoming budget period. The rate per cost driver has been established as £100. The budgeted cost of the ordering activity is therefore 500 × £100 = £50,000.

Activity based budgeting (ABB) involves defining the activities that underlie the financial figures in each function. The level of activity in terms of cost drivers is used to decide how much resource should be allocated and how well the activity is being managed, and to explain differences between the budget and actual results.

Implementing ABB leads to the realisation that the **business as a whole** needs to be **managed** with more reference to the behaviour of activities and cost drivers identified.

(a) **Traditional budgeting may make managers 'responsible' for activities that are driven by factors beyond their control**: the cost of setting up new personnel records and of induction training would traditionally be the responsibility of the personnel manager even though such costs are driven by the number of new employees required by managers other than the personnel manager.

(b) The **budgets for costs not directly related to production** are often traditionally set using an **incremental approach** because of the difficulty of linking the activity driving the cost to production level. However, this assumes that all of the cost is unaffected by any form of activity level, which is often not the case in reality. Some of the costs of the purchasing department, for example, will be fixed (such as premises costs) but some will relate to the number of orders placed or the volume of production, say. In an ABB framework the budget for the purchasing department can take account of the expected number of orders.

Summary

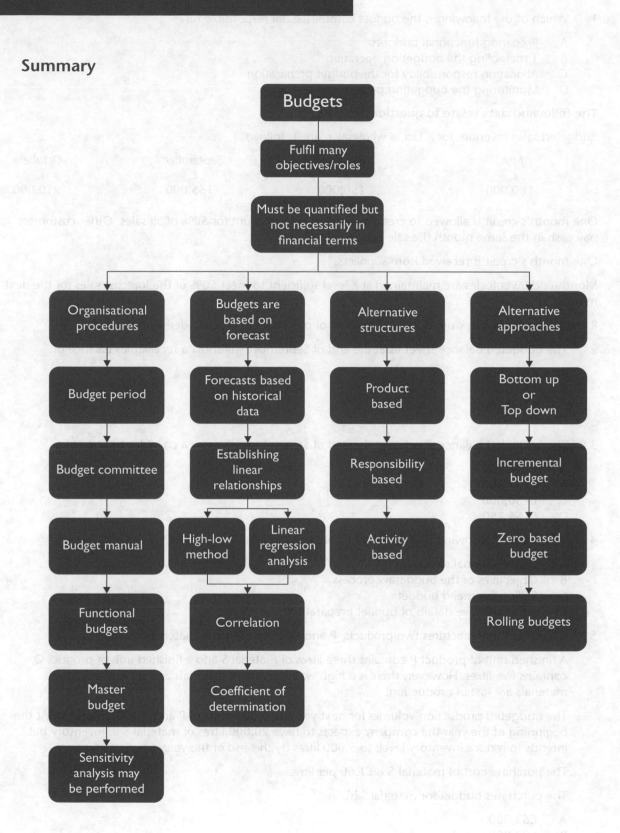

```
                          Budgets

                          Fulfil many
                          objectives/roles

                       Must be quantified but
                       not necessarily in
                       financial terms
```

Organisational procedures	Budgets are based on forecast	Alternative structures	Alternative approaches
Budget period	Forecasts based on historical data	Product based	Bottom up or Top down
Budget committee	Establishing linear relationships	Responsibility based	Incremental budget
Budget manual	High-low method / Linear regression analysis	Activity based	Zero based budget
Functional budgets	Correlation		Rolling budgets
Master budget	Coefficient of determination		
Sensitivity analysis may be performed			

Self-test

Answer the following questions.

1   Which of the following is the budget committee *not* responsible for?

    A   Preparing functional budgets
    B   Timetabling the budgeting operation
    C   Allocating responsibility for the budget preparation
    D   Monitoring the budgeting process

The following data relate to questions 2 and 3.

Budgeted sales revenues for R Ltd, a wholesaler, are as follows.

July £	August £	September £	October £
180,000	150,000	165,000	210,000

One month's credit is allowed to credit customers, who account for 50% of all sales. Other customers pay cash in the same month the sale occurs.

One month's credit is received from suppliers.

Month-end inventories are maintained at a level sufficient to meet 50% of the forecast sales for the next month.

R Ltd adds a profit mark-up of 20% to the cost of purchases in order to derive the selling price.

2   The budgeted balance sheet as at the end of September will show a receivables balance of:

    A   £75,000
    B   £82,500
    C   £150,000
    D   £165,000

3   The budgeted balance sheet as at the end of September will show a payables balance of:

    A   £118,750
    B   £137,500
    C   £150,000
    D   £156,250

4   Which of the following is unlikely to be contained in a budget manual?

    A   Organisational structures
    B   Objectives of the budgetary process
    C   Selling overhead budget
    D   Administrative details of budget preparation

5   Cassius Ltd manufactures two products, P and Q, from the same material, S.

    A finished unit of product P contains three litres of material S and a finished unit of product Q contains five litres. However, there is a high wastage rate of materials and 25% of the input materials are lost in production.

    The budgeted production volumes for next year are 6,000 units of P and 8,100 units of Q. At the beginning of the year the company expects to have 20,000 litres of material S in inventory but intends to reduce inventory levels to 5,000 litres by the end of the year.

    The purchase cost of material S is £1.60 per litre.

    The purchases budget for material S is:

    A   £63,000
    B   £93,000
    C   £100,800
    D   £148,800

6   Which TWO of the following are included in the master budget?

    A   Cash budget
    B   Sales budget
    C   Capital expenditure budget
    D   Budgeted balance sheet

7   A retailing company is preparing its annual budget. It plans to make a profit of 25% on the cost of sales. Inventories will be maintained at the end of each month at 30% of the following month's sales requirements.

Details of budgeted sales are as follows

	Credit sales – gross £	Cash sales £
December	1,900,000	400,000
January	1,500,000	250,000
February	1,700,000	350,000
March	1,600,000	300,000

(a)   Budgeted inventory levels at the end of December are £ [   ]

(b)   Budgeted inventory purchases for January are £ [   ]

8   The coefficient of correlation between advertising expenditure and the number of theatre tickets sold is 0.97. Which TWO of the following statements are correct?

    A   97% of the variation in ticket sales can be explained by variations in advertising expenditure

    B   94% of the variation in ticket sales can be explained by variations in advertising expenditure

    C   A 97% increase in advertising expenditure will result in a 97% increase in ticket sales

    D   There is a fairly high degree of positive correlation between advertising expenditure and ticket sales

9   A transport company has recorded the following maintenance costs for the last two periods.

	Period 7	Period 8
Miles travelled	30,000	50,000
Maintenance cost per mile	£1.90	£1.30

The forecast maintenance cost for period 9, when 38,000 miles will be travelled, is £ [   ]

10   In what circumstances might participative or bottom-up budgets *not* be effective?

    A   In centralised organisations
    B   In well-established organisations
    C   In very large businesses
    D   During periods of economic affluence

Now go back to the Learning Objectives in the Introduction. If you are satisfied you have achieved these objectives, please tick them off.

Answer to Interactive question 1

	Before	After	Doesn't matter
Sales revenue; sales quantities		✓	
Finished goods inventories; production volume	✓		
Materials usage; labour hours			✓
Materials usage; materials purchases	✓		

The sales revenue budget is derived by multiplying the budgeted sales quantities by the standard selling price. Therefore the sales revenue budget must be prepared **after** the budget for sales quantities.

The production volume budget is derived by adjusting the budgeted sales quantities for budgeted changes in finished goods inventories. Therefore the budget for finished goods inventories must be prepared before the production volume budget.

The materials usage budget and the labour hours budget are derived from the production volume budget, **independently** of each other.

The materials purchases budget is derived by adjusting the materials usage budget for budgeted changes in materials inventories. Therefore the material usage budget must be prepared **before** the materials purchases budget.

Answer to Interactive question 2

(a) **Sales budget**

	Product X	Product Y	Product Z	Total
Sales quantity	2,000	4,000	3,000	
Sales price	£100	£130	£150	
Sales value	£200,000	£520,000	£450,000	£1,170,000

(b) **Production budget**

	Product X	Product Y	Product Z
Sales quantity	2,000	4,000	3,000
Closing inventories	600	1,000	800
	2,600	5,000	3,800
Less opening inventories	(500)	(800)	(700)
Budgeted production	2,100	4,200	3,100

(c) **Material usage budget**

	Production Units	RM11 Units	RM22 Units	RM33 Units
Product X	2,100	10,500	4,200	–
Product Y	4,200	12,600	8,400	8,400
Product Z	3,100	6,200	3,100	9,300
Budgeted material usage		29,300	15,700	17,700

(d) **Material purchases budget**

	RM11 Units	RM22 Units	RM33 Units
Budgeted material usage	29,300	15,700	17,700
Closing inventories	18,000	9,000	12,000
	47,300	24,700	29,700
Less opening inventories	(21,000)	(10,000)	(16,000)
Budgeted material purchases	26,300	14,700	13,700
Cost per unit of material	£5	£3	£4
Budgeted material purchases	£131,500	£44,100	£54,800

(e) **Labour budget**

Product	Production	Hours required per unit	Labour budget Total hours	Rate per hour	Cost
	Units			£	£
X	2,100	4	8,400	9	75,600
Y	4,200	6	25,200	9	226,800
Z	3,100	8	24,800	9	223,200
Budgeted total wages					525,600

Answer to Interactive question 3

TC = £ $\boxed{46,500}$ + £ $\boxed{85}$ V

Although we only have two activity levels in this question we can still apply the high/low method.

	Valuations	Total cost £
Period 2	515	90,275
Period 1	420	82,200
Change due to variable cost	95	8,075

∴ Variable cost per valuation = £8,075/95 = £85.

Period 2: fixed cost = £90,275 – (515 × £85)

= £46,500

Answer to Interactive question 4

Statement (a) is true. The coefficient of determination is r^2.

Statement (b) is false. r can reach 1 or –1, therefore r^2 can reach 1.

Statement (c) is false. A high coefficient of determination means it is very likely that variations in one variable cause variations in the other. The high degree of correlation may, however, be due to chance (ie spurious correlation).

1   A   The budget committee is not responsible for preparing functional budgets. The manager responsible for implementing the budget must prepare it, not the budget committee.

           Since the committee is a co-ordinating body it is definitely responsible for timetabling and allocating responsibility for budget preparation. It is also responsible for monitoring the whole budgetary planning and control process.

2   B   The budgeted receivables balance at the end of September is £82,500.

           Since one month's credit is given to credit customers, the outstanding receivables balance at the end of each month is equal to the credit sales for that month.

           Credit sales for September = 50% × £165,000 = £82,500

           If you answered £165,000 you did not allow for the fact that only 50% of sales are made on credit.

           If you answered £75,000 or £150,000 you based your answer on the sales revenue for August, all of which will have been received from customers by the end of September.

3   D   The budgeted payables balance at the end of September is £156,250.

           Since one month's credit is received from suppliers the payables balance at the end of each month is equal to the credit purchases for that month.

           The budgeted cost of goods sold in each month is derived by multiplying each sales figure by (100/120) to remove the profit mark-up.

	September £
Budgeted cost of goods sold (£165,000 × 100/120)	137,500
Budgeted closing inventory (£210,000 × 100/120 × 50%)	87,500
	225,000
Less budgeted opening inventory (£165,000 × 100/120 × 50%)	(68,750)
Budgeted purchases = budgeted payables	156,250

           If you answered £118,750 you reversed the budgeted opening and closing inventory.

           The option of £137,500 is incorrect because the purchases are not equal to the cost of goods sold since there are budgeted changes in inventory.

           If you answered £150,000 you treated the 20% profit as a margin on the sales price rather than as a mark-up on the cost of purchases.

4   C   The selling overhead budget is unlikely to be contained in a budget manual. All of the other items are concerned with the organisation and co-ordination of the budgetary process, therefore they would be included in the budget manual.

5 C

	Material S litres
Material S required for production:	
Product P: 6,000 units × 3 × 100/75	24,000
Product Q: 8,100 units × 5 × 100/75	54,000
Total material S required for production	78,000
Plus budgeted closing inventory	5,000
	83,000
Less budgeted opening inventory	(20,000)
Budgeted material purchases in litres	63,000
× purchase cost per litre	× £1.60
Budgeted material purchases in £	£100,800

If you answered £63,000 you selected the figure for purchases in litres rather than the value of the budgeted purchases.

If you answered £93,000 you did not deal correctly with the losses. The 25% loss is based on the input materials. You calculated a 25% loss based on the output.

If you answered £148,800 you reversed the opening and closing inventory.

6 A,D The cash budget and the budgeted balance sheet form a part of the master budget, together with the budgeted income statement.

The sales budget and the capital expenditure budget are subsidiary budgets that provide the basic data for consolidation into the master budget.

7 (a) Budgeted inventory levels at the end of December are £420,000.

(b) Budgeted inventory purchases for January are £1,472,000.

WORKINGS

(a) Sales in January = £1,500,000 + £250,000

= £1,750,000

Cost of sales (×100/125) = £1,400,000

End of December inventory = 30% × £1,400,000

= £420,000

(b) Sales in February = £1,700,000 + £350,000

= £2,050,000

Cost of sales (×100/125) = £1,640,000

End of January inventory = 30% × £1,640,000

= £492,000

	January £
Cost of goods sold	1,400,000
Budgeted closing inventory	492,000
	1,892,000
Less budgeted opening inventory	(420,000)
Budgeted purchases	1,472,000

8 B,D A is incorrect and B is correct. The coefficient of determination $(r^2) = (0.97)^2 = 0.9409$, therefore 94% of the variation in the value of y (ticket sales) can be explained by a linear relationship with x (advertising expenditure).

C is incorrect because it misinterprets the meaning of the coefficient of correlation.

D is correct. There is a fairly high degree of positive correlation because r, the coefficient of correlation, is close to 1.

9 The forecast maintenance cost for period 9 is £60,200.

To use the high-low method we need to know the total cost incurred at each activity level.

	Miles travelled		Total cost incurred £
Period 8	50,000	(× £1.30)	65,000
Period 7	30,000	(× £1.90)	57,000
Variable cost	20,000		8,000

Variable cost per mile = £8,000/20,000 = £0.40

Fixed cost = £65,000 − (50,000 miles × £0.40) = £45,000

Forecast maintenance cost for 38,000 miles:	£
Variable cost (38,000 × £0.40)	15,200
Fixed cost	45,000
	60,200

10 A Participative (bottom-up) budgets might not be effective in centralised organisations. An imposed or top-down budgeting system is likely to be most effective in this situation.

CHAPTER 7

Working capital

Introduction

Examination context

Topic List

1   What is 'working capital'?

2   Balancing liquidity and profitability

3   Balancing short-term and long-term finance for working capital

4   The cash operating cycle

5   Managing inventory

6   Managing trade payables

7   Managing trade receivables

8   Treasury management

9   Cash budgets

Summary and Self-test

Answers to Interactive questions

Answers to Self-test

Introduction

Learning objectives

- Identify the constituent elements of working capital and treasury
- Specify the methods by which each element can be managed by the finance function to optimise working capital and cash flow
- Prepare a cash budget for a business, which highlights the quantity and timing of cash surpluses and deficits
- Calculate the cash cycle for a business and recognise its significance
- Recognise how a business manages surpluses and deficits predicted in cash budgets

The specific syllabus references for this chapter are: 2d, e, f, g.

Syllabus links

As with Chapter 6, this budgeting chapter will underpin your study of planning within the Business Strategy syllabus. You will study working capital again in the Strategic Business Management syllabus at Advanced level.

Examination context

You will not be asked to prepare a full cash budget in the exam. However, you could be asked to prepare an extract from information provided. For example, you may be asked to calculate the budgeted receipts from customers or the budgeted payments made to suppliers, taking account of the budgeted activity and planned credit periods.

In the examination, candidates may be required to:

- Use data supplied to prepare extracts from cash budgets
- Select appropriate actions to be taken in the light of information provided by a cash budget
- Calculate and interpret the cash cycle for a business
- Assess the liquidity of a business using current and quick ratios

Questions on working capital and treasury management could easily appear in the exam. They are likely to be set in a scenario context. Knowledge-type questions are also likely, set on particular principles or definitions.

1 What is 'working capital'?

Section overview

- The components of working capital are inventory, receivables, cash and payables.

Definition

Working capital: is the total of the current assets of a business less its current liabilities.

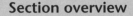

Net working capital is made up of current assets less current liabilities:

> Receivables + Inventory + Cash – Payables

Investment in working capital is needed to 'oil the wheels' of business.

It is essential to consider working capital as a whole and how the components all fit together. The management of working capital is concerned with the **liquidity** position of the company, so the main aim is to turn the cash round as quickly as possible whilst ensuring that **profitability** is not thereby undermined: it is a **trade-off**.

2 Balancing liquidity and profitability

Section overview

- All businesses face a trade off between being profitable (providing a return) and being liquid (staying in business).

Alternative policies in working capital management need to be reviewed in terms of their relative **risk** and **return**. An important aspect of the **risk** associated with various options is the effect it has on the company's **liquidity** position. Liquidity is obviously of crucial importance to the **financial stability** of a business; mismanagement of a firm's liquidity position may result in it being unable to pay its debts which, in turn, may result in corporate insolvency. A business's liquidity determines its ability to survive. This can be illustrated by looking at each component of working capital in turn.

- **Cash**. A business requires a particular level of cash (or overdraft facility) in order to pay debts when they fall due, and particularly to take advantage of any generous discounts offered for prompt payment. However, a better return could be earned by investing any cash surplus in a high-yielding investment. By ensuring that it has sufficient liquid assets (cash), therefore, a business is reducing its chance of owning more profitable assets.

- **Receivables**. A business could decide that it does not want to offer credit to customers, because the delay in payment jeopardises its liquidity position. If it tried to adopt this policy however, customers would be driven away, revenue would fall and profits would fall.

- **Inventory**. In order to satisfy customer demand, manufacturing and retailing firms need to maintain finished goods inventory; to keep production runs moving without disruption, raw materials inventories also need to be maintained. This means that a business will have money tied up in inventories that, again, it might feel it could use more profitably elsewhere. However, if inventories were not available when required, a potential sale might be lost; the cost of a broken production facility may be higher than the cost of holding inventory.

- **Payables**. To improve its cash position a business might decide not to pay suppliers until after two or three months, rather than after the normal one month. Apart from the obvious cost of lost discount opportunities, the business runs the risk of alienating its suppliers and even losing sources of supply.

In each of the above instances the business must weigh up **profitability versus liquidity**. Since ultimately a business aims to maximise profits, it must establish the financial costs and benefits of

different liquidity positions. Inevitably all working capital decisions reduce to decisions over cash levels, since current assets should eventually be turned into cash.

Remember that profit and cash flows are not the same. It is possible to make accounting profits while suffering a dramatic decline in the cash balance (and *vice versa*). In consequence, history is littered with examples of companies which have gone insolvent while reporting accounting profits. Since the consequences of compulsory liquidations are invariably catastrophic for all concerned, it is crucial for a business to maintain a sound liquidity position. **Cash budgeting** and **performance measurement** are key techniques in monitoring and controlling that position.

3 Balancing short-term and long-term finance for working capital

Section overview

- Every business faces risk in the way it finances working capital. The more long-term finance is used to finance trading activities, the lower the risk and therefore the lower the return.

- Businesses may be aggressive, average or defensive in their financing policies.

- Ratios can be used to assess a business's liquidity position.

3.1 Financing current assets

For most businesses a proportion of current assets will effectively be **permanent**. The method of financing this level is best seen diagrammatically.

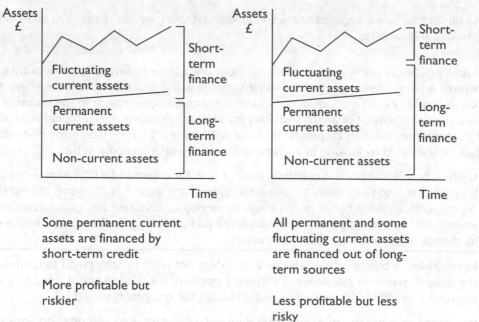

Some permanent current assets are financed by short-term credit

More profitable but riskier

All permanent and some fluctuating current assets are financed out of long-term sources

Less profitable but less risky

Figure 7.1: Financing working capital investment

The options set out in Figure 7.1 are only two of many possible approaches. For example, the use of short-term credit could be extended to finance a proportion of the non-current assets or, alternatively, all of the business's finance requirements could be provided by long-term finance.

The choice is a matter for managerial judgement of the trade-off between the relative **cheapness** of short-term finance versus its **risks**.

3.1.1 The cost of short-term finance

Short-term finance is usually **cheaper** than long-term finance due to the risks taken by lenders. For example, if a bank were considering two loan applications, one for one year and the other for 20 years, all other things being equal it would demand a higher interest rate on the 20-year loan. This is because it feels more exposed to **risk** on long-term loans, as more could possibly go wrong over a period of 20 years than over a period of one year.

Occasionally this situation can be reversed. Sometimes short-term interest rates will be higher than long-term rates, as when the market expects interest rates to fall in the long run. But if funds have been borrowed long-term, early repayment may not be possible or, if allowed, early repayment penalties may be experienced. **The flexibility of short-term finance may, therefore, reduce its overall cost**.

Finally, short-term finance also includes items such as trade payables; it can therefore have a low average cost (interest is charged by banks on overdrafts but not by ordinary suppliers unless an agreed credit period has been exceeded). Long-term finance includes equity finance which is particularly expensive; because of the **risk they suffer shareholders expect high returns**, and dividends are not tax deductible.

3.1.2 The risks of short-term finance

The price paid for the reduced cost of short-term finance is an increase in risk.

- **Renewal risk**

    Being short-term it has to be continually renegotiated as the various facilities expire. Either because of economic conditions (eg a credit squeeze) or because of the financial situation of the business, such renewal may be difficult to obtain.

- **Interest rate risk**

    If the business is constantly having to renew its funding arrangements, it will be at the mercy of fluctuations in short-term interest rates.

3.2 Making the working capital financing decision

No single ideal financing package can be recommended as it all depends upon the risk/return trade-offs of individual businesses.

Businesses may be categorised as having **aggressive**, **average** or **defensive** positions in this area, and the **current ratio** (current assets ÷ current liabilities) can indicate which financing policy is adopted.

Worked example: Aggressive, average and defensive positions

The following three companies have asset financing structures which may be considered as aggressive, average and defensive:

Balance sheet (statement of financial position)

	Aggressive £'000	Average £'000	Defensive £'000
Non-current assets	50	50	50
Current assets	50	50	50
Total assets	100	100	100
Equity (£1 shares)	30	50	50
Long-term borrowings (average cost 10% pa)	–	20	40
Current liabilities (average cost 3% pa)	70	30	10
Total equity and liabilities	100	100	100
Current ratio	0.7:1	1.7:1	5:1

Income statement (statement of comprehensive income)

	Aggressive £	Average £	Defensive £
PBIT	15,000	15,000	15,000
Less finance costs			
(10% × long term, 3% × current)	(2,100)	(2,900)	(4,300)
	12,900	12,100	10,700
Tax @ 30%	(3,870)	(3,630)	(3,210)
Net profit for the period = earnings available to shareholders	9,030	8,470	7,490
Earnings per share (30,000 or 50,000 shares)	30.1p	16.94p	14.98p

The **aggressive company**, which has more short-term credit than equity in its structure, returns a higher profit but at the cost of greater risk revealed in its relatively poor current ratio.

The **average company** matches its maturities; permanent current assets are financed by long-term debt, while fluctuating current assets are financed by short-term credit. There is less risk here than in the aggressive company, as shown by the healthy current ratio, but considerably less return as well, as seen in the EPS.

The **defensive company** has sacrificed profitability for liquidity by using a very small amount of short-term credit, which finances only some of the fluctuating current assets. This is a low-risk, low return company.

The financing choice must be made by the management of the individual company, bearing in mind the **willingness of creditors to lend** and the **risk of its industrial sector**.

3.3 Financing growth in working capital

The level of working capital directly affects the amount of growth the business can sustain organically from its own internal resources. Growth in sales volume means additional inventories and receivables. Even if no further capital expenditure is required to achieve the growth, the underlying working capital invested in a business will still need to increase.

How much growth a business can sustain out of its own resources, before issuing new long-term capital, is constrained both by:

- Its anticipated rate of **profitability** and
- The underlying **asset requirement**

If a business is to grow without borrowing or issuing further capital, it needs to **increase its profitability** and/or to **make better use of its assets**.

3.4 Assessing the liquidity position via ratios

A secure liquidity position is desirable. The business's liquidity position can be assessed in **two** ways: by **ratios**, and via the **cash operating cycle**.

```
                                    Ratios
                                      |
       ┌───────────────────┬──────────────────────┬───────────────────┐
   Inventory           Receivables            Payables            Liquidity
   turnover            collection             payment              ratios
                         period                period

   Inventory          Receivables            Payables           Current assets
  ─────────── × 365   ─────────── × 365      ───────── × 365    ──────────────
  Cost of sales        Revenue               Purchases          Current liabilities
  (Inventory turnover                                           (current ratio)
      period)

   Cost of sales                                                * Current assets – inventory
   ───────────                                                    ──────────────────────
    Inventory                                                      Current liabilities
  (Inventory turnover                                             (quick ratio or
       ratio)                                                      liquidity ratio)
```

These can be compared with:

- The same company in previous periods
- Other companies in the same industry

to see whether they are getting better or worse, and how they look against industry averages.

For an individual business, we can gain a better understanding of the effects of funding and operational decisions on its liquidity position by manipulating its ratios.

For the following ratios averages should be used where they are available, but the year-end figure should be used if not.

3.4.1 Inventory turnover period

This measure shows the average length of time that inventory is held for.

$$\text{Inventory turnover period} = \frac{\text{Inventory}}{\text{Cost of sales}} \times 365$$

If the inventory is held for a shorter period, the costs of holding the stock will decrease. A similar insight is obtained by calculating the inventory turnover ratio – see below.

3.4.2 Rate of inventory turnover

The rate of inventory turnover monitors how many times inventory turns over during the trading period.

$$\text{Rate of inventory turnover} = \frac{\text{Cost of sales}}{\text{Average inventory}}$$

In general **the rate of turnover should be as high as possible** since this means that the inventory is lower, thus reducing costs such as space costs, insurance, obsolescence write-offs and the cost of capital being tied up. However, potential sales might be forgone if inventory is so low that customer's needs cannot be met.

3.4.3 Receivables collection period

This KPI monitors how long on average it takes to collect debts.

$$\text{Receivables collection period (in days)} = \frac{\text{Average receivables}}{\text{Annual sales revenue}} \times 365$$

The collection period can also be measured in months, in which case the ratio calculation would be multiplied by 12 instead of by 365.

The lower this period, the lower the capital cost of the money invested in receivables balances and the lower the risk of bad debts. However, customers may go elsewhere if the credit period offered is too low.

3.4.4 Payables payment period

This KPI monitors how long on average the company waits before paying its suppliers.

$$\text{Payables payment period} = \frac{\text{Average payables}}{\text{Annual purchases}} \times 365$$

In general **this period should be as high as possible**. However supplier goodwill may be lost if the period of credit taken is too long. Continuity of supply could also be disrupted if suppliers place overdue accounts on stop.

The payment period can also be measured in months, in which case the ratio calculation would be multiplied by 12 instead of by 365.

The purchases figure should be used where this is available. If not then cost of sales should be used as an alternative.

Worked example: Working capital ratios

Division S is a retail operation. Its year-end working capital comprises inventory valued at cost, trade receivables of £90,000, cash and trade payables. Its financial performance ratios include the following.

Gross profit margin	25%
Current ratio	2.3:1
Receivables collection period	30 days
Payables payment period	40 days
Rate of inventory turnover	18 times

The opening inventory, receivables and payables balances are the same as the closing balances.

Requirement

Calculate the division's year-end cash balance.

Solution

Step 1
Calculate the annual sales revenue

$$\text{Receivables collection period (in days)} = \frac{\text{Average receivables}}{\text{Sales revenue}} \times 365$$

$$\text{Sales revenue} = \frac{£90,000}{30} \times 365$$

$$= £1,095,000$$

Step 2
Calculate the cost of sales/purchases

Since the opening and closing inventories are equal, the cost of sales is equal to the purchases.

$$\text{Cost of sales} = £1,095,000 \times 0.75$$

$$= £821,250$$

Step 3
Calculate the inventory balance

$$\text{Rate of inventory turnover} = \frac{\text{Cost of sales}}{\text{Average inventory}}$$

$$\text{Inventory} = \frac{£821,250}{18}$$

$$= £45,625$$

Step 4
Calculate the trade payables balance

Payables payment period $= \dfrac{\text{Average payables}}{\text{Purchases}} \times 365$

Trade payables $= \dfrac{40 \times £821{,}250}{365}$

$= £90{,}000$

Step 5
Calculate the current assets balance

Current ratio $= \dfrac{\text{Current assets}}{\text{Current liabilities}}$

Current assets $= 2.3 \times £90{,}000$

$= £207{,}000$

Step 6
Calculate the cash balance

		£	£
Total current assets			207,000
Less:	Inventory	45,625	
	Receivables	90,000	
			135,625
Cash balance			71,375

Worked example: Manipulating working capital ratios 1

Right Ltd currently has inventory and payables of £15,000 and receivables of £30,000. It pays its suppliers one month after receiving goods from them but allows its customers two months' credit. Right Ltd does not expect any change to its level of business, but it now proposes to reduce its receivables credit period to one month to bring it in line with its payables payment period. It also proposes an increase in its inventory levels, such that its inventory turnover period will increase from 30 days to 60 days. What will be the effect of these decisions on Right Ltd's ratios?

	Current policy days		Proposed policy days	
		£		£
Inventory turnover/Inventory	30	15,000	60	30,000
Payables period/Payables	(30)	(15,000)	(30)	(15,000)
Receivables period/Receivables	60	30,000	30	15,000
Cash operating cycle/Net current assets	60	30,000	60	30,000
Current ratio		3:1		3:1
Quick ratio		2:1		1:1

Interactive question 1: Risk in working capital decisions   [Difficulty level: Intermediate]

Is Right Ltd's proposal more or less risky than its current operation?

See **Answer** at end of this chapter.

4 The cash operating cycle

Section overview

- The cash operating cycle is the length of time between paying out cash for raw materials and other input costs and receiving the cash for goods or services supplied.

- The length of each element of working capital (receivables, payables and so on) can be calculated in days and then summed to determine the length of the cash operating cycle.

- Liquidity problems can be caused if the cash cycle becomes too long. The forecasting and control of working capital requirements is critical to the management of the cash operating cycle.

- Liquidity can be assessed using the current and quick ratios.

4.1 What is the cash operating cycle?

It is important to note that movements in working capital will have an impact on an organisation's cash balance. The efficient control of working capital is therefore vital in the management of an organisation's cash.

The measurement of the cash operating cycle focuses on the length of time between an organisation paying out cash for its raw materials and other input costs and receiving the cash for goods or services supplied.

The cash operating cycle is normally measured in days and it may be referred to as the working capital cycle. It can be depicted in Figure 7.2 below.

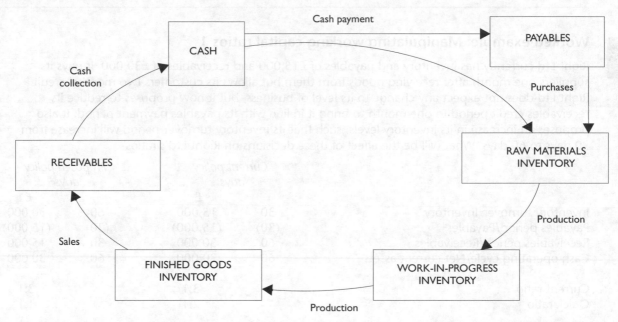

Figure 7.2: The cash operating cycle

4.2 Calculating the length of the cash operating cycle

The length of the cash cycle and its component parts can be calculated as follows

			Days
Raw materials holding period	$\dfrac{\text{Average inventory of raw materials}}{\text{Annual usage}}$	× 365 =	X
Average payables payment period	$\dfrac{\text{Average trade payables}}{\text{Annual purchases}}$	× 365 =	(X)
Average production period	$\dfrac{\text{Average inventory of work in progress}}{\text{Annual cost of sales}}$	× 365 =	X
Average inventory-holding period	$\dfrac{\text{Average inventory of finished goods}}{\text{Annual cost of sales}}$	× 365 =	X
Average receivables collection period	$\dfrac{\text{Average receivables}}{\text{Annual sales revenue}}$	× 365 =	X
Length of cycle			X

Where averages cannot be calculated or are not available then period-end balances should be used.

Interactive question 2: Calculating the cash operating cycle [Difficulty level: Intermediate]

Marlboro Ltd has the following estimated figures for the coming year:

Sales	£3,600,000
Average receivables	£306,000
Gross profit margin	25% on sales
Average inventories	
Finished goods	£200,000
Work in progress	£350,000
Raw materials	£150,000
Average payables	£130,000

Inventory levels are constant.

Raw materials represent 60% of total production cost.

Requirement

Complete the table to calculate the company's cash operating cycle. Use the space provided in the table for your workings.

Cost of sales	=		
			Days
Raw materials in inventory	=		
Credit taken from suppliers	=		( )
WIP in inventory	=		
Finished goods in inventory	=		
Credit given to customers	=		
Number of days between payment and receipt			

See **Answer** at the end of this chapter.

Worked example: Manipulating working capital ratios 2

A profitable business's inventory turnover ratio of 20 rises by 20%. Its number of receivables days rises by 10% from 70 days, but its cost of goods sold and payables days remain the same. The effect on its cash operating cycle is as follows:

		Period 1	Days	*Period 2*	Days
Inventory turnover period	Cost of sales/Inventory	365/20	18	365/(20 × 1.2)	15
Receivables days	Receivables/Revenue		70	70 × 1.1	77
			88		92

The cash operating cycle will therefore lengthen.

4.3 Investment in working capital

The level of **investment in working capital** increases considerably over the period of the cycle, as seen in Figure 7.3, which highlights the situation where raw materials are bought, processed into work in progress, then finally into finished goods. Cash paid out for labour and overheads during this time increases the investment.

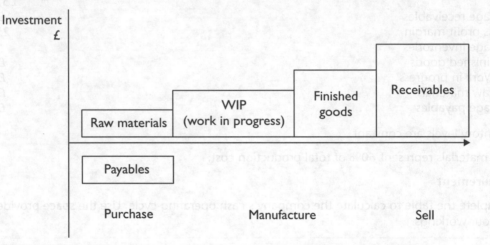

Figure 7.3: Investment in working capital

A business with inventory days of 50 and receivables days of 60 might appear to have the same working capital investment (110 days) as a company with 90 days' inventory and 20 days' receivables. In practice, the level of investment in the latter business is lower, as less capital is tied up in inventories (particularly raw materials) than in receivables.

The total investment is also influenced by:

- **Growth** (see overtrading below)

- **Inflation**. As the price of raw material inputs rises, together with labour and overhead costs in production, a firm is likely to put up its selling prices. Thus, the monetary investment in inventory + receivables – payables increases

4.4 Variations between businesses

Different types of business have different working capital requirements.

A large national supermarket chain	A civil engineering firm with many large projects, eg constructing buildings for 2012 Olympics	Manufacturer of toys or artificial Christmas trees
• High investment in inventory (for example non-food items such as clothing and electrical goods) in shops and warehouses.	• Relatively low investment in raw material inventory as each job is unique and supplies may be bought when needed.	• Due to the seasonal nature of the business, working capital requirements will fluctuate significantly during the year.
• Low investment in receivables (as most sales are in cash).	• Long WIP and receivables days. Progress payments are used to offset outflows but there may be money held back by the customer until the job is deemed satisfactory.	• Receivables will increase as customers (retailers) stock up for Christmas but will be much lower earlier in the year.
• Ability to take long credit terms from suppliers by applying various sorts of pressure. Cash operating cycle may be negative ie cash comes in before it is paid out to suppliers.		• The manufacturer is likely to spread its production process over the year to smooth production, with inventory building in the run-up to the peak period.
• Cash operating cycle relatively stable as there is not that much seasonal activity. Non-food may have a longer cycle where items spend longer in inventory (turnover is less frequent) ie overall cycle may be made up of distinct elements.		• Cash flow is likely to be disjointed – outflows whilst inventory is built up with the majority of inflows concentrated in a later period of the year. Cash operating cycle therefore likely to vary significantly depending on the time of year.

4.5 Limitations of working capital performance measures

The measures must be used with care, because:

- The balance sheet values at a particular point in time **may not be typical**.

- Balances used for **a seasonal business** will not represent average levels, eg Christmas tree manufacturer.

- Such measures concern the **past** not the future.

Therefore, measures should not be considered in isolation. **Trends** and **industry averages** are important.

4.6 Overtrading

The amount of cash required to fund the cash operating cycle will **increase** as:

- The cycle gets longer
- Sales (and hence purchases of inventory required) increase

This can often happen at the start of a new business, since

- There is **no trading record**, so suppliers are likely to insist on a very short credit period.

- There is **no reputation** to draw in customers, so a long credit period is likely to be extended to customers in order to break into the market.

- If the business has found a **'niche market'**, rapid sales expansion may occur.

This can lead to the cycle being 'out of balance', **so short**-term financing may be necessary to get over the initial period. If this finance is unavailable it may be necessary to **sell non-current assets** to pay debts or, at the extreme, to go into **insolvent liquidation**. The forecasting of working capital so as to avoid overtrading is thus of particular importance for new businesses.

4.7 Solutions to liquidity problems

The aim must be to reduce the length of the cash operating cycle by:

- **Reducing the inventory-holding period**

- **Reducing the production period** – not easy to do but it might be worth investigating different machinery or different working methods

- **Reducing customers' credit** period and tightening up on **cash collection**

- **Extending the period of credit taken from suppliers** – again, not easy to do as the business has to comply with their terms, but it is worth considering the advantages and disadvantages of taking early settlement discounts

4.8 Assessing the liquidity position

In addition to forecasting and controlling working capital it is important that the business should monitor its liquidity position on a regular basis. Two important measures that can be used to assess the liquidity position are the current ratio and the quick (liquidity) ratio.

4.8.1 Current ratio

This ratio measures the ability to meet short-term liabilities from easily or quickly realisable current assets. It is calculated as follows.

$$\text{Current ratio} = \frac{\text{Current assets}}{\text{Current liabilities}}$$

A higher value for the ratio indicates that the business is more liquid and is able more easily to meet its current liabilities from its available current assets.

In general a **higher ratio is preferable to a lower one**. However, if a business has a very high ratio this may indicate that funds are tied up in current assets, such as inventory and cash that may be used more productively elsewhere in the business.

The most appropriate level for the current ratio will depend on the type of business. For example a supermarket will have a relatively low current ratio because it does not hold inventories of raw materials and work in progress and a large proportion of its sales to customers are made for cash, with consequently a low investment in receivables.

On the other hand a manufacturer will have a relatively high current ratio because of the need to invest in inventories of raw materials and work-in-progress and to provide credit to customers.

4.8.2 Quick (liquidity) ratio

The nature of the inventory in some types of business means that it cannot be easily or quickly converted into cash. **This inventory cannot be relied upon as a liquid asset** when it is necessary to meet short-term liabilities.

The quick ratio therefore excludes inventory from the current assets as follows.

$$\text{Quick (liquidity) ratio} = \frac{\text{Current assets less inventories}}{\text{Current liabilities}}$$

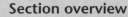

Interactive question 3: Calculating ratios to assess the liquidity position

[Difficulty level: Easy]

The following balances were recorded for a business at the end of last week.

	£'000
Inventories	982
Receivables	648
Cash	78
Payables	653

Requirement

Complete the table below to compare the current ratio and quick (liquidity) ratio with the average for businesses in the industry. Comment on the results.

	Ratio for this business	Industry average
Current ratio		2.5:1
Quick (liquidity) ratio		1.4:1

Comments on the results:

See **Answer** at the end of this chapter.

5 Managing inventory

Section overview

- There are many, usually non-financial, reasons for a business to hold inventory, but it does so at considerable cost.

- As a result, businesses try to keep inventory levels down as far as possible, using a variety of inventory control systems: re-order level, periodic review, ABC, economic order quantity (EOQ), just-in-time (JIT) and perpetual inventory.

5.1 Why hold inventory?

Inventory is an idle resource costing the business money, so there must be good reasons for holding it. Again there are trade offs:

Profitability	v	Liquidity
Higher inventories may give higher sales	v	Higher inventories mean more finance is needed

Reasons for holding inventory:

- To **meet demand** by acting as a **buffer** in times of unusually high consumption, to reduce the risk of stockouts or where supplier delivery times (lead times) are uncertain

- To **ensure continuity of production**

- To take advantage of **quantity discounts** by ordering more at a time

- To buy in ahead of a **shortage** or ahead of a **price rise**

- For **technical reasons**, such as maturing whisky or keeping oil in pipelines

- To **reduce ordering costs** by ordering more items on fewer occasions

- Because of **seasonality of demand** (eg Christmas trees) or supply
- Because suppliers insist on **minimum order quantities**
- Because **special promotions** are being offered, eg 10p off a can of beans

5.2 Costs associated with holding inventory

- **Purchase price**, ie the cost of the inventory itself
- **Holding costs**:
  - Opportunity cost of capital tied up
  - Cost of insurance
  - Risk of deterioration, obsolescence and pilferage
  - Cost of the warehousing function
  - Cost of stores administration
- **Re-order costs**:
  - Transport costs
  - Clerical and administrative expenses
  - Batch set-up costs for goods produced internally

  These costs vary with the number of orders which will increase as inventory levels are reduced.

- **Shortage costs**:
  - Production stoppages caused by lack of raw materials
  - Stockout costs for finished goods – anything from a delayed sale to a lost customer
  - Emergency re-order costs

The benefits of holding inventory must outweigh the costs.

5.3 Inventory control systems

For both finance and operational reasons it is therefore very important to control inventory levels effectively. There is a wide range of inventory control systems available.

- **Re-order level system.** A fixed quantity (the optimum order quantity – models exist for determining this) will be ordered whenever inventory falls to a pre-determined level (the re-order level). One way of doing this is to put inventory in two receptacles or 'bins'. When one empties, the next order is placed with the supplier, which should arrive by the time the second bin empties. This system aims to minimise costs while providing the necessary supply to users.

- **Periodic review system.** Inventory levels are reviewed at fixed time intervals to fit in with production schedules, and variable quantities are ordered as appropriate. This is a very simple method of inventory control.

- **ABC system.** The aim here is to reduce the work involved in inventory control in a business which may have several thousand types of inventory item. Inventory is categorised into classes A, B or C according to the annual cost of the usage of that inventory item, or the difficulty of replacements, or the importance to the production process. Class A will then take most of the inventory control effort, Class B less and Class C less still. While this seems acceptable for inventories of finished goods, it may cause problems for raw materials. There may be an item which has a very small cost but which is vital for the manufacture of the finished product. Such an item would have to be included in the Class A items because of its inherent importance, rather than its cost.

- **Economic order quantity system (EOQ).** The EOQ model for inventory control approaches mathematically the problem of when to order inventory and how much to order. The formula is:

$$EOQ = \sqrt{\frac{2cd}{h}}$$

where c = cost of placing one order

  d = estimated usage of the inventory item over a particular period

  h = cost of holding one unit of inventory for that period

The purchase price of the item is not included in the calculation; what this method attempts to do is minimise the costs and maximise the benefit of ordering and holding inventory. It does not concern itself with whether the best price is being obtained.

Worked example: Economic order quantity (EOQ)

Material X costs £100 per kg. 2,000 kgs are to be used per year, and holding costs per kg per year are £5. Each order placed costs £200 in administration time.

$$\text{EOQ for material}: \sqrt{\frac{2 \times 200 \times 2,000}{5}} = 400 \, \text{kgs}$$

Annual usage is 2,000 kgs, so 2,000/400 = 5 orders per year will be placed.

While EOQ appears to be a satisfactorily precise model, it has some serious limitations:

- It is cumbersome to apply

- Some simplifying assumptions are made about usage and a constant purchase price that may be unjustified

- It ignores the potential benefit of taking advantage of bulk discounts

- It can be very difficult in practice to estimate holding costs and the cost of placing each order

- **Just-in-time (JIT) manufacturing systems.** Production and purchasing are linked closely to sales demand on a week-to-week basis so there is a fairly continuous flow of raw materials inventories into work in progress, which becomes finished goods to go straight to a customer. This means that negligible inventories of raw materials and finished goods need to be held. Features of JIT systems include:

  - The need for flexibility of both suppliers and the workforce to expand and contract output at short notice.

  - Guaranteed quality of raw materials. Quality must be maintained at every stage. There are no inventories in reserve should one batch of raw materials prove to be faulty, so production would stop until a further delivery can be made.

  - Close working relationship between suppliers and users including geographical proximity in order to be able to make immediate deliveries.

  - Willingness of the workforce to increase or decrease working hours from one period to another. This could be done by having a core workforce with a group of part-time or freelance workers.

  - Rationalised factory layout systems to minimise movements between stages.

- **Perpetual inventory methods.** Where a business keeps perpetual inventory records, there will frequently be a replenishment point that triggers off an order. This may be by way of an exception report for a computerised system. Such a system relies upon the accuracy of the records, not on physical measures such as the two-bin system. Point of sale terminals in shops automatically update inventory records as each sale is made. One advantage of such a system is the data it provides to management to determine which product lines are moving rapidly. Marketing managers may also use the data to make tactical decisions on special prices and promotions to sell slow-moving items.

- **Other ways to manage inventory:**

  - Sub-contract (**outsource**) non-core processes, passing on the inventory holding problem to another business.

  - Obtain **progress payments** from customers, thus reducing the net capital required to finance inventory.

  - Reduce the number of product lines, eg drop products near the end of their **product life cycle**.

6 Managing trade payables

Section overview

• Trade credit is generally a cheap source of finance.

Credit periods for the buyer are a source of short-term finance. For example, if a buyer decides not to pay its trade debts for a further month, it has obtained a further month's use of its cash.

Trade payables are not, however, without cost:

• **Credit status** may be lost so the supplier gives low priority to the buyer's future orders, with consequent disruption of activities.

• The supplier may **raise prices** in order to compensate for the finance which he is involuntarily supplying.

• The buyer will lose any **cash discount** for prompt payment; the cost of the lost discount should be compared with other short-term sources of finance, eg overdrafts.

The advantages of trade credit are that:

• It is **convenient and informal** (ie it is unusual to tell your suppliers that you do not intend to pay them on time, though after a while they will realise anyway).

• It can be used by businesses which **do not qualify for credit** from a financial institution.

• It does not prevent advantage being taken of **settlement discounts** (which can result in a very cheap source of financing) because a period of time is still allowed before payment has to be made.

• Trade credit can represent a **virtual subsidy or sales promotion device** offered by the seller – for example, favourable terms may be offered when a new company is set up.

• It can be used on a **very short-term basis** to overcome unexpected cash flow crises.

Because of these advantages, a business should:

• Consider **switching suppliers** if better credit terms are available or if better terms exist for sole supplier relationships.

• Negotiate better terms for buying **large quantities**.

• **Reconcile statements** (make sure that what the supplier says a company owes agrees with what the company thinks it owes).

• Pay only on completion of **correct delivery**.

7 Managing trade receivables

Section overview

• The cost of granting credit to customers has to be balanced against the benefits of doing so.
• Proper management of trade receivables should ensure an adequate level of collections.
• Trade receivables may be financed by invoice discounting or factoring.

7.1 What is the ideal level of trade receivables?

The management of trade receivables involves the business trading-off:

• The **costs of extending credit** to customers – these include finance costs, irrecoverable debts and administrative costs of the credit control department.

• The **benefits of granting credit** – in their simplest form these are larger profits due to the increased sales generated because of the credit terms offered.

The costs of extending credit can be difficult to quantify (particularly the administrative costs) and the benefits are also difficult to measure. Most firms would find it very difficult to forecast the precise effect on sales of, for example, increasing credit terms by ten days. Nevertheless, the trade-off must be considered when making credit management decisions.

Managing the level of trade receivables involves some very practical issues, usually undertaken by the receivables ledger and credit control sections of the business's finance function.

7.2 Credit control and collection policies

Credit control and collection policies should be set at **board level**. Implementation of the policies may fall outside the remit of the finance function itself, but the **treasury management** section could certainly be involved in credit control.

7.2.1 Credit terms and settlement discounts

Credit terms can be changed and must respond to competition, new markets etc but they will be influenced largely by **trade custom** which may, for example, be payment within 60 days.

Settlement discounts are again influenced largely by custom and practice within the industry. The business must ensure the cost does not outweigh the benefit, and should compare it with the cost of other sources of short-term finance, eg overdraft. Offering discounts can be expensive. For example, if it costs a company 2% discount per month to get receipts early from customers, the annual cost is $1.02^{12} - 1 = 26.8\%$.

Worked example: Settlement discount

Left Ltd has monthly sales of £20,000. 25% of receivables are paid within one month of a sale, and 70% are paid within two months, but 5% of receivables are never paid. Left Ltd proposes offering a 3% discount to receivables settling invoices within one month of the invoice date. As a result, monthly sales are predicted to rise to £25,000, and 50% of trade receivables will pay within one month. 44% will pay within two months but irrecoverable debts will rise to 6%. All sales are invoiced at the end of each month. The discount will be offered for all invoices issued from Month 1. By how much will total cash inflows from trade receivables in Months 1 and 2 change as a result, and what will be the effect on profit?

	Sales	Cash received Month 1	Month 2	Irrecoverable debts	Discount allowed
	£	£	£	£	£
Current policy		25%	70%	5%	
Sales M1	20,000	5,000	14,000	1,000	0
Sales M2	20,000	0	5,000	0	0
Total cash		5,000	19,000	1,000	0
Proposed policy		50% × 97%	44%	6%	50% × 3%
Sales M1	25,000	12,125	11,000	1,500	375
Sales M2	25,000	0	12,125	0	0
		12,125	23,125	1,500	375

There is a large cash flow benefit of £7,125 in Month 1, and a benefit of £4,125 per month once the normal pattern is established. The reduction in monthly profits caused by increased irrecoverable debts is £500, while profits are further reduced by £375 with respect to the discount allowed.

The company must **communicate its terms** to customers clearly and unambiguously:

- On orders
- On invoices
- On statements

The settlement discount policy must be **enforced**, otherwise most customers will continue to take the settlement discount as a matter of course, whether or not they pay on time.

7.2.2 Credit rating

The risk that a customer will not pay its debts can be indicated by giving each customer a **credit rating**. Customers who pay on time are given a high credit rating, but those who pay slowly are given a low one; some customers may be refused credit altogether, so supplies are only made against cash.

Credit ratings should be based on:

- An assessment of the **ability of the customer** to meet the liabilities.

- An assessment of **financial statements**, particularly for major customers.

- The use of **credit-rating agencies** (eg Dun and Bradstreet) who rate the customer according to a number of factors related to its ability to pay.

- An analysis of **on going trading experience** with each customer.

- The practice in some industries whereby **credit managers liaise regularly** to exchange information with other businesses. This is very useful, since members will alert each other as soon as problems are identified.

- **Credit limits** on how much can be outstanding on a customer's account at any time. These should be reviewed frequently and reported immediately if exceeded so that necessary action can be taken.

- **Trade and bank references**, although these may be so bland as to be of limited value; these references may provide valuable corroboration of other sources of information however.

Credit ratings should be **reviewed regularly**.

Interactive question 4: Collection procedures [Difficulty level: Exam standard]

You are employed in the receivables ledger section of Kott plc. Your manager has asked you to help in a project to improve the cash operating cycle of Kott plc.

Requirement

Identify **three** ways in which collection of amounts owed by customers could be speeded up.

See **Answer** at the end of this chapter.

7.3 Financing trade receivables

Receivables are an asset, and so can be **'sold'** like any other asset by means of invoice discounting or factoring.

7.3.1 Invoice discounting

This involves selling the invoices to a discounting company for a **cash sum**, then repaying the discounter when the debtor pays the invoice. Note that the business retains full responsibility for sales ledger, credit control and collection functions. However, the discounting company may perform certain credit checks and ratings before entering the agreement. This form of discounting is effectively a form of overdraft facility as the discounter makes a charge for lending the money.

7.3.2 Receivables factoring

This contains three closely integrated elements:

- **Accounting and collection** – the business is paid by the factor as customers settle their invoices or after an agreed settlement period. The factor maintains the sales ledger accounting function.

- **Credit control** – the factor is responsible for chasing the customers and speeding up the collection of debts. Recourse factoring means that any bad debts are passed back to the client company. Non-recourse factoring provides 100% bad debt insurance, that is the client does not suffer from the cost of bad debts.

- **Finance against sales** – the factor advances, say, 80% of the value of sales immediately on invoicing.

Factoring is becoming increasingly competitive; generally, factors will act for customers with revenue in excess of £100,000 and invoices over £100. The usual fees are about 2-3% of invoice value as an administration charge, plus a charge for cash advances. The major disadvantage is the loss of immediate contact with the customer, who may see factoring as a sign of financial problems.

7.4 Good practice in receivables management

Good practice can be summarised as: **look after key accounts** and **manage time scales**.

7.4.1 Look after key accounts

It frequently happens that 20% of customers represent 80% of the debts. These customers, and their debts, must receive **special attention**.

7.4.2 Manage time scales

Attempt to reduce all time scales between **placement of an order** and **receipt of cash from the customer**, and eliminate any causes of disputes or non-payments. This should serve to tighten up the cash operating cycle in general.

The following are some practical examples.

- To reduce the time between the placement of the order and the receipt of goods by the customer:
  - Encourage customers to switch to the quickest method of ordering such as internet ordering.
  - Make sure orders are taken accurately.
  - Clear orders for creditworthiness as soon as possible.
  - Make the despatch as quickly as possible, supported/accompanied by accurate despatch documentation; a computerised online order processing and invoicing system will reduce delays.
  - Use efficient carriers.

- To reduce the time taken to **bill your customer**:
  - Issue invoices on time – customers will not pay without them.
  - Ensure disputed invoices are agreed as soon as possible.
  - Issue statements promptly each month, as many customers pay only on statement; acknowledge disputed items on the statement, so that the 'agreed' items will be paid more quickly.
  - Be flexible, and invoice to meet the customer's requirements (eg provide duplicate copies if requested).

- To reduce the time taken **to collect debts**:
  - Credit control reports must state the age of each transaction and the number of days overdue for payment. These aged lists should help detect changes in the length of time taken to collect debts and can be prepared in total and/or by customer.

Worked example: Total receivables ageing

	November 20X1 Outstanding £	% of total	December 20X1 Outstanding £	% of total
0-30 days	10,000	86.2	12,000	80.5
31-60 days	1,000	8.6	2,000	13.4
61-90 days	500	4.3	750	5.0
90+ days	100	0.9	150	1.1
	11,600	100.0	14,900	100.0

The changes from November to December show customers taking longer to pay. It might be a normal seasonal pattern. If not, the customers who are responsible need to be identified.

Worked example: Customer ageing, December 20

Customer	0 – 30 days £	31 – 60 days £	61 – 90 days £	90+ days £
Sid plc	200	–	–	–
Snow plc	150	20	–	–
Gizzard Ltd	120	80	60	40
⋮	⋮	⋮	⋮	⋮
	12,000	2,000	750	150

Gizzard Ltd appears to be one of the problem customers; perhaps it is time to start more aggressive collection procedures?

7.4.3 Other ideas

- **Issue credit notes promptly**

- **Deal personally** with those people who pass invoices or sign cheques. Do not be fobbed off too often with 'the cheque's in the mail!'

- Pay **commission** to salespeople on cash collected, not on sales so that they will be motivated to ensure their contacts pay up

- Set **targets** for receivables days or percentage overdue accounts; report actual performance against targets and review performance regularly: set incentives and pay bonuses to credit managers

7.5 Trade credit insurance

Trade credit insurance insures a business against the possible **default and insolvency of its credit customers** and, where exports are involved, **political risk**. It is therefore a useful tool in credit management, helping to minimise possible problems from late payment and bad debts.

Credit insurance means a business can:

- Insure all or part of its receivables ledger against default by a customer
- Include a 'first loss' (or excess) on its accounts to be insured
- Be insured only up to a ceiling ('credit limit')

The premium paid will vary in accordance with the above factors.

The insurer invariably sets a credit limit on the maximum amount that can be insured. Policies cost between 0.20% and 0.50% of annual revenue on accounts to be insured. However, premiums are also influenced by factors such as effectiveness of credit control systems, length of credit given and previous experience of irrecoverable debts. The policyholder will have to accept part of any loss; credit insurers will typically accept 75% to 95% of any loss, the balance being taken by the policyholder. Insurance brokers or insurance intermediaries usually arrange policies.

8 Treasury management

> **Section overview**
>
> - The risks of running out of cash have to be balanced against the costs of holding cash, just like with inventory.
> - Businesses have four motives for holding cash: transactions, finance, precautionary and investment motives.
> - Short term surpluses of cash should be invested; short term shortages of cash need to be funded.
> - Effective transmission of cash will improve the promptness with which the business benefits from having cash.

8.1 The basic trade-off: cost of holding v cost of running out of cash

To manage its cash position successfully the business must trade off the cost of holding cash against the cost of running out of cash.

The **cost of holding cash**, either as a cash float or in a current account, is the opportunity cost of what else could be done with the money. Cash is an idle asset and earns little or no return. If the funds were put to work elsewhere (ie invested) they could generate profits.

The **costs of running out of cash** vary, depending upon the circumstances of the business. Cash shortages result in the business not being able to pay its payables on time, and this could have many implications. Examples include:

- **Loss of settlement discounts** from trade suppliers
- Loss of **supplier goodwill**, eg refusal of further credit, higher prices, poor delivery
- Poor **industrial relations** if wage payments are delayed
- Creditors petitioning for **winding-up** the business

Although the above costs may be difficult to quantify the business must at all times ensure that it has sufficient liquidity, in the form of cash balances or overdraft/loan facilities, to maintain its solvency.

8.2 Influences on cash balances

There are a number of motives underlying how much a business would wish to hold as cash:

- **Transactions motive** – to meet current day-to-day financial obligations, eg payroll, the purchase of raw materials, etc.

- **Finance motive** – to cover major items such as the repayment of loans and the purchase of non-current assets.

- **Precautionary motive** – to give a cushion against unplanned expenditure, rather like buffer inventory.

- **Investment motive** – to take advantage of market opportunities.

8.3 Aim of good cash management

The primary aim of good cash management is to **have the right amount of cash available at the right time**. This involves:

- Accurate **cash budgeting/forecasting**, so that shortfalls and surpluses can be anticipated
- **Planning short-term finance** when necessary
- **Planning investment of surpluses** when necessary
- Cost-efficient **cash transmission**

8.4 Short-term finance

- **Receivable factoring** and **invoice discounting**;

- **Bank overdrafts**:

  - May be used to fund fluctuating working capital

  - Are technically repayable on demand, so carry some risk

  - Normally carry a flat charge for the facility and variable interest on the balance, eg 1–5% above base rate

  - Are flexible in that the business borrows only when it needs to (unlike a fixed term loan)

- **Short-term bank loans**:

  - Should ideally match the term of the loan with the duration of the project
  - Can have fixed or variable rates of interest

- **Operating leases** allow the business to have use of long-term assets such as plant or vehicles without paying the full amount of their cost. Instead, a regular amount is paid out each month to give use of the asset, while the risks of ownership remain with the lessor.

8.5 Investing surplus funds

If a business identifies a **short-term surplus of funds** it should aim to invest it to earn a return. If the surplus is of a **longer-term** nature it should be invested in longer-term projects to increase shareholder wealth, or returned to shareholders as dividends.

Surplus funds can be invested in various financial products:

- **Treasury bills** issued by the Bank of England on behalf of the government, which have a minimum investment of £50,000+, run for three months and are highly secure and liquid, but offer low returns.

- **Deposits**, which offer investment periods ranging from overnight to five years. They are available from banks, local authorities and building societies with yields exceeding that of Treasury bills.

- **Gilts** (longer-term government debt), which offer a large range of maturities and rates based on money market rates; they can have capital gains tax advantages.

- **Bonds**, which are debentures and loans of companies quoted on the stock market; rates fluctuate with general interest rates and there is good liquidity.

- **Equities** dealt on the Stock Exchange offer good marketability and liquidity but relatively high risk.

Most businesses will be looking for a variety of investments in order to minimise the risks involved, and also to ensure that some cash is available at short notice and some is invested longer term to obtain higher interest rates.

When choosing investments from the list above the following factors should be considered:

- The amount of funds available
- The length of time for which the funds are available
- The likelihood of needing early withdrawal (consider liquidity)
- The notice period for withdrawal, and penalties
- The risk and the return of the investment

8.6 Transmission of cash

Making sure that funds such as cash, cheques and automated receipts go promptly into a business's bank account is very important.

The interval between when funds are paid into a bank and when they can be drawn upon depends on the **clearing mechanism** used.

- **General clearing** (mainly of cheques, but most internet transfers still take the same amount of time!) – this covers items of any size but there is generally a three to four day delay before funds are cleared (ie can be drawn upon).

- **Clearing House Automated Payment System (CHAPS)** – this covers items ≥ £10,000 and provides same-day clearing, so funds have value more quickly.

- **Banks Automated Clearing System (BACS)** – this deals with salaries, standing orders and direct debits. The account of the payer is debited on the same day as the account of the recipient is credited.

Practical matters should be managed carefully:

- Banking routines – bank regularly
- Banking procedure, eg varying the route taken for security
- Analysis of clearing times, eg a percentage of dividend cheques may take up to six months to be banked so funds are not needed immediately the cheque is written
- Same day clearing is available if both parties bank at the same branch

9 Cash budgets

Section overview

- A cash budget shows the cash effect of all the decisions taken in the budgetary planning exercise.

- It is a statement tabulating future cash receipts and payments to show the forecast cash balance of a business at defined intervals.

- The appropriate management action to be taken in response to forecast cash deficits or surpluses will depend on whether the situation is expected to be short term or longer term.

- Certain non-cash items such as depreciation are not included in a cash budget.

A **cash budget** is a statement in which estimated future cash receipts and payments are tabulated in such a way as to show the forecast cash balance of a business at defined intervals.

9.1 Preparing cash budgets

For example, in December 20X2 an accounts department might wish to estimate the cash position of the business during the three following months, January to March 20X3. A cash budget might be drawn up in the following format.

	Jan £	Feb £	Mar £
Estimated cash receipts			
From accounts payable	14,000	16,500	17,000
From cash sales	3,000	4,000	4,500
Proceeds on disposal of non-current assets		2,200	
Total cash receipts	17,000	22,700	21,500
Estimated cash payments			
To suppliers of goods	8,000	7,800	10,500
To employees (wages)	3,000	3,500	3,500
Purchase of non-current assets		16,000	
Rent and rates			1,000
Other overheads	1,200	1,200	1,200
Repayment of loan	2,500		
	14,700	28,500	16,200
Net surplus/(deficit) for month	2,300	(5,800)	5,300
Opening cash balance	1,200	3,500	(2,300)
Closing cash balance	3,500	(2,300)	3,000

In this example the accounts department has calculated that the cash balance at the beginning of the budget period, 1 January, will be £1,200. Estimates have been made of the cash that is likely to be received by the business (from cash and credit sales, and from a planned disposal of non-current assets in February). Similar estimates have been made of cash due to be paid out by the business (payments to suppliers and employees, payments for rent, rates and other overheads, payment for a planned purchase of non-current assets in February and a loan repayment due in January).

From these estimates it is a simple step to calculate the net cash movement in each month. In some months the budgeted cash payments may exceed cash receipts and there will be a **deficit** for the month; this occurs during February in the above example because of the large investment in non-current assets in that month.

The last part of this cash budget shows how the business's estimated cash balance can then be rolled along from month to month. Starting with the opening balance of £1,200 at 1 January a cash surplus of £2,300 is generated in January. This leads to a closing January balance of £3,500, which becomes the opening balance for February. The deficit of £5,800 in February throws the business's cash position into **overdraft** and the overdrawn balance of £2,300 becomes the opening balance for March. Finally, the cash surplus of £5,300 in March leaves the business with a favourable cash position of £3,000 at the end of the budget period.

9.2 The usefulness of cash budgets

Cash budgets enable management to make any **forward planning decisions** that may be needed, such as advising their bank of estimated overdraft requirements or strengthening their credit control procedures to ensure that customers pay more quickly.

The cash budget can also give management an indication of **potential problems** that could arise and allows them the opportunity to take action to avoid such problems. A cash budget can show **potential cash positions** as explored in Section 9.3 below. Management will need to take appropriate action depending on the potential position.

9.3 Potential cash positions

Interactive question 5: Cash budget [Difficulty level: Easy]

Tick to show which of the following should be included in a **cash** budget.

	Include	Do not include
Funds from the receipt of a bank loan		
Revaluation of a non-current asset		
Receipt of dividends from outside the business		
Depreciation of distribution vehicles		
Bad debts written off		
Share dividend paid		

See **Answer** at the end of this chapter.

Worked example: Preparing a cash budget

Penny operates a retail business. Purchases are sold at cost plus 331/3%.

(a)

	Budgeted sales in month £	Labour cost in month £	Expenses incurred in month £
January	40,000	3,000	4,000
February	60,000	3,000	6,000
March	160,000	5,000	7,000
April	120,000	4,000	7,000

(b) It is management policy to have sufficient inventory in hand at the end of each month to meet half of next month's sales demand.

(c) Suppliers for materials and expenses are paid in the month after the purchases are made/expenses incurred. Labour is paid in full by the end of each month.

(d) Expenses include a monthly depreciation charge of £2,000.

(e) (i) 75% of sales are for cash.
(ii) 25% of sales are on one month's credit.

(f) The company will buy equipment costing £18,000 for cash in February and will pay a dividend of £20,000 in March. The opening cash balance at 1 February is £1,000.

Requirement

Prepare a cash budget for February and March and comment on the result.

Solution

Cash budget

	February £	March £
Receipts		
Receipts from sales	55,000 (W1)	135,000 (W2)
Payments		
Trade payables	37,500 (W3)	82,500 (W3)
Expense payables	2,000 (W4)	4,000 (W4)
Labour	3,000	5,000
Equipment purchase	18,000	–
Dividend	–	20,000
Total payments	60,500	111,500
Receipts less payments	(5,500)	23,500
Opening cash balance b/f	1,000	(4,500)
Closing cash balance c/f	(4,500)	19,000

WORKINGS

(1)

		£
Receipts in February	75% of Feb sales (75% × £60,000)	45,000
	25% of Jan sales (25% × £40,000)	10,000
		55,000

(2)

		£
Receipts in March	75% of Mar sales (75% × £160,000)	120,000
	25% of Feb sales (25% × £60,000)	15,000
		135,000

(3) **Purchases**

	January		February	
		£		£
For Jan sales	(50% of £30,000)	15,000		
For Feb sales	(50% of £45,000)	22,500	(50% of £45,000)	22,500
For Mar sales		–	(50% of £120,000)	60,000
		37,500		82,500

These purchases are paid for in February and March.

(4) **Expenses**

Cash expenses in January (£4,000 – £2,000) and February (£6,000 – £2,000) are paid in February and March respectively. Depreciation is not a cash item.

Note: Steps should be taken either to ensure that an **overdraft facility** is available for the cash shortage at the end of February, or to **defer certain payments** so that the overdraft is avoided. Some payments must be made on due dates (payroll, taxation and so on) but it is possible that other payments can be delayed, depending on the requirements of the business and/or the goodwill of suppliers.

Interactive question 6: Cash budget   [Difficulty level: Intermediate]

You are presented with the budgeted data shown in Annex A for the period November 20X1 to June 20X2 by your firm. It has been extracted from the other functional budgets that have been prepared.

You are also told the following.

(a) Sales are 40% cash, 60% credit. Credit sales are paid two months after the month of sale.

(b) Purchases are paid in the month following purchase.

(c) 75% of wages are paid in the current month and 25% the following month.

(d) Overheads are paid the month after they are incurred. The overhead figures include monthly depreciation of £2,000.

(e) Dividends are paid three months after they are declared.

(f) Capital expenditure is paid two months after it is incurred.

(g) The opening cash balance is £15,000.

Annex A

	Nov X1	Dec X1	Jan X2	Feb X2	Mar X2	Apr X2	May X2	June X2
	£	£	£	£	£	£	£	£
Sales	80,000	100,000	110,000	130,000	140,000	150,000	160,000	180,000
Purchases	40,000	60,000	80,000	90,000	110,000	130,000	140,000	150,000
Wages	10,000	12,000	16,000	20,000	24,000	28,000	32,000	36,000
Overheads	12,000	12,000	17,000	17,000	17,000	22,000	22,000	22,000
Dividends declared		20,000						40,000
Capital expenditure			30,000			40,000		

Use the following framework to prepare the cash budget.

	January £'000	February £'000	March £'000	April £'000	May £'000	June £'000
Receipts						
Sales revenue:						
Cash						
Credit						

	January £'000	February £'000	March £'000	April £'000	May £'000	June £'000
Payments						
Purchases						
Wages						
75%						
25%						
Overheads						
Dividends						
Capital						
expenditure	___	___	___	___	___	___
	===	===	===	===	===	===
Net cash flow						
Opening balance	___	___	___	___	___	___
Closing balance	===	===	===	===	===	===

See **Answer** at the end of this chapter.

Summary and Self-test

Summary

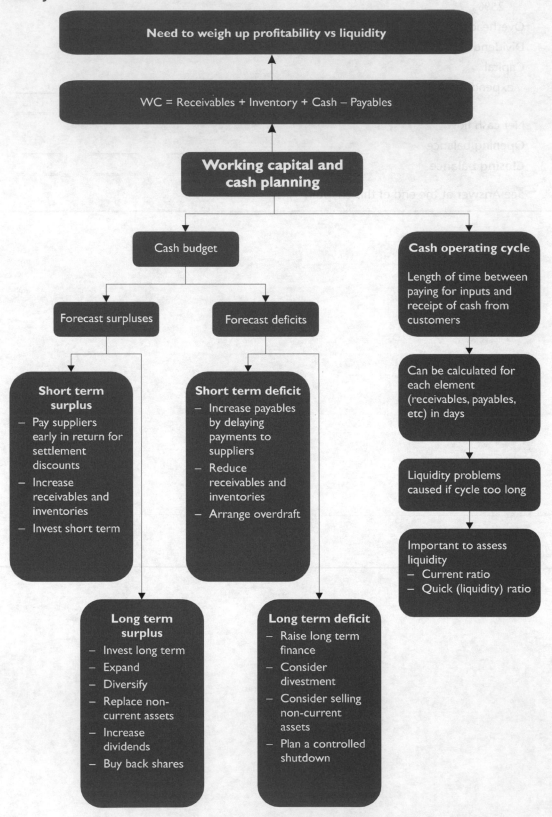

Need to weigh up profitability vs liquidity

WC = Receivables + Inventory + Cash − Payables

Working capital and cash planning

Cash budget

Cash operating cycle

Length of time between paying for inputs and receipt of cash from customers

Forecast surpluses

Forecast deficits

Can be calculated for each element (receivables, payables, etc) in days

Short term surplus
- Pay suppliers early in return for settlement discounts
- Increase receivables and inventories
- Invest short term

Short term deficit
- Increase payables by delaying payments to suppliers
- Reduce receivables and inventories
- Arrange overdraft

Liquidity problems caused if cycle too long

Important to assess liquidity
- Current ratio
- Quick (liquidity) ratio

Long term surplus
- Invest long term
- Expand
- Diversify
- Replace non-current assets
- Increase dividends
- Buy back shares

Long term deficit
- Raise long term finance
- Consider divestment
- Consider selling non-current assets
- Plan a controlled shutdown

ICAEW

Self-test

Answer the following questions.

1   X will begin trading on 1 January 20X3. The following sales revenue is budgeted for January to March 20X3.

January	February	March
£13,000	£17,000	£10,000

Five per cent of sales will be for cash. The remainder will be credit sales. A discount of 5% will be offered on all cash sales. The payment pattern for credit sales is expected to be as follows.

Invoices paid in the month after sale	75%
Invoices paid in the second month after sale	23%
Bad debts	2%

Invoices are issued on the last day of each month.

The amount budgeted to be received from customers in March 20X3 is:

A   £15,428
B   £15,453
C   £15,618
D   £16,215

2   The amount of working capital is most likely to increase when

A   Work-in-progress falls
B   Selling prices increase
C   The credit period allowed to customers is reduced
D   The credit period taken from suppliers is increased

3   A retailing company earns a gross profit margin of 37.5% on its monthly sales of £20,000. In order to generate additional cash, the following changes are proposed:

	Present	Proposed
Inventory holding period	1.5 months	1.0 month
Trade payable payment period	1.0 month	1.3 months

How much additional cash will be generated at the end of the month in which these changes take place?

A   £2,500
B   £3,750
C   £6,250
D   £10,000

4   Selected figures from a firm's budget for next month are as follows:

Sales	£450,000
Gross profit on sales	30%
Decrease in trade payables over the month	£10,000
Increase in cost of inventory held over the month	£18,000

What is the budgeted payment to trade payables?

A   £343,000
B   £323,000
C   £307,000
D   £287,000

5   A company's cash budget for next year shows a cash deficit for the months of April and May. For the remaining months there will be a cash surplus.

Which TWO of the following management actions would be most appropriate in response to the expected cash position in April and May?

A   Increase inventories of raw materials
B   Arrange a bank overdraft
C   Delay the payment of suppliers as much as possible
D   Issue additional share capital
E   Offer additional credit to customers

6   The following are items from APC Ltd's opening and closing balance sheet and income statements for the year 20X8.

	1 January £'000	31 December £'000
Receivables	800	900
Inventory	600	700
Payables	200	250

Credit sales	£10,000,000
Cost of goods sold	£6,000,000

What is the approximate length of the cash operating cycle?

A   54 days
B   57 days
C   61 days
D   84 days

7   Gemstrong Ltd is a retail company that has average sales of £14.6m per annum and earns a mark-up of 25%. Inventory averages £2.0m, receivables average £0.9m and trade payables £0.6m.

If all sales and purchases are on credit, how long is the company's cash operating cycle (to the nearest day)?

A   58 days
B   66 days
C   69 days
D   104 days

8   A company sells inventory at a profit to a customer on credit. How will this transaction affect each of the following ratios immediately after the transaction?

Current ratio	☐ Increase	☐ Decrease	☐ Stay the same
Quick (liquidity) ratio	☐ Increase	☐ Decrease	☐ Stay the same

9   A subsidiary which sells goods wholesale has a year-end trade payables balance of £192,000. The remainder of the working capital items consist of trade receivables, inventories and cash.

The inventory, receivables and payables balances were the same at the year end as at the beginning of the year.

Relevant financial ratios for the year are as follows:

Quick (liquidity) ratio	1.7:1
Rate of inventory turnover	6 times p.a.
Payables payment period	1.5 months

The current ratio to the nearest whole number at the year end is ☐

10 A retailing company's working capital consists of inventory, trade receivables, cash and trade payables. All working capital balances were the same at the beginning and the end of the year. The sales revenue for the year was £900,000.

The financial ratios for the year include the following.

Current ratio	3.4:1
Rate of inventory turnover	15 times p.a.
Receivables collection period	73.0 days
Payables payment period	36.5 days
Gross profit margin	20.0%

The closing cash balance was £ [   ]

Now go back to the Learning Objectives in the Introduction. If you are satisfied you have achieved these objectives, please tick them off.

Answers to Interactive questions

Answer to Interactive question 1

While liquidity as seen in the current ratio is unaffected by the decisions, when we look at the quick ratio, which treats inventory as non-current in the short term, we can clearly see that Right Ltd's short-term liquidity will decrease as a result of the proposed changes, so it is a riskier policy.

Answer to Interactive question 2

Cost of sales = 75% × £3,600,000 = £2,700,000

		Days
Raw materials in inventory	$= \dfrac{150,000}{2,700,000 \times 60\%} \times 365$	34
Credit taken from suppliers	$= \dfrac{130,000}{*2,700,000 \times 60\%} \times 365$	(29)
WIP in inventory	$= \dfrac{350,000}{2,700,000} \times 365$	47
Finished goods in inventory	$= \dfrac{200,000}{2,700,000} \times 365$	27
Credit given to customers	$= \dfrac{306,000}{3,600,000} \times 365$	31
Number of days between payment and receipt		110

* Since inventory levels are constant, annual purchases = annual usage.

Answer to Interactive question 3

	Ratio for this business	Industry average
Current ratio	$\dfrac{(982 + 648 + 78)}{653} = \dfrac{1,708}{653} = 2.6{:}1$	2.5:1
Quick (liquidity) ratio	$\dfrac{(1,708 - 982)}{653} = 1.1{:}1$	1.4:1

Comments on the results:

The current ratio is close to the industry average, which appears to suggest an adequate level of liquidity. However when inventory is deducted from the current assets the quick ratio is below the industry average. This business is more reliant than average on liquidating its inventory in order to meet its current liabilities. The importance of this will depend upon how quickly the inventory can be turned into cash, ie the length of the cash operating cycle. Moreover, the business has relatively little cash and its liquidity as measured by the quick ratio relies on the quality of its receivables, ie how likely customers are to pay their debts and how quickly they will pay.

Answer to Interactive question 4

- Set clearly defined procedures to be followed. Establish timings for issuing letters of demand and the point when further deliveries should stop.

- Ensure the receivables ledger section liaises with marketing management to see if the latter can assist.

- Consider creating a stop list ie suspending supplies, etc.

- Decide whether outside assistance, such as solicitors, trade associations and debt collection agencies are needed earlier in the cycle to collect overdue debts.

- Assess whether it may be cheaper to collect debts through the court system than through outside help.

Answer to Interactive question 5

Any item that is a cash flow will be included. Non-cash items are excluded from a cash budget.

	Include	Do not include
Funds from the receipt of a bank loan	✓	
Revaluation of a non-current asset		✓
Receipt of dividends from outside the business	✓	
Depreciation of distribution vehicles		✓
Bad debts written off		✓
Share dividend paid	✓	

Answer to Interactive question 6

	January £'000	February £'000	March £'000	April £'000	May £'000	June £'000
Receipts						
Sales revenue:						
Cash	44	52	56	60	64	72
Credit	48	60	66	78	84	90
	92	112	122	138	148	162
Payments						
Purchases	60	80	90	110	130	140
Wages:						
75%	12	15	18	21	24	27
25%	3	4	5	6	7	8
Overheads	10	15	15	15	20	20
Dividends			20			
Capital expenditure			30			40
	85	114	178	152	181	235
Net cash flow	7	(2)	(56)	(14)	(33)	(73)
Opening balance	15	22	20	(36)	(50)	(83)
Closing balance	22	20	(36)	(50)	(83)	(156)

Answers to Self-test

1 A

	Received in March
	£
Cash sales (5% × £10,000) × 95%	475.00
February sales (£17,000 × 95%) × 75%	12,112.50
January sales (£13,000 × 95%) × 23%	2,840.50
	15,428.00

If you answered B you forgot to allow for five per cent discount on cash sales.

If you selected C as the correct answer you have included the bad debts for March as a cash receipt.

If you answered D you forgot that credit sales amounted to only 95 per cent of each month's budgeted sales revenue.

2 B

A, C and D will cause a fall. B may increase receivables.

3 D

Monthly cost of sales = £20,000 × 62.5%
= £12,500

	£	£
Existing inventory level 1.5 × £12,500		18,750
New inventory level 1 × £12,500		(12,500)
Change in inventory level		6,250
Existing payables 1 × £12,500	12,500	
New payables 1.3 × £12,500	16,250	
Change in payables		3,750
Total change in working capital		10,000

If you answered A you treated the change in payables as a cause of a reduction in cash. However, if payables increase this will increase their cash inflow. The other two incorrect options considered each of the changes separately, but their effects must be combined to derive the correct answer.

4 A

	£'000
Cost of sales for month = £450,000 × 70%	315
Decrease in trade payables	10
Increase in inventory	18
Budgeted payment to trade payables	343

If you selected an incorrect option you did not treat the change in trade payables and inventory balances correctly.

An increase in inventory indicates that budgeted purchases are greater than the budgeted cost of goods to be sold in the month, which would increase the amount payable to suppliers. Since the balance owed to suppliers is budgeted to decrease, this further increases the amount budgeted to be paid to suppliers.

5   B,C

The budget forewarns of a short term deficit and these are the two most appropriate responses to this situation.

Action taken to increase inventories or to offer additional credit to customers will result in cash outflows. These are not appropriate actions in the light of a short term deficit.

Although the issue of additional share capital would help to reduce or eliminate a cash deficit, this would be a more appropriate action to take if the predicted deficit were expected to continue in the longer term.

6   B

Average inventory	= £650,000		
Inventory period	$= \dfrac{650 \times 365}{6,000}$	=	39.54 days
Average receivables	= £850,000		
Receivables period	$= \dfrac{850 \times 365}{10,000}$	=	31.03 days
Average payables	= £225,000		
Purchases	= cost of goods sold plus increase in inventory		
	= £6,000,000 + £100,000		
	= £6,100,000		
Payables period	$= \dfrac{225 \times 365}{6,100}$	=	(13.46) days
Cash operating cycle			57 days

If you selected 84 days you added together the days for each element of working capital. However, the payable period, during which the company takes credit from suppliers, reduces the length of the cycle and hence should be deducted.

7   B

		Days
Receivable days	$(0.9/14.6) \times 365$	22.5
Payable days	$(0.6/(14.6 \div 1.25)) \times 365$	(18.8)
Inventory days	$(2.0/(14.6 \div 1.25)) \times 365$	62.5
		66.2

If you selected 58 days you based your calculations of payables days and inventory days on the sales revenue rather than on the cost of sales.

If you arrived at an answer of 69 days you performed your calculations using a margin of 25 per cent of sales, rather than a mark up of 25 per cent of cost.

If you selected 104 days you added together the days for each element of working capital. The payables days should be subtracted, since credit from suppliers reduces the cash operating cycle.

8   Both ratios will increase. The current liability figure used as the denominator will stay the same in both cases. The total of the current assets will increase because of the profit element in receivables, therefore the current ratio will increase. The total of the liquid assets will also increase therefore the quick (liquidity) ratio will increase.

9   The current ratio at the year end is $\boxed{3:1}$

WORKING

Payables payment period (in months) $= \dfrac{\text{Average payables}}{\text{Purchases}} \times 12$

$$1.5 = \dfrac{£192,000}{\text{Purchases}} \times 12$$

Purchases $= £1,536,000$

Inventory = unchanged $\therefore$ cost of sales $= $ Purchases

Rate of inventory turnover $= \dfrac{\text{Cost of sales}}{\text{Average inventory}}$

$$6 = \dfrac{£1,536,000}{\text{Inventory}}$$

Inventory $= £256,000$

From the quick ratio, receivables and cash $= 1.7 \times £192,000$

$= £326,400$

$\therefore$ Current ratio $= \dfrac{£256,000 + £326,400}{£192,000}$

$= 3:1$

10   The closing cash balance was £ $\boxed{16,800}$

WORKING

Since gross profit margin $= 20\%$

Cost of sales $= 80\% \times £900,000$

$= £720,000$

Inventory = unchanged $\therefore$ cost of sales $= $ purchases

Payables payment period (in days) $= \dfrac{\text{Average trade payables}}{\text{Purchases}} \times 365$

$$36.5 = \dfrac{\text{Trade payables}}{£720,000} \times 365$$

Trade payables $= £72,000$

Since current ratio $= \dfrac{\text{Current assets}}{\text{Current liabilities}} = 3.4:1$

Current assets $= 3.4 \times £72,000$

$= £244,800$

Rate of inventory turnover $= \dfrac{\text{Cost of sales}}{\text{Average inventory}}$

$$15 = \dfrac{£720,000}{\text{Inventory}}$$

Inventory $= £48,000$

Receivables collection period (in days)
$$= \frac{\text{Average trade receivables}}{\text{Sales revenue}} \times 365$$

$$73 = \frac{\text{Trade receivables}}{£900{,}000} \times 365$$

Trade receivables = £180,000

Current assets = Inventory + Receivables + Cash

£244,800 = £48,000 + £180,000 + Cash

Cash = £16,800

CHAPTER 8

Performance management

Introduction
Examination context
Topic List
    1 Performance evaluation
    2 Responsibility centres
    3 Performance measures
    4 The balanced scorecard
    5 Budgetary control
Summary and Self-test
Answers to Interactive questions
Answers to Self-test

Introduction

Learning objectives

- Identify the reasons for and key features of effective performance management systems

- Select appropriate financial and non-financial performance measures which effectively encourage the business as a whole to meet its objectives

- Identify the role of controls in ensuring effective performance management

- Identify how performance measures and compliance measures are integrated into the general systems of control in businesses

The specific syllabus references for this chapter are: 3a, b, c, d, e.

Syllabus links

Decentralisation and an understanding of responsibility centres also feature in the Business and Finance syllabus, in the context of appreciating how these structures help to achieve business objectives. You will also study internal controls in more depth in the context of your Assurance syllabus and some of the performance measures covered in this chapter will be met again when you are studying the interpretation of financial information for the Financial Accounting and Reporting syllabus.

Examination context

It is important to appreciate that both numerical and written questions will be set on performance measures and a thorough understanding of flexed budgets is required as a basis for variance analysis in the next chapter.

In the examination, candidates may be required to:

- Identify the most appropriate performance measure in a given situation

- Demonstrate an understanding of the effect of management actions on specific performance measures

- Demonstrate an understanding of the purpose and operation of a responsibility accounting system

- Interpret the information provided by specific performance measures

- Calculate the flexed cost budget for a given level of activity

- Interpret the information provided by a flexed budget comparison

1 Performance evaluation

Section overview

- The term 'feedback' is used to describe both the process of reporting back control information to management and the control information itself.

- Effective feedback information should have the following features.

    - Clear and comprehensive

    - Use an exception reporting format

    - Identify separately the controllable costs and revenues

    - Prepared on a regular basis

    - Timely

    - Sufficiently accurate for the purpose intended (not containing irrelevant detail)

    - Communicated to the manager who has authority and responsibility to act on the information

- Inappropriate performance measures can lead to a lack of goal congruence and may introduce budget bias.

- Hopwood identified three styles of evaluation: budget constrained; profit conscious; non-accounting.

1.1 Feedback control

The term 'feedback' is used to describe both the process of reporting back control information to management and the control information itself. In a business organisation, it is information produced from within the organisation (management control reports) with the purpose of helping management and other employees with control decisions.

The feedback loop can be depicted as follows.

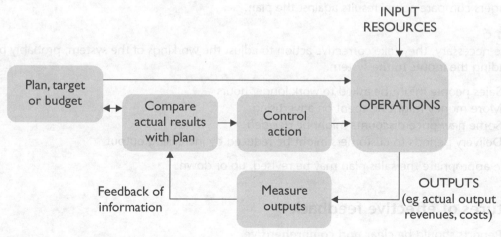

Figure 8.1: Feedback loop in the control cycle

The elements in the control cycle, illustrated in Figure 8.1, are as follows.

Step 1

Plans and targets are set for the future. These could be long , medium or short term plans. Examples include budgets, profit targets and standard costs (which we will learn more about in the next chapter).

Step 2

Plans are put into operation. As a consequence, resources are consumed and costs are incurred.

Step 3
Actual results are recorded and analysed.

Step 4
Information about actual results is fed back to the management concerned, often in the form of accounting reports. This reported information is **feedback**.

Step 5
The feedback is used by management to compare actual results with the plan or targets (what should be or should have been achieved).

Step 6
By comparing actual and planned results, management can then do one of three things, depending on how they see the situation.

(1) **They can take control action**. By identifying what has gone wrong, and then finding out why, corrective measures can be taken.

(2) **They can decide to do nothing**. This could be the decision when actual results are going better than planned, or when poor results were caused by something which is unlikely to happen again in the future.

(3) **They can alter the plan or target** if actual results are different from the plan or target, and there is nothing that management can do (or nothing, perhaps, that they want to do) to correct the situation.

It may be helpful at this stage to relate the control system to a practical example, such as monthly sales.

Step 1
A sales budget or plan is prepared for the year.

Step 2
Management organises the business's resources to achieve the budget targets.

Steps 3 and 4
At the end of each month, actual results are reported back to management.

Step 5
Managers compare actual results against the plan.

Step 6
Where necessary, they take corrective action to adjust the workings of the system, probably by amending the inputs to the system.

- Sales people might be asked to work longer hours
- More money might be spent on advertising
- Some new price discounts might be decided
- Delivery periods to customers might be reduced by increasing output

Where appropriate the sales plan may be revised, up or down.

1.2 Features of effective feedback

(a) Reports should be **clear and comprehensive**.

(b) The **'exception principle'** should be applied so that significant differences between the target and the actual results are highlighted for investigation. Areas that are conforming to plan should be given less prominence in the management control reports.

(c) The **controllable costs and revenues should be separately identified**. These are the items that can be directly influenced by the manager who receives the report. It can be demotivating if managers feel that they are being held responsible for items which are outside their control and which they are unable to influence. Uncontrollable items might be included for information (rather than action).

(d) Reports should be **produced on a regular basis** to ensure that continual control is exercised.

(e) Reports should be **made available to managers in a timely fashion**. This means they must be produced in good time to allow the manager to take control action before any adverse results get much worse.

(f) Information should be **sufficiently accurate** for the purpose intended.

(g) **Irrelevant detail should be excluded** from the report.

(h) Reports should be **communicated to the manager who has responsibility and authority** to act on the information.

1.3 The behavioural impact of performance measurement

Research evidence suggests that all too often performance measures lead to a lack of goal congruence. Managers seek to improve their performance on the basis of the indicator used, even if this is not in the best interests of the organisation as a whole.

For example, a production manager may be encouraged to achieve and maintain high production levels and to reduce costs, particularly if his or her bonus is linked to these factors. Such a manager is likely to be highly motivated. However, the need to maintain high production levels could lead to high levels of slow-moving inventory, resulting in an adverse effect on the company's cash flow. Thus **the manager's behaviour has been distorted by the control system**.

The impact of an accounting system on managerial performance depends ultimately on how the information is used. Research by Hopwood has shown that there are three distinct ways of using budgetary information to evaluate managerial performance.

Style of evaluation	Comment
Budget constrained	'The manager's performance is primarily evaluated upon the basis of his ability to continually meet the budget on a short term basis. This criterion of performance is stressed at the expense of other valued and important criteria and the manager will receive unfavourable feedback from his superior if, for instance, his actual costs exceed the budgeted costs, regardless of other considerations.'
Profit conscious	'The manager's performance is evaluated on the basis of his ability to increase the general effectiveness of his unit's operations in relation to the long term purposes of the organisation. For instance, at the cost centre level one important aspect of this ability concerns the attention which he devotes to reducing long run costs. For this purpose, however, the budgetary information has to be used with great care in a rather flexible manner.'
Non accounting	'The budgetary information plays a relatively unimportant part in the superior's evaluation of the manager's performance.'

A summary of the effects of the three styles of evaluation is as follows.

	Style of evaluation		
	Budget constrained	Profit conscious	Non-accounting
Involvement with costs	High	High	Low
Job-related tension	High	Medium	Medium
Manipulation of the accounting reports (bias)	Extensive	Little	Little
Relations with the supervisor	Poor	Good	Good
Relations with colleagues	Poor	Good	Good

Research has shown no clear preference for one style over another.

1.4 Budget bias

In the table above we have indicated that bias or **manipulation of accounting reports is more likely to occur if the manager is under pressure to achieve short-term budget targets**.

In the process of preparing budgets, managers might introduce budget slack into their estimates. This is when a manager deliberately overestimates costs and/or underestimates revenues, so that they will not be blamed in the future for overspending and/or poor results.

In controlling actual operations, managers might ensure that their spending rises to meet their inflated budget, otherwise they will be 'blamed' for careless budgeting.

A typical situation is for a manager to pad the budget and waste money on non-essential expenses so that all budget allowances are used. The reason behind the manager's action is the fear that unless the allowance is fully spent it will be reduced in future periods, thus making the manager's job more difficult as the future reduced budgets will not be so easy to attain. Because inefficiency and slack are allowed for in budgets, achieving a budget target means only that costs have remained within the accepted levels of inefficient spending.

Budget bias can work in the other direction too. It has been noted that, after a run of mediocre results, some managers deliberately overstate revenues and understate cost estimates, no doubt feeling the need to make an immediate favourable impact by promising better performance in the future. They may merely delay problems, however, as the managers may well be censured when they fail to hit these optimistic targets.

This is another example of management's reaction to control systems distorting the processes that the control systems are meant to serve.

2 Responsibility centres

Section overview

- Divisionalisation involves splitting the organisation into separate divisions, for example according to location or the product or service provided.

- In a decentralised organisation the authority for certain decisions is delegated to less senior managers. The most appropriate degree of decentralisation depends on a range of factors.

- There are a number of advantages and disadvantages of decentralisation.

- Responsibility accounting is the term used to describe decentralisation of authority, with the performance of the decentralised units measured in terms of accounting results.

- With a system of responsibility accounting there are four types of responsibility centre: cost centre, revenue centre, profit centre, investment centre.

- An investment centre manager has responsibility for capital investment in the centre.

- The performance of the responsibility centre manager should be monitored and based only on those items over which the manager can exercise control:

  - Controllable costs and revenues should be separated from non-controllable costs and revenues.

  - Controllable elements of divisional investment should be separated from non-controllable elements.

2.1 Divisionalisation

As companies grow, and possibly also spread geographically, it is likely that they will consider some form of divisionalisation. This involves splitting the company into divisions, for example according to location or according to the product or service provided. Divisional managers are then given the authority to make decisions concerning the activities of their divisions.

2.2 Decentralisation

In general, a **divisional structure will lead to decentralisation of the decision making process**. Divisional managers may have the freedom to set selling prices, choose suppliers, make output decisions and so on. Later in this section we will see that the degree of decentralisation depends on how much freedom managers are given to make decisions.

2.2.1 Factors affecting the degree of decentralisation

- **Management style**. An authoritarian style is likely to mean that decision making is centralised.

- **The size of the organisation**. Decentralisation tends to increase as an organisation grows.

- **The extent of activity diversification**. A greater diversification of activities will lead to more decentralisation.

- **Effectiveness of communications**. Decentralisation can only operate if information is communicated effectively both up and down the organisation.

- **The ability of management**. The more able the management team, the more decentralisation is likely to result.

- **The speed of technological advancement**. Managers lower down the organisation are more likely to be familiar with changing technology, therefore decentralisation would be more appropriate.

- **The geography of locations and the extent of local knowledge needed**. If an organisation is spread over a wide range of locations then decentralisation is likely to be most effective. Local managers would make more effective decisions based on their knowledge of local markets.

2.2.2 The advantages of decentralisation

- **Senior managers are freed from detailed involvement in day to day operations** and can devote more time to strategic issues.

- **The quality of decisions is likely to improve** because local managers may be able to make more informed judgements based on local knowledge.

- **The increased responsibility should motivate managers** in decentralised organisations.

- **Decisions should be taken more quickly** in response to changing conditions.

- Decentralised operations provide **valuable training grounds for future senior managers** by giving them experience of managerial skills in what may be a less complex environment than that faced by more senior managers.

2.2.3 The disadvantages of decentralisation

- **It can be difficult to coordinate the activities of the organisation** since several people are making decisions rather than just a few.

- **The organisation might effectively divide into a number of self-interested segments**, leading to a lack of goal congruence in decision making.

- **Senior managers lose control over day to day activities**.

- **Evaluating the performance of managers and their area of responsibility becomes difficult**.

- There may be a **duplication of some roles**, for example administration, with consequent increased costs.

2.3 Responsibility accounting

We have already discussed responsibility accounting in outline in the context of cost classification in the first chapter of this Study Manual.

Responsibility accounting is the term used to describe decentralisation of authority, with the performance of the decentralised units or responsibility centres measured in terms of accounting results.

Within a system of responsibility accounting there are **four main types of responsibility centre**: cost centre, revenue centre, profit centre and investment centre.

Decentralisation is a matter of degree, depending on how much freedom and authority is given to managers. In the weakest form of decentralisation a system of cost centres or revenue centres might be used. As decentralisation becomes stronger the responsibility accounting framework will be based around profit centres. Decentralisation in its strongest form means that investment centres are used.

Type of responsibility centre	Manager has control over	Principal performance measures
Cost centre	Controllable costs	Variance analysis
		Efficiency measures
Revenue centre	Revenues only	Revenues
Profit centre	Controllable costs	Profit
	Sales prices (including transfer prices)	Profit margins
Investment centre	Controllable costs	Return on investment
	Sales prices (including transfer prices)	Residual income
	Output volumes	Other financial ratios
	Investment in non-current assets and working capital	

2.4 Cost centres

A cost centre manager is responsible for, and has control over, the costs incurred in the cost centre. The manager has **no responsibility for earning revenues or for controlling the assets and liabilities of the centre**.

Functional departments such as production and personnel might be treated as cost centres and made responsible for their costs.

It is important that control reports for a cost centre show a clear distinction between **controllable costs**, over which the cost centre manager can exercise some control, and **uncontrollable costs**, which cannot be controlled by the cost centre manager.

2.5 Revenue centres

The manager of a revenue centre **is responsible only for raising revenue** but has no responsibility for forecasting or controlling costs. An example of a revenue centre is a sales centre where a sales manager might be responsible for achieving a budgeted level of sales revenue.

2.6 Profit centres

A profit centre is a part of a business accountable for both costs and revenues.

For a profit centre organisation structure to be established it is necessary to identify units of the organisation to which both revenues and costs can be separately attributed. Revenues might come from sales of goods and services to external customers, or from goods and services provided to other responsibility centres within the organisation. These internal 'sales' are charged at a transfer price, which you learned about in Chapter 5.

A profit centre's performance report, in the same way as that for a cost centre, would **identify separately the controllable and non-controllable costs as well as the controllable and non-controllable revenues**. A profit centre performance report might look like this.

PROFIT CENTRE Y
INCOME STATEMENT FOR THE PERIOD

	Budget £'000	Actual £'000	Variance £'000
Sales revenue	X	X	
Variable cost of sales	(X)	(X)	
Contribution	X	X	
Directly attributable/controllable fixed costs			
Salaries	(X)	(X)	
Stationery costs	(X)	(X)	
	etc	etc	
Gross profit (directly attributable/controllable)	X	X	
Share of uncontrollable costs (eg head office costs)	(X)	(X)	
Net profit	X	X	

The budget for the sales revenue and variable cost of sales will be flexed according to the activity level achieved. You will learn how to do this later in this chapter.

The variances (differences between budgeted and actual results) could be analysed in further detail for the profit centre manager.

Notice that three different 'profit levels' are highlighted in the report.

(a) Contribution, which is within the control of the profit centre manager.

(b) Directly attributable gross profit, which is also within the manager's control.

(c) Net profit, which is after charging certain uncontrollable costs and which is therefore not controllable by the profit centre manager.

2.7 Investment centres

Where a manager of a division is allowed some discretion about the amount of investment undertaken by the division, assessment of results by profit alone (as for a profit centre) is clearly inadequate. **The profit earned must be related to the amount of capital invested.** Such divisions are sometimes called investment centres for this reason.

Performance can be measured by return on capital employed (ROCE), often referred to as return on investment (ROI) and other subsidiary ratios, or by residual income (RI).

The amount of capital employed attributed to an investment centre should consist only of directly attributable non-current assets and working capital (net current assets).

(a) Subsidiary companies that are treated as investment centres are often required to remit spare cash to the central treasury department at group head office. In this situation the directly attributable working capital would normally consist of inventories and receivables less payables, but minimal amounts of cash.

(b) If an investment centre is apportioned a share of head office non-current assets, the amount of capital employed in these assets should be recorded separately because it is not directly attributable to the investment centre or controllable by the manager of the investment centre.

Interactive question 1: Controllable investment in division [Difficulty level: Easy]

The manager of division D has complete autonomy regarding the purchase and use of non-current assets and inventory but the payment of all suppliers is undertaken by head office which maintains a central bank account. The manager also has authority to establish the division's own credit policy with regard to its customers. The division operates a credit control department but all cash received from customers is remitted immediately to head office.

Classify the following assets and liabilities to indicate whether or not they are a part of the divisional investment that is within the control of the manager of division D.

Item	Part of controllable divisional investment	Not part of controllable divisional investment
Non-current assets	☐	☐
Trade receivables	☐	☐
Trade payables	☐	☐
Inventory	☐	☐

See **Answer** at the end of this chapter.

3 Performance measures

Section overview

- Effective performance measures should promote goal congruence, incorporate only controllable factors and encourage the pursuit of longer term as well as short-term objectives.

- Inappropriate performance measures may lead to sub-optimal behaviour.

- Two performance measures for investment centres that relate the profit earned to the capital invested are Return on Investment (ROI) and Residual Income (RI).

- In certain circumstances the use of ROI as a performance measure might not lead to goal congruent decisions.

- ROI tends to focus attention on short-term performance.

- RI is a measure of an investment centre's profits after deducting a notional or imputed interest cost of the capital invested in the centre.

- RI is less useful as a comparative measure because it is absolute.

- RI will encourage marginally profitable investments because it will increase if a proposed project earns a return which is higher than the cost of capital.

3.1 General requirements for effective performance measures

One or more performance measures, or key performance indicators (KPIs), might be used to monitor the performance of each responsibility centre. Before going on to consider some of the individual measures in detail it will be useful to summarise the features of effective performance measures.

- They should **promote goal congruence** by providing an incentive to promote the responsibility centre's performance in line with overall company objectives.

- The measures should incorporate **only those factors over which the responsibility centre manager has control**.

- They should **encourage the pursuit of longer term objectives** as well as short-term, budget-constrained objectives.

3.2 Potential problems with inappropriate performance measures

Problems that may arise through the use of inappropriate measures include the following.

- Managers may **manipulate information** in order to ensure achievement of the KPIs.

- The measures might **cause demotivation and stress-related conflict** between a manager and the manager's subordinates, superiors or fellow managers.

- The measures might **promote excessive concern for the control of short-term costs,** possibly at the expense of longer term profitability.

- They may lead to the **assessment of a responsibility centre as an isolated unit,** rather than as an integral part of the whole organisation.

3.3 Performance measures for a cost centre

Since the manager of a cost centre has responsibility for the costs incurred within the centre, appropriate performance measures could be as follows.

- Cost variances, which are the differences between the budgeted or standard costs and the actual costs

- Cost per unit

- Cost per employee

- Other non-financial measures such as the rate of labour turnover or staff absenteeism

3.4 Performance measures for a revenue centre

Appropriate performance measures would be related to the revenue earned.

- Revenue variances, which are the differences between the budgeted or standard revenue and the actual revenue achieved

- Revenue earned per employee

- Percentage market share achieved

- Growth in revenue

3.5 Performance measures for a profit centre

Since the manager of a profit centre has responsibility for the revenue earned and the costs incurred within the centre all of the above performance measures would be suitable. Additional measures might include the following.

- Gross profit margin, which is the difference between the selling price and the direct costs incurred, often expressed as a percentage of the selling price

- Operating profit margin, which is the gross profit less indirect costs incurred such as administrative salaries, often expressed as a percentage of the selling price

3.6 Performance measures for an investment centre

All of the measures appropriate for a cost, revenue and profit centre would be suitable for monitoring the performance of an investment centre. In addition, certain measures related to the management of the investment in the division would also be useful. Such measures might include a number of working capital ratios.

- Liquidity measures such as the current ratio and the quick (liquidity) ratio
- Rate of inventory turnover
- Receivables and payables periods

Two other measures monitor the return achieved in the division in relation to the level of investment.

- Return on investment (ROI)
- Residual income (RI)

We studied the working capital ratios in detail in Chapter 7. Now we will go on to look at ROI and RI.

3.7 Return on investment (ROI)

ROI is often used as a measure to monitor the performance of an investment centre. It shows how much profit has been earned in relation to the amount of capital invested in the centre.

$$ROI = \frac{Controllable\ divisional\ profit}{Divisional\ capital\ employed} \times 100\%$$

The main reason for the widespread use of ROI is that it **ties in directly with the accounting system** and is identifiable from the income statement and balance sheet.

Use of the ROI facilitates comparisons but ranking is difficult as the measure is a relative percentage. For example, is a five per cent return on £1 (20p) really better than a one per cent return on £1 million (£10,000)?

Worked example: Ranking using ROI

Suppose that a company has two investment centres, A and B, which show results for the year as follows.

	A £	B £
Profit	60,000	30,000
Capital employed	400,000	120,000
ROI	15%	25%

Investment centre A has generated double the profits of investment centre B, and in terms of profits alone has therefore been more 'successful'. However, B has achieved its profits with a much lower capital investment, and so has earned a much higher ROI. This suggests that B has been a more successful investment than A.

3.7.1 Capital employed

A decision needs to be taken on which assets to include in capital employed. Leased assets, shared assets, idle assets and goodwill need to be given careful consideration. Centrally-controlled assets are excluded because the investment centre manager cannot exercise control over their use.

Usually, opening capital employed or an average of opening and closing capital is used, on the grounds that this has been generating the year's profits.

The use of historical cost/carrying amount may lead to problems as shown below.

Worked example: The effect of changing the capital employed base

An asset costs £100,000, has a life of four years, and its scrap value is nil. The asset generates annual cash flows of £34,000 and straight line depreciation is used.

Requirements

(a) Calculate annual ROI using opening carrying amount (ie depreciation is deducted from the asset value).

(b) Calculate annual ROI using historical cost (ie no depreciation is deducted from the asset value).

(c) Comment on any problems identified by these calculations.

Solution

ROI using opening carrying amount

Year 1: (34 − 25) ÷ 100 = 9%

Year 2: (34 − 25) ÷ 75 = 12%

Year 3: (34 − 25) ÷ 50 = 18%

Year 4: (34 − 25) ÷ 25 = 36%

ROI improves despite constant annual profits. Consequently divisional managers may hold assets for too long.

ROI using historical cost

Years 1 − 4: (34 − 25) ÷ 100 = 9%

ROI using historical cost overcomes the increasing return problem of using the carrying amount. However, it is not perfect.

Using the historical cost/carrying amounts may be misleading, particularly when **comparing** divisions, if:

- Assets have been bought at different points in time and prices have changed due to inflation
- Assets of one division are older than those of another and have been written down to a lower value
- Different depreciation policies are applied by different divisions.

To resolve this, one solution would be to use a **replacement cost valuation**.

3.7.2 Profit

Usually the profit figure taken as the numerator in the ROI calculation is after depreciation, but this may lead to distortion, as discussed above.

It is common for divisions and managers to be assessed on pre-tax profit, since the company's ultimate tax charge is likely to be significantly affected by central decisions and is therefore not controllable by divisional managers.

However, it is important that managers are made aware of the tax implications of their operational decisions.

3.7.3 ROI and goal congruence

In certain circumstances the **use of ROI as a performance measure might not lead to goal congruent decisions**.

Worked example: ROI and goal congruence

Data for an investment centre are as follows.

Target ROI (= cost of capital)	20%
Divisional profit	£300,000
Capital employed	£1m

Requirement

Would the division manager accept a project requiring capital of £100,000 and generating profits of £25,000, if the manager were paid a bonus based on ROI?

Solution

Divisional ROI without the project	=	$\dfrac{£300{,}000}{£1m} \times 100\%$
	=	30.0%
Divisional ROI with the project	=	$\dfrac{£325{,}000}{£1.1m} \times 100\%$
	=	29.5%
ROI of the project	=	25.0%

Although the project ROI is acceptable to the company (25%), the manager would not be motivated to accept a project which lowers divisional ROI.

A limitation of ROI is that it **tends to focus attention on short-term performance**, whereas investment decisions should be evaluated over their full life.

3.8 Residual income (RI)

An alternative way of measuring the performance of an investment centre is residual income (RI). RI is a measure of the centre's profits **after deducting a notional or imputed interest cost of the capital invested in the centre**.

RI can avoid some of the behavioural problems of dysfunctionality that arise with the use of ROI.

Worked example: Residual income and goal congruence

Returning to the data in the previous example, would the division manager accept the proposed project if the manager's bonus was based on RI?

Solution

	£'000
Divisional RI without the project:	
Divisional profit	300
Imputed interest charge (20% × £1m)	200
	100
Divisional RI with the project:	
Divisional profit	325
Imputed interest charge (20% × £1,100,000)	220
	105
RI of the project	
Profit	25
Imputed interest charge (20% × £100,000)	20
	5

The RI would increase therefore the manager would accept the project. In this particular circumstance, RI would lead to the correct decision since the project ROI of 25% is acceptable to the company.

Note that the ROI and the RI are both based on the same figures for profits and capital employed. The difference is that ROI is a relative measure whereas RI is an absolute measure.

3.8.1 RI and comparisons

RI is less useful as a comparative measure because it is absolute.

Worked example: Using ROI and RI to measure comparative performance

A company has a target ROI and an imputed interest charge of 20% for each of its investment centres. Which of the two divisions is performing better, using the following performance measures?

(a)   Residual income
(b)   Return on investment

	Division 1	Division 2
Capital employed	£1,000,000	£100,000
Controllable profits:		
Year 1	£200,000	£20,000
Year 2	£220,000	£40,000

Solution

(a)   **Residual income**

	Division 1 £'000	Division 2 £'000
Year 1		
Divisional profit	200	20
Imputed interest charge		
(£1,000,000 × 20%)	200	
(£100,000 × 20%)		20
RI	—	—
Year 2		
Divisional profit	220	40
Imputed interest charge	200	20
	20	20

Using RI the relative performance of the two divisions appears to be the same. Both divisions have increased the annual RI by £20,000.

(b)   **Return on investment**

		Division 1	Division 2
Year 1	£200,000/£1,000,000	20%	
	£20,000/£100,000		20%
Year 2	£220,000/£1,000,000	22%	
	£40,000/£100,000		40%

Return on investment shows that division 2 is out performing division 1. Despite earning the same absolute increase in RI it is much easier for the larger division to generate a further £20,000 of RI. **Hence using RI to compare divisions of different sizes is misleading.**

Interactive question 2: ROI and RI   [Difficulty level: Intermediate]

An investment centre with capital employed of £570,000 is budgeted to earn a profit of £119,700 next year. A proposed non-current asset investment of £50,000, not included in the budget at present, will earn a profit next year of £8,500 after depreciation. The company's cost of capital is 15%.

Complete the boxes to show the budgeted ROI and RI for next year, both with and without the investment.

	ROI	RI
Without investment	[ ] %	£ [ ]
With investment	[ ] %	£ [ ]

See **Answer** at the end of this chapter.

3.8.2 The advantages and disadvantages of RI compared with ROI

The advantages of using RI

(a) Residual income will **increase** when investments earning above the cost of capital are undertaken and investments earning below the cost of capital are eliminated.

(b) Residual income is **more flexible** since a different cost of capital can be applied to investments with **different risk** characteristics.

The **disadvantages** of RI are that it **does not facilitate comparisons** between investment centres nor **does it relate the size of a centre's income to the size of the investment**.

3.8.3 RI versus ROI: marginally profitable investments

Residual income will increase if a new investment is undertaken which earns a profit in excess of the imputed interest charge on the value of the asset acquired. Residual income will go up even if the profit from the investment only just exceeds the imputed interest charge, and this means that 'marginally profitable' investments are likely to be undertaken by the investment centre manager.

In contrast, when a manager is judged by ROI, a marginally profitable investment would be less likely to be undertaken because it would reduce the average ROI earned by the centre as a whole.

4 The balanced scorecard

Section overview

- The balanced scorecard approach to the provision of information focuses on four different perspectives: customer, innovation and learning, financial and internal business.

- The information provided in the balanced scorecard includes both financial and non-financial elements.

- As with all techniques, problems can arise when the balanced scorecard approach is applied.

4.1 Introduction

The balanced scorecard was developed to help companies manage the multiple objectives they have to satisfy to compete in today's markets. Traditional accounting measures have a number of weaknesses that make them less relevant today.

- They **tend to concentrate on a single factor**, eg profit, revenue, ROI or RI
- They are **primarily historical**, eg how have we done compared with last year
- They are **capable of distortion**
- There is often **confusion between measures and objectives**
- Traditional accounting performance measures are of **little use as a guide to action**

4.2 The balanced scorecard approach

The balanced scorecard involves the following steps:

- Identify the **critical success factors** for the business from four perspectives:

    - Financial perspective – how do we create value for our shareholders?
    - Customer perspective – what do new and existing customers value from us?
    - Innovation and learning perspective – can we continue to improve and create value?
    - Internal business perspective – at what must we excel?

- Identify the **core competences and resources required to achieve them**

- Develop the **key performance indicators** (financial and non-financial – see below) to best measure progress towards achieving the necessary competences and resources

- Set targets

- Monitor performance

4.3 Non-financial performance measures

It is important to realise that financial measures will only tell part of the story. To minimise the risk of suboptimal decisions, a company should **use as broad a range of measures as possible**, both quantitative and qualitative.

Other measures to consider could include:

- The number of new products developed
- The rate of employee turnover
- Customer praise/complaints
- The number of outstanding orders
- The number of warranty claims
- Health and safety incident statistics

4.4 Potential measures

A selection of potential measures is detailed below. These would obviously need adapting for the circumstances of the individual company concerned.

Financial perspective

Possible financial measures include:

- Survival, eg cash flows
- Growth, eg sales revenue
- Cost reduction, eg unit costs
- Asset utilisation, eg working capital ratios
- Risk, eg order books

Customer perspective

Possible customer perspective measures include:

- Time, eg product delivery lead times
- Quality, eg defect rates
- Price, eg compared with the prices of competitors
- Satisfaction, eg repeat purchases

Innovation and learning perspective

Possible measures include:

- Employees, eg the rate of staff turnover
- Learning, eg the number of days spent on staff training
- Products and services, eg the percentage of revenue generated by new products and services

Internal business perspective

Possible measures include:

- The number or percentage of quality control rejects
- The average set-up time
- The speed of producing management information

The scorecard is 'balanced' in the sense that managers are required to think in terms of all four perspectives, to **prevent improvements being made in one area at the expense of another**.

Interactive question 3: Balanced scorecard evaluation   [Difficulty level: Intermediate]

Radlan & Dunne are a firm of High Street solicitors. They have traditionally measured their success in terms of ROI. They have decided to modernise their approach and plan to use the Balanced Scorecard to measure performance. Suggest three measures they could use under each of the four balanced scorecard perspectives.

Perspective	Measures
Financial	1
	2
	3
Customer	1
	2
	3
Innovation and learning	1
	2
	3
Internal business	1
	2
	3

See **Answer** at the end of this chapter.

4.5   Problems

As with all techniques, problems can arise when the balanced scorecard is applied.

Problem	Explanation
Conflicting measures	Some measures in the scorecard such as research funding and cost reduction may naturally conflict. It is often difficult to determine the balance which will achieve the best results.
Selecting measures	Not only do appropriate measures have to be devised but the number of measures used must be agreed. Care must be taken that the impact of the results is not lost in a sea of information.
Expertise	Measurement is only useful if it initiates appropriate action. Non-financial managers may have difficulty with the usual profit measures. With more measures to consider this problem will be compounded.
Interpretation	Even a financially-trained manager may have difficulty in putting the figures into an overall perspective.
Too many measures	The ultimate objective for commercial organisations is to maximise profits or shareholder wealth. Other targets should offer a guide to achieving this objective and not become an end in themselves.

5 Budgetary control

Section overview

- A fixed budget is a budget which is set for a single activity level.

- A flexible budget recognises different cost behaviour patterns and is designed to change as the volume of activity changes.

- Effective budgetary control involves comparing a flexible budget (based on the actual activity level) with the actual results. The differences between the flexible budget figures and the actual results are called budget variances.

5.1 Effective budgetary control

We have seen that the performance of all types of responsibility centres may be monitored by the comparison of actual costs and revenues with the budget for the period.

However if activity levels fluctuate then **the comparison of the actual results with a budget prepared for a different activity level might not be valid for control purposes**.

To be more meaningful, the actual results should be compared with a realistic budget for the actual activity level achieved.

5.2 Fixed budgets

The master budget prepared before the beginning of the budget period is known as the **fixed** budget. By the term 'fixed', we do not mean that the budget is kept unchanged. Revisions to a fixed master budget will be made if the situation so demands. The term 'fixed' means the following.

(a) The budget is prepared on the basis of an estimated volume of production or output and an estimated volume of sales, but no plans are made for the event that actual volumes of production and sales may differ from budgeted volumes.

(b) When actual volumes of production and sales during a control period (month or four weeks or quarter) are achieved, a fixed budget is not adjusted (in retrospect) to represent a new target for the new levels of activity.

The major purpose of a fixed budget lies in its use at the planning stage, when it seeks to define the broad objectives of the organisation.

Fixed budgets (in terms of a **pre-set expenditure limit**) are also useful for **controlling any fixed cost**, and **particularly non-production fixed costs** such as advertising, because such costs should be unaffected by changes in activity level (within a certain range).

5.3 Flexible budgets

A **flexible budget** recognises different cost behaviour patterns and is designed to change as the volume of activity changes.

A **flexible budget** has two advantages.

(a) At the **planning** stage, it may be helpful to know what the effects would be if the actual outcome differs from the prediction. For example, a company may budget to sell 10,000 units of its product, but may prepare flexible budgets based on sales of, say, 8,000 and 12,000 units. This would enable **contingency plans** to be drawn up if necessary, and is an example of sensitivity analysis which we discussed in Chapter 6.

(b) At the end of each month or year, actual results may be compared with the relevant activity level in the flexible budget as a **control** procedure.

5.4 Preparation of flexible budgets

Step 1

The first step in the preparation of a flexible budget is the determination of cost behaviour patterns, which means deciding whether costs are fixed, variable or semi-variable.

- Fixed costs are easy to spot. **They remain constant as activity levels change.**

- For non-fixed costs, divide each cost figure by the related activity level. If the cost is a variable cost, the cost per unit will remain constant. If the cost is a semi-variable cost, the unit rate will reduce as activity levels increase.

Step 2

The second step in the preparation of a flexible budget is to calculate the budget cost allowance for each cost item.

Budget cost allowance = Budgeted fixed cost + (Number of units × Variable cost per unit)

Semi-variable costs therefore need splitting into their fixed and variable components so that the budget cost allowance can be calculated.

Interactive question 4: Analysing semi-variable costs   [Difficulty level: Intermediate]

One method for splitting semi-variable costs is the high/low method, which we covered in Chapter 6. Attempt the following question to make sure you remember how to do this.

The cost of factory power has behaved as follows in past years.

	Units of output produced	Cost of factory power £
20X1	7,900	38,700
20X2	7,700	38,100
20X3	9,800	44,400
20X4	9,100	42,300

Budgeted production for 20X5 is 10,200 units.

Ignoring inflation, the cost of factory power which will be incurred is estimated to be £ ⬚.

See **Answer** at the end of this chapter.

Worked example: Preparing a flexible budget

(a) Prepare a budget for 20X6 for the variable direct labour costs and overhead expenses of a production department flexed at the activity levels of 80%, 90% and 100%, using the information listed below.

    (i)   The variable direct labour hourly rate is expected to be £7.50

    (ii) 100% activity represents 60,000 direct labour hours

    (iii) Variable costs

Indirect labour	£0.75 per direct labour hour
Consumable supplies	£0.375 per direct labour hour
Canteen and other welfare services	6% of direct and indirect labour costs

(iv) Semi variable costs are expected to relate to the direct labour hours in the same manner as for the last five years.

Year	Direct labour hours	Semi-variable costs £
20X1	64,000	20,800
20X2	59,000	19,800
20X3	53,000	18,600
20X4	49,000	17,800
20X5	40,000 (estimate)	16,000 (estimate)

(v) Fixed costs

	£
Depreciation	18,000
Maintenance	10,000
Insurance	4,000
Rates	15,000
Management salaries	25,000

(vi) Inflation is to be ignored.

(b) Calculate the budget cost allowance (ie expected expenditure) for 20X6 assuming that 57,000 direct labour hours are worked.

Solution

(a)

	80% level 48,000 hrs £'000	90% level 54,000 hrs £'000	100% level 60,000 hrs £'000
Variable direct labour	360.00	405.00	450.00
Other variable costs			
Indirect labour	36.00	40.50	45.0
Consumable supplies	18.00	20.25	22.5
Canteen etc	23.76	26.73	29.7
Total variable costs (£9.12 per hour)	437.76	492.48	547.2
Semi-variable costs (W)	17.60	18.80	20.0
Fixed costs			
Depreciation	18.00	18.00	18.0
Maintenance	10.00	10.00	10.0
Insurance	4.00	4.00	4.0
Rates	15.00	15.00	15.0
Management salaries	25.00	25.00	25.0
Budgeted costs	527.36	583.28	639.2

WORKING

Using the high/low method:

	£
Total cost of 64,000 hours	20,800
Total cost of 40,000 hours	16,000
Variable cost of 24,000 hours	4,800
Variable cost per hour (£4,800/24,000)	0.20

	£
Total cost of 64,000 hours	20,800
Variable cost of 64,000 hours (× £0.20)	12,800
Fixed costs	8,000

Semi variable costs are calculated as follows.

			£
60,000 hours	(60,000 × £0.20) + £8,000	=	20,000
54,000 hours	(54,000 × £0.20) + £8,000	=	18,800
48,000 hours	(48,000 × £0.20) + £8,000	=	17,600

(b) The budget cost allowance for 57,000 direct labour hours of work would be as follows.

		£
Variable costs	(57,000 × £9.12)	519,840
Semi-variable costs	(£8,000 + (57,000 × £0.20))	19,400
Fixed costs		72,000
		611,240

5.5 Flexible budgets and control

Suppose W Co manufactures a single product, the CL. Budgeted results and actual results for June 20X2 are shown below.

	Budget	Actual results	Variance*
Production and sales of the CL (units)	2,000	3,000	
	£	£	£
Sales revenue (a)	20,000	30,000	10,000 (F)
Direct materials	6,000	8,500	2,500 (A)
Direct labour	4,000	4,500	500 (A)
Maintenance	1,000	1,400	400 (A)
Depreciation	2,000	2,200	200 (A)
Rent and rates	1,500	1,600	100 (A)
Other costs	3,600	5,000	1,400 (A)
Total costs (b)	18,100	23,200	5,100 (A)
Profit (a) – (b)	1,900	6,800	4,900 (F)

* The variance is the difference between the budget and the actual results. A favourable variance (F) indicates that the difference would result in a higher profit (higher sales revenue or lower cost). An adverse variance (A) indicates that the difference would result in a lower profit (lower sales revenue or higher cost).

(a) In this example, the variances are meaningless for purposes of control. Costs were higher than budget because the **volume of output was also higher**; variable costs would be expected to increase above the budgeted costs in the fixed budget. There is no information to show whether control action is needed for any aspect of costs or revenue.

(b) For control purposes, it is necessary to know the answers to questions such as the following.

- Were actual costs higher than they should have been to produce and sell 3,000 CLs?
- Was actual revenue satisfactory from the sale of 3,000 CLs?

5.5.1 The correct approach to control

The **correct approach** to control is as follows.

- Identify fixed and variable costs.
- Produce a **flexible budget** based on the **actual activity level**.

In the previous example of W Co, let us suppose that we have the following estimates of cost behaviour.

(a) Direct materials, direct labour and maintenance costs are variable.
(b) Rent and rates and depreciation are fixed costs.
(c) Other costs consist of fixed costs of £1,600 plus a variable cost of £1 per unit made and sold.

The control analysis should therefore be based on a flexible budget as follows.

	Fixed budget (a)	Flexible budget (b)	Actual results (c)	Budget variance (c)-(b)	
Production & sales (units)	2,000	3,000	3,000		
	£	£	£	£	
Sales revenue	20,000	30,000	30,000	0	
Variable costs					
Direct materials	6,000	9,000	8,500	500	(F)
Direct labour	4,000	6,000	4,500	1,500	(F)
Maintenance	1,000	1,500	1,400	100	(F)
Semi-variable costs					
Other costs	3,600	4,600	5,000	400	(A)
Fixed costs					
Depreciation	2,000	2,000	2,200	200	(A)
Rent and rates	1,500	1,500	1,600	100	(A)
Total costs	18,100	24,600	23,200	1,400	(F)
Profit	1,900	5,400	6,800	1,400	(F)

£3,500 (F)
Volume variance

£1,400 (F)
Expenditure variance

£4,900 (F)
Total variance

Notice that the total variance has not altered. It is still £4,900 (F) as before. The flexible budget comparison merely analyses the total variance into two separate components.

5.5.2 Interpretation of the control statement

We can analyse the above as follows.

(a) In selling 3,000 units the expected profit is shown by the flexible budget. This is not the fixed budget profit of £1,900, but the flexible budget profit of £5,400. Instead, actual profit was £6,800, ie £1,400 more than we should have expected. This is the £1,400 favourable expenditure variance. The reason for this £1,400 improvement is that, given output and sales of 3,000 units, overall costs were lower than expected (and sales revenue was exactly as expected). For example, the direct material cost was £500 lower than expected.

(b) Another reason for the improvement in profit above the fixed budget profit is the **sales volume**. W Co sold 3,000 units of CL instead of 2,000, with the following result.

	£	£
Budgeted sales revenue increased by		10,000
Budgeted variable costs increased by:		
Direct materials	3,000	
Direct labour	2,000	
Maintenance	500	
Variable element of other costs	1,000	
		6,500
Budgeted fixed costs are unchanged		–
Budgeted profit increased by		3,500

Budgeted profit was therefore increased by £3,500 because sales volume increased. This is the £3,500 favourable volume variance.

(c) A full variance analysis statement would be as follows.

	£	£	£
Fixed budget profit			1,900
Variances			
Sales volume			3,500 (F)
Direct materials cost		500 (F)	
Direct labour cost		1,500 (F)	
Maintenance cost		100 (F)	
Other costs	400 (A)		
Depreciation	200 (A)		
Rent and rates	100 (A)		
Total expenditure variance	700 (A)	2,100 (F)	1,400 (F)
Actual profit			6,800

If management believes that any of these variances are large enough to justify it, they will investigate the reasons for them to see whether any corrective action is necessary.

Interactive question 5: Budget cost allowances   [Difficulty level: Intermediate]

WL Co manufactures and sells a single product, R. Since the R is highly perishable, no inventories are held at any time. WL Co's management uses a flexible budgeting system to control costs. Extracts from the flexible budget are as follows.

Output and sales (units)	4,000	5,500
Budget cost allowances	£	£
Direct material	16,000	22,000
Direct labour	20,000	24,500
Variable production overhead	8,000	11,000
Fixed production overhead	11,000	11,000
Selling and distribution overhead	8,000	9,500
Administration overhead	7,000	7,000
Total expenditure	70,000	85,000

Production and sales of product R amounted to 5,100 units during period 5.

The total budget cost allowances in the flexible budget for period 5 will be:

(a) Direct material £ ☐

(b) Direct labour £ ☐

(c) Variable production overhead £ ☐

(d) Fixed production overhead £ ☐

(e) Selling and distribution overhead £ ☐

(f) Administration overhead £ ☐

(g) Production and sales of product R in period 6 amounted to 5,500 units. Budgeted output for the period was 4,000 units. Actual total expenditure was £82,400.

(i) The total expenditure variance for period 6 was £ ☐ favourable/adverse (delete as necessary)

(ii) The volume variance for period 6 was £ ☐ favourable/adverse (delete as necessary)

See **Answer** at the end of this chapter.

Summary

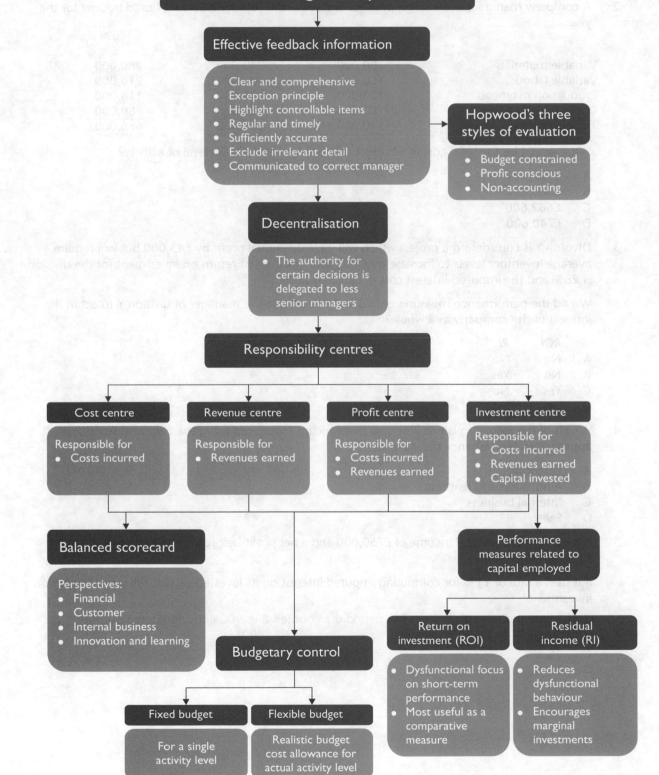

Performance management systems

Effective feedback information

- Clear and comprehensive
- Exception principle
- Highlight controllable items
- Regular and timely
- Sufficiently accurate
- Exclude irrelevant detail
- Communicated to correct manager

Hopwood's three styles of evaluation

- Budget constrained
- Profit conscious
- Non-accounting

Decentralisation

- The authority for certain decisions is delegated to less senior managers

Responsibility centres

Cost centre	Revenue centre	Profit centre	Investment centre
Responsible for - Costs incurred	Responsible for - Revenues earned	Responsible for - Costs incurred - Revenues earned	Responsible for - Costs incurred - Revenues earned - Capital invested

Balanced scorecard

Perspectives:
- Financial
- Customer
- Internal business
- Innovation and learning

Performance measures related to capital employed

Budgetary control

Fixed budget

For a single activity level

Flexible budget

Realistic budget cost allowance for actual activity level

Return on investment (ROI)

- Dysfunctional focus on short-term performance
- Most useful as a comparative measure

Residual income (RI)

- Reduces dysfunctional behaviour
- Encourages marginal investments

Self-test

Answer the following questions.

1   Which of the following items would be excluded in the calculation of controllable divisional profit?

    A   Sales to external customers
    B   Head office costs
    C   Variable divisional expenses
    D   Controllable divisional fixed costs

2   A company manufactures a single product and has drawn up the following flexed budget for the year.

	50%	60%	70%
	£	£	£
Variable materials	200,000	240,000	280,000
Variable labour	150,000	180,000	210,000
Production overhead	100,000	108,000	116,000
Other overhead	80,000	80,000	80,000
Total cost	530,000	608,000	686,000

What would be the total cost in a budget that is flexed at the 67% level of activity?

    A   £626,600
    B   £660,600
    C   £662,600
    D   £740,600

3   Division Y is considering a project which will increase annual profit by £45,000 but will require average inventory levels to increase by £180,000. The current return on investment for the division is 28% and the imputed interest cost of capital is 20%.

Would the performance measures of ROI and RI motivate the manager of division Y to act in the interest of the company as a whole?

	ROI	RI
A	No	No
B	No	Yes
C	Yes	No
D	Yes	Yes

4   Which of the following is **not** a perspective which is monitored using the balanced scorecard approach to performance measurement?

    A   Financial
    B   Innovation and learning
    C   Internal business
    D   Sales

5   A division has a residual income of £750,000 and a net profit before imputed interest of £1,850,000.

If it uses a rate of 11% for computing imputed interest on its invested capital, what is its return on investment?

    A   7.5%
    B   11%
    C   18.5%
    D   26%

6   A division currently has an investment base of £2,400,000 and annual profits of £480,000. The following additional investments are being considered.

	Outlay £000	Annual profit £000
Investment Q	1,400	350
Investment R	600	200
Investment S	400	88

Which combination of investments will maximise the division's return on investment?

A   Investment Q only
B   Investment R only
C   Investments Q and R
D   Investments Q, R and S

7   On the last day of the financial year an investment centre has net assets with a total carrying amount of £1.2 million, with a return on investment (ROI) of 15%.

The manager of this division is considering selling one of its non-current assets immediately prior to the year end. The non-current asset has a carrying amount of £105,000 and a net realisable value of £80,000.

What would be the division's ROI immediately after the sale of the asset at the end of the year?

A   13.2%
B   14.2%
C   15.3%
D   16.4%

8   A divisionalised company uses return on investment (ROI) and residual income (RI) to assess the performance of its divisions. Straight-line depreciation is used and assets are valued at net book value. If the cash flows from a new investment in a depreciable non-current asset are likely to be constant over the life of the investment, what will be the effect of the investment on the ROI and RI over the life of the asset?

	ROI	RI
A	Increase	Increase
B	Increase	No change
C	No change	No change
D	Decrease	Decrease

9   What is a budget cost allowance?

A   A budget of expenditure applicable to a particular function

B   A budget allowance which is set without permitting the ultimate budget manager the opportunity to participate in setting the budget

C   The budgeted cost expected for the actual level of activity achieved during the period

D   A fixed budget allowance for expenditure which is expected every period, regardless of the level of activity

10   BF Limited manufactures and sells a single product. An extract from the flexed budget for production costs is as follows.

	Activity level 80% £	90% £
Direct material	3,200	3,600
Direct labour	2,800	2,900
Production overhead	5,400	5,800
Total production cost	11,400	12,300

The total production cost in a budget that is flexed at the 88% level of activity will be £ ☐

Now, go back to the Learning Objectives in the Introduction. If you are satisfied you have achieved these objectives, please tick them off.

Answers to Interactive questions

Answer to Interactive question 1

Item	Part of controllable divisional investment	Not part of controllable divisional investment
Non-current assets	☑	☐
Trade receivables	☑	☐
Trade payables	☐	☑
Inventory	☑	☐

Answer to Interactive question 2

	ROI	RI
Without investment	21.0%	£34,200
With investment	20.7%	£35,200

WORKINGS

	Without investment	With investment
ROI		
£119,700/£570,000	21.0%	
£128,200/£620,000		20.7%
RI	£	£
Profit	119,700	128,200
Imputed interest charge:		
£570,000 × 15%	85,500	
£620,000 × 15%		93,000
	34,200	35,200

Answer to Interactive question 3

Many answers are possible. They could include:

Financial perspective

All the standard measures plus:

- Proportion of income from legal aid
- Regularity of income paid in prolonged cases
- Net fee income from 'No Win, No Fee' litigation

Customer perspective

- Number of cases won
- Number of new clients won through recommendations
- Cost of key services (eg conveyancing) compared to other local firms

Innovation and learning

- Continuing Professional Development (CPD) courses attended
- New services offered
- New methods of service delivery introduced (eg online Wills)

Internal business perspective

- Time taken to process key services (eg to draft and type Wills)
- Administration cost (eg courier services, website maintenance)
- Speed of accessing archives
- Ease of access to legislative and case law databases

Answer to Interactive question 4

The cost of factory power is estimated to be £ | 45,600 |.

WORKINGS

	Units	£
20X3 (highest output)	9,800	44,400
20X2 (lowest output)	7,700	38,100
	2,100	6,300

The variable cost per unit is therefore £6,300/2,100 = £3.

The level of fixed cost can be calculated by looking at any output level.

	£
Total of factory power in 20X3	44,400
Less variable cost of factory power (9,800 × £3)	29,400
Fixed cost of factory power	15,000

An estimate of costs in 20X5 is as follows.

	£
Fixed cost	15,000
Variable cost of budgeted production (10,200 × £3)	30,600
Total budgeted cost of factory power	45,600

Answer to Interactive question 5

(a) Direct material £ | 20,400 |

(b) Direct labour £ | 23,100 |

(c) Variable production overhead £ | 10,200 |

(d) Fixed production overhead £ | 11,000 |

(e) Selling and distribution overhead £ | 9,100 |

(f) Administration overhead £ | 7,000 |

(g) (i) The total expenditure variance for period 6 was £ | 2,600 | favourable

 (ii) The volume variance for period 6 was £ | 15,000 | adverse

WORKINGS

(a) Direct material is a variable cost of £16,000/4,000 = £4 per unit.

Budget cost allowance for 5,100 units = 5,100 × £4 = £20,400.

(b) Direct labour is a semi-variable cost which can be analysed using the high-low method.

	Output units	£
High	5,500	24,500
Low	4,000	20,000
Change	1,500	4,500

Variable cost per unit	= £4,500/1,500 = £3
Substituting in high output, fixed cost	= £24,500 – (5,500 × £3)
	= £8,000

Budget cost allowance for 5,100 units:

	£
Variable cost = 5,100 × £3	15,300
Fixed cost	8,000
	23,300

(c) Variable production overhead per unit = £8,000/4,000 = £2 per unit.

Budget cost allowance for 5,100 units = 5,100 × £2 = £10,200.

(d) Fixed production overhead cost allowance is fixed at £11,000.

(e) Selling and distribution is a semi-variable cost which can be analysed using the high-low method.

	Output units	£
High	5,500	9,500
Low	4,000	8,000
Change	1,500	1,500

Variable cost per unit	= £1,500/1,500 = £1
Substituting in high output, fixed cost	= £9,500 – (5,500 × £1)
	= £4,000

Budget cost allowance for 5,100 units:

	£
Variable cost = 5,100 × £1	5,100
Fixed cost	4,000
	9,100

(f) Administration overhead cost allowance is fixed at £7,000.

(g) The budgeted and actual output volumes correspond to the two activity levels provided in the question data. The total budget cost allowance for each activity level can be used as the basis for the variance calculations.

(i) Expenditure variance = Budget cost allowance for 5,500 units – actual expenditure for 5,500 units

= £85,000 – £82,400

= £2,600 favourable

(ii) Volume variance = budget cost allowance for original budget of 4,000 units – budget cost allowance for actual volume of 5,500 units

= £70,000 – £85,000 = £15,000 adverse

1   B   Head office costs are not controllable by the divisional manager and should be excluded from the calculation of controllable divisional profit.

2   C   £662,600

Variable material cost per 1% activity =		£4,000
Variable labour cost per 1% activity		£3,000

Production overhead

		£
At	50% activity	100,000
At	70% activity	116,000
Change	20%	16,000

Variable cost per 1% change in activity is (£16,000 / 20) = £800

	£
Substituting in 70% activity	
Variable cost = 70 × £800	56,000
Total cost	116,000
Therefore fixed cost	60,000

Other overhead is a wholly fixed cost.

Budget flexed at 67% level of activity

	£'000
Variable material 67 × £4,000	268.0
Variable labour 67 × £3,000	201.0
Production overhead	
Variable 67 × £800	53.6
Fixed	60.0
Other overhead	80.0
	662.6

3   B   ROI on marginal investment   = £45,000/£180,000

= 25%

This is higher than the cost of capital therefore it would be acceptable to the company as a whole. However, the manager would reject the project based on ROI because it is lower than the current divisional ROI.

Incremental RI   = £45,000 – (£180,000 × 20%)

= £9,000

Therefore the manager would accept the project if performance was assessed on the basis of residual income. This would be acting in the interest of the company as a whole.

4   D   The sales perspective is not one of the four perspectives of the balanced scorecard approach. The four perspectives are financial, innovation and learning, internal business and customer.

5   C   Imputed interest is £1,850,000 - £750,000 = £1,100,000. With interest at 11%, capital must be £10m. ROI = £1,850,000/£10,000,000 = 18.5%.

6   C   Investment Q only $= \dfrac{£480,000 + £350,000}{£2,400,000 + £1,400,000}$ = 21.8%

Investment R only $= \dfrac{£480,000 + £200,000}{£2,400,000 + £600,000}$ = 22.7%

Investments Q and R $= \dfrac{£480,000 + £350,000 + £200,000}{£2,400,000 + £1,400,000 + £600,000}$ = 23.4%

Investments Q, R and S $= \dfrac{£480,000 + £350,000 + £200,000 + £88,000}{£2,400,000 + £1,400,000 + £600,000 + £400,000}$ = 23.3%

CHAPTER

8

7 A

	£
Original profits = 15% × £1.2 million	180,000
Loss on sale of asset = £105,000 − £80,000	25,000
Revised profits	155,000

Revised investment base = £(1,200,000 − 105,000 + 80,000)

= £1,175,000

$$\text{Revised ROI} = \frac{£155,000}{£1,175,000}$$

= 13.2%

8 A If returns are constant and the value of the asset base is falling, both ROI and RI will increase.

9 C A budget cost allowance is the expected expenditure in a budget which has been flexed to the actual level of activity. It includes a basic, unchanged allowance for fixed costs and an amount for variable costs according to the level of activity.

Option A describes a functional budget and option B is an imposed or top-down budget. A budget cost allowance **includes an amount for variable overhead** therefore option D is not correct.

10 The total production cost in a budget that is flexed at the 88% level of activity will be £ 12,120 .

WORKING

Direct material cost per 1% activity = £40

Direct labour cost per 1% activity is not a constant amount at both activity levels, so this must be a semi-variable cost. Since production overhead is also a semi-variable cost the two costs can be analysed together, to save time (since the question asks only for a total cost in the answer).

			£
Direct labour and production overhead			
At	80%	activity	8,200
At	90%	activity	8,700
Change	10%		500

$$\text{Variable cost per 1\% change in activity} = \frac{£500}{10\%} = £50$$

Substituting in 80% activity:

	£
Variable cost = 80 × £50	4,000
Total cost	8,200
∴ Fixed cost	4,200

Flexed budget cost at 88% level of activity is as follows.

		£
Direct material (88 × £40)		3,520
Direct labour and production overhead:	Variable (88 × £50)	4,400
	Fixed	4,200
		12,120

CHAPTER 9

Standard costing and variance analysis

Introduction

Examination context

Topic List

1 Standard costing and standard costs

2 Cost variances

3 Sales variances and operating statements

4 Interpreting variances and deriving actual data from variance detail

Summary and Self-test

Answers to Interactive question

Answers to Self-test

Introduction

Learning objectives

- Calculate differences between actual performance and standards in terms of price and volume effects and identify possible reasons for those differences

- Calculate and reconcile budgeted and actual profits using standard marginal costing.

The specific syllabus reference for this chapter is: 3e.

Syllabus links

An understanding of variance analysis as a part of the work of the finance function will be necessary for your Business and Finance syllabus and as a part of performance measurement within that syllabus.

Examination context

20% of the marks in the examination will be allocated in one scenario-based question. Calculation of variances, covered in this chapter, may be examined in this form.

You may also be examined on the contents of this chapter by multiple choice, multi-part multiple choice or multiple response questions.

The calculation and analysis of variances lends itself well to numerical exam questions. However you are also likely to be presented with narrative questions, perhaps testing your understanding of the meaning of calculated variances.

The examiner is also likely to ask you to 'work backwards' from variance information to derive extracts from the actual results or the original standards. This requires a thorough understanding of the methods of variance calculation and of the meaning of the results of the calculations.

In the examination, candidates may be required to:

- Calculate and interpret variances for variable costs
- Calculate and interpret contribution-based variances for sales
- Derive actual cost and standard cost data from calculated variances
- Demonstrate an understanding of the meaning and use of standard cost operating statements

Traditionally students find variances a difficult area. They can be approached in a tabular manner or using formulae – find the one that suits you best. Understanding the meaning can help with understanding and remembering the calculations.

1 Standard costing and standard costs

Section overview

- Standard costing is the preparation of standard costs to use in variance analysis, a key management control tool.

- Standards for each cost element are made up of a monetary component and a resources requirement component.

- Standard costing enables the principle of management by exception to be practised.

- If they are to continue to be useful for control purposes, standard costs must be revised whenever there are changes in required resource inputs or in the price of resources.

1.1 Standard costing

Definition

Standard costing is defined by the Chartered Institute of Management Accountants as a 'control technique that reports variances by comparing actual costs to pre-set standards so facilitating action through management by exception'.

Standard costing (for control) therefore involves the following.

- The establishment of predetermined estimates of the costs of products or services
- The collection of actual costs
- The comparison of the actual costs with the predetermined estimates

1.2 Standard costs

A standard cost per unit is the expected, or normal, cost per unit, based on expectations (standards) for:

- The usage of resources; and
- The price per unit of resource.

A simple standard cost card, taking account of only variable costs, is shown below.

Standard cost: Widget

	Units of resource	Price per unit of resource	£
Material	6 kg	£5	30
Labour	2.5 hours	£8	20
Variable production overhead	2.5 hours	£2	5
Standard variable production cost			55

Standards provide an expected cost for **one unit** of output. A budget is a financial plan for a **period of time**. However, standard costs can be used in the preparation of budgets.

When standard costs are used, budgetary control variance analysis is based on a comparison between actual results and a flexed budget that uses standard costs. The particular advantage of standard costs is that the cost information consists of a quantity of resources (units of raw material, hours of direct labour and variable overheads) and a price per unit of resource (cost per kilogram of material or cost per hour for labour, etc).

As a result of this additional information, the analysis of the cost variances can be more detailed, and so can provide more control information to management.

C H A P T E R

9

1.3 Standard costing and management by exception

Standard costs, when established, are **average expected unit costs**. Because they are only averages and not a rigid specification, actual results will vary to some extent above or below the average. Standard costs can therefore be viewed as **benchmarks for comparison purposes**, and variances should only be reported and investigated if there is a significant difference between actual and standard. The problem is in deciding whether a variation from standard should be considered significant and worthy of investigation. Tolerance limits can be set and only variances that exceed such limits would require investigation.

Standard costing therefore enables the principle of **management by exception** to be practised.

Definition

Management by exception is defined by CIMA as the 'practice of concentrating on activities that require attention and ignoring those which appear to be conforming to expectations. Typically standard cost variances or variances from budget are used to identify those activities that require attention.'

1.4 Setting standard costs

Standards for units of production or service should be based on careful investigation and research, and standards should be **continually monitored to ensure that they are reasonable and reliable**. If there is an inaccuracy in the standard cost, a comparison of actual results against the standard will provide meaningless and unhelpful variance information.

A possible reason for a variance may be that the standard is unreliable or inaccurate, rather than that actual results were worse or better than they should have been. Companies that use standard costs therefore try to make their standard costs as reliable as possible, and will revise the standard whenever there are changes in resource inputs required or in the price per unit of resource.

1.5 The advantages of standard costing

- Carefully planned standards are an **aid to more accurate budgeting**.

- Standard costs provide a **yardstick** against which actual costs can be measured.

- The setting of standards involves determining the **most appropriate materials and methods** which may lead to economies.

- A target of efficiency is set for employees to reach and **cost consciousness is stimulated**.

- Variances can be calculated which enable the principle of '**management by exception**' to be operated. Only the variances which exceed acceptable tolerance limits need to be investigated by management with a view to control action.

- Standard costs **simplify the process of bookkeeping in cost accounting**, because they are easier to use than LIFO, FIFO and weighted average costs.

- Standard times **simplify the process of production scheduling**.

- Standard performance levels might provide an **incentive for individuals** to achieve targets for themselves at work.

2 Cost variances

Section overview

- Variances measure the difference between actual results and expected results. The process by which the total difference between standard and actual results is analysed is known as variance analysis.

- The material total variance can be divided into the material price variance and the material usage variance.

- Since material inventories are usually valued at standard cost in a standard costing system, material price variances are usually extracted at the time of purchase of the materials, rather than at the time of usage.

- The labour total variance can be divided into the labour rate variance and the labour efficiency variance.

- The variable overhead total variance can be divided into the variable overhead expenditure variance and the variable overhead efficiency variance.

- If the variable overhead rate is stated in terms of a rate per labour hour, then the variable overhead efficiency variance, in hours, is exactly the same as the labour efficiency variance in hours, and it occurs for the same reasons.

- The fixed overhead expenditure variance is the difference between the budgeted and actual fixed overhead expenditure in the period.

2.1 Variances

Definition

Variance: A cost variance is defined by CIMA as 'the difference between a planned, budgeted, or standard cost and the actual cost incurred. The same comparisons may be made for revenues.'

Variance analysis: Variance analysis is defined as the 'evaluation of performance by means of variances, whose timely reporting should maximise the opportunity for managerial action'.

As we saw in Chapter 8, when actual results are better than expected results, we have a **favourable variance** (F). If, on the other hand, actual results are worse than expected results, we have an **adverse variance** (A).

2.2 Material variances

Definition

Material total variance: The material total variance 'measures the difference between the standard material cost of the output produced and the actual material cost incurred' (CIMA).

The **material total variance** can be divided into the **material price variance** and the **material usage variance**.

(a) **The material price variance**

This is the difference between the standard cost and the actual cost for the actual quantity of material used or purchased. In other words, it is the difference between what the material did cost and what it should have cost.

C
H
A
P
T
E
R

9

(b) **The material usage variance**

This is the difference between the standard quantity of materials that should have been used for the number of units actually produced, and the actual quantity of materials used, valued at the standard price per unit of material. In other words, it is the difference between how much material should have been used and how much material was used, valued at standard price.

 ## Worked example: Material variances

Product X has a standard material cost as follows.

10 kilograms of material Y at £10 per kilogram = £100 per unit of X.

During period 4, 1,000 units of X were manufactured, using 11,700 kilograms of material Y which cost £98,631.

Requirement

Calculate the following variances.

(a) The material total variance
(b) The material price variance
(c) The material usage variance

Solution

(a) **The material total variance**

This is the difference between what 1,000 units should have cost and what they did cost.

	£
1,000 units should have cost (× £100)	100,000
but did cost	98,631
Material total variance	1,369 (F)

The variance is favourable because the units cost less than they should have cost.

Now we can break down the material total variance into its two constituent parts: the material price variance and the material usage variance.

(b) **The material price variance**

This is the difference between what 11,700 kgs should have cost and what 11,700 kgs did cost.

	£
11,700 kgs of Y should have cost (× £10)	117,000
but did cost	98,631
Material Y price variance	18,369 (F)

The variance is favourable because the material cost less than it should have.

(c) **The material usage variance**

This is the difference between how many kilograms of Y should have been used to produce 1,000 units of X and how many kilograms were used, valued at the standard cost per kilogram.

1,000 units should have used (× 10 kgs)	10,000 kgs
but did use	11,700 kgs
Usage variance in kgs	1,700 kgs (A)
× Standard price per kilogram	× £10
Usage variance in £	£17,000 (A)

The variance is adverse because more material was used than should have been used.

(d) **Summary**

	£
Price variance	18,369 (F)
Usage variance	17,000 (A)
Total variance	1,369 (F)

2.2.1 Using formulae to calculate materials variances

You may prefer to use formulae to calculate standard cost variances. The formulae for the material cost variances are as follows.

Material price variance	=	(Standard price per unit of materials – Actual price per unit of materials) × Actual quantity of materials
		$(SP - AP) \times AQ$
Material usage variance	=	(Standard quantity of materials for actual output – Actual quantity used) × Standard price per unit of material
		$(SQ - AQ) \times SP$

The total material cost variance in formula terms is:

(Standard price per unit of materials × Standard quantity of materials)

less

(Actual price per unit of materials × Actual quantity of materials)

ie $(SP \times SQ) - (AP \times AQ)$

Algebraically, material price variance + material usage variance

$= (SP - AP) \times AQ + (SQ - AQ) \times SP$

$= (SP \times AQ) - (AP \times AQ) + (SQ \times SP) - (AQ \times SP)$

$= (SP \times SQ) - (AP \times AQ)$

(as above)

Worked example: Using formulae to calculate material variances

Using the data in the last example the formulae would be applied as follows.

Materials price variance	=	$(SP - AP) \times AQ$
	=	$[£10 - (£98,631/11,700)] \times 11,700$
	=	£18,369 (F)
Materials usage variance	=	$(SQ - AQ) \times SP$
	=	$[(1,000 \times 10kg) - 11,700kg] \times £10$
	=	£17,000 (A)

2.2.2 Materials variances and opening and closing inventory

Suppose that a company uses raw material P in production, and that this raw material has a standard price of £3 per metre. During one month 6,000 metres are bought for £18,600, and 5,000 metres are used in production. At the end of the month, inventory will have been increased by 1,000 metres. In variance analysis, the problem is to decide the **material price variance**. Should it be calculated on the basis of **materials purchased** (6,000 metres) or on the basis of **materials used** (5,000 metres)? The answer to this problem depends on how **closing inventories** of the raw materials will be valued.

(a) If closing inventories of raw materials are valued at **standard cost**, (1,000 units at £3 per unit) then the price variance is calculated on material **purchases** in the period.

(b) If closing inventories of raw materials are valued at **actual cost** (FIFO) (1,000 units at £3.10 per unit) then the price variance is calculated on materials **used in production** in the period.

2.2.3 When to calculate the material price variance

A **full standard costing system** is usually in operation and therefore the price variance is usually calculated on **purchases** in the period. The variance on the full 6,000 metres will be written off to the costing income statement, even though only 5,000 metres are included in the cost of production.

There are two main advantages in extracting the material price variance at the time of **purchase**.

(a) If variances are extracted at the time of purchase they will be **brought to the attention of managers earlier** than if they are extracted as the material is used. If it is necessary to correct any variances then management action can be more timely, such as negotiating the price down with the supplier.

(b) Since variances are extracted at the time of purchase, **all inventories will be valued at standard price**. This is administratively easier and it means that all issues from inventories can be made at standard price. If inventories are held at actual cost it is necessary to calculate a separate price variance on each batch as it is issued. Since issues are usually made in a number of small batches this can be a time-consuming task, especially with a manual system.

The price variance would be calculated as follows.

	£
6,000 metres of material P purchased should cost (× £3)	18,000
but did cost	18,600
Price variance	600

2.3 Labour variances

The calculation of **labour variances** is very similar to the calculation of material variances.

Definition

Labour total variance: The labour total variance measures the difference between the standard labour cost of the output produced and the actual labour cost incurred.

The **labour total variance** can be divided into the **labour rate variance** and the **labour efficiency variance**.

(a) **The labour rate variance**

This is similar to the material price variance. It is the difference between the standard cost and the actual cost for the actual number of hours paid for.

In other words, it is the difference between what the actual labour used did cost and what it should have cost.

(b) **The labour efficiency variance**

This is similar to the material usage variance. It is the difference between the hours that should have been worked for the number of units actually produced, and the actual number of hours worked, valued at the standard rate per hour.

Worked example: Labour variances

The standard labour cost of product X is as follows.

2 hours of grade Z labour at £10 per hour = £20 per unit of product X.

During period 4, 1,000 units of product X were made, and the labour cost of grade Z labour was £17,825 for 2,300 hours of work.

Requirement

Calculate the following variances.

(a) The labour total variance
(b) The labour rate variance
(c) The labour efficiency variance

Solution

(a) **The labour total variance**

This is the difference between what 1,000 units should have cost and what they did cost.

	£
1,000 units should have cost (× £20)	20,000
but did cost	17,825
Labour total variance	2,175 (F)

The variance is favourable because the units cost less than they should have done.

Again we can analyse this total variance into its two constituent parts.

(b) **The labour rate variance**

This is the difference between what 2,300 hours should have cost and what 2,300 hours did cost.

	£
2,300 hours of work should have cost (× £10)	23,000
but did cost	17,825
Labour rate variance	5,175 (F)

The variance is favourable because the labour cost less than it should have cost.

(c) **The labour efficiency variance**

1,000 units of X should have taken (× 2 hours)	2,000 hrs
but did take	2,300 hrs
Efficiency variance in hours	300 hrs (A)
× Standard rate per hour	× £10
Efficiency variance in £	£3,000 (A)

The variance is adverse because more hours were worked than should have been worked.

(d) **Summary**

	£
Rate variance	5,175 (F)
Efficiency variance	3,000 (A)
Total variance	2,175 (F)

2.3.1 Using formulae to calculate labour variances

The formulae that you may wish to use to calculate the labour cost variances are as follows.

Labour rate variance = (Standard rate of pay per hour – Actual rate of pay per hour) × Actual labour hours

= (SR – AR) × AH

Labour efficiency variance = (Standard labour hours for actual output – Actual labour hours) × Standard rate of pay per hour

= (SH – AH) × SR

As with the materials variances, the total labour cost variance can be shown algebraically to be (SR × SH) – (AR × AH).

Worked example: Using formulae to calculate labour variances

Using the data in the last example the formulae would be applied as follows.

Labour rate variance = (SR – AR) × AH

= [£10 – £17,825/2,300] × 2,300

= £5,175 (F)

$$\text{Labour efficiency variance} \quad = \quad (\text{SH} - \text{AH}) \times \text{SR}$$
$$= \quad [(1,000 \times 2 \text{ hours}) - 2,300] \times £10$$
$$= \quad £3,000 \text{ (A)}$$

2.4 Variable production overhead variances

Definition

Variable production overhead total variance: Variable production overhead total variance measures the difference between the variable production overhead that should be used for actual output and the variable production overhead actually used.

Variable production overhead expenditure variance: Variable production overhead expenditure variance measures the actual cost of any change from the standard variable overhead rate per hour.

Variable production overhead efficiency variance: Variable production overhead efficiency variance is the standard variable production overhead cost of any change from the standard level of efficiency.

The variable overhead total variance can be subdivided into the variable overhead expenditure variance and the variable overhead efficiency variance.

Worked example: Variable overhead variances

Suppose that the variable overhead cost of product X is as follows.

    2 hours at £1.50 = £3 per unit

During the latest period, 400 units of product X were made. The labour force worked 760 hours. The variable overhead cost was £1,672.

Calculate the following variances.

(a)   The variable overhead total variance
(b)   The variable overhead expenditure variance
(c)   The variable overhead efficiency variance

Solution

(a)   **The variable overhead total variance**

This is similar to the labour total variance. It is the difference between the standard variable overhead cost of 400 units and the actual variable overhead cost incurred.

	£
400 units of product X should cost (× £3)	1,200
but did cost	1,672
Variable overhead total variance	472 (A)

(b)   **The variable overhead expenditure variance**

This is the difference between the amount of variable overhead that should have been incurred in the actual hours worked, and the actual amount of variable overhead incurred.

	£
760 hours of variable overhead should cost (× £1.50)	1,140
but did cost	1,672
Variable overhead expenditure variance	532 (A)

ICAEW

(c) **The variable overhead efficiency variance**

400 units of product X should take (× 2 hrs)	800 hrs
but did take	760 hrs
Variable overhead efficiency variance in hours	40 hrs (F)
× Standard rate per hour	× £1.50
Variable overhead efficiency variance in £	£60 (F)

If the variable overhead rate is stated in terms of a rate per labour hour, the variable overhead efficiency variance is exactly the same, in hours, as the labour efficiency variance, and occurs for the same reasons.

However, the variable overhead rate is sometimes stated in terms of a rate per machine hour, in which case the difference must be calculated between the actual machine hours and the standard machine hours for the output achieved.

The difference in hours, whether expressed in terms of labour hours or in terms of machine hours, is evaluated at the standard variable overhead rate per hour.

(d) **Summary**

	£
Variable overhead expenditure variance	532 (A)
Variable overhead efficiency variance	60 (F)
Variable overhead total variance	472 (A)

2.4.1 Using formulae to calculate variable overhead variances

The formulae that you may wish to use to calculate the variable overhead cost variances are as follows.

Variable overhead expenditure variance	=	(Standard variable overhead rate per hour – Actual variable overhead rate per hour) × Actual hours
	=	(SR – AR) × AH
Variable overhead efficiency variance	=	(Standard hours for actual output – Actual hours) × Standard variable overhead rate per hour
	=	(SH – AH) × SR

The standard rate per hour, and the actual and standard hours, can be expressed in terms of labour or in terms of machine hours.

The same algebraic breakdown of variable overhead variances can be derived as for materials and labour variances.

Worked example: Using formulae to calculate variable overhead variances

Using the data from the last example the formulae would be applied as follows.

Variable overhead expenditure variance	=	(SR – AR) × AH
	=	[£1.50 – (£1,672/760)] × 760
	=	£532 (A)
Variable overhead efficiency variance	=	(SH – AH) × SR
	=	[(400 × 2) – 760] × £1.50
	=	£60 (F)

2.5 Fixed overhead expenditure variance

The **fixed overhead expenditure variance** is simply the difference between the budgeted and actual fixed overhead expenditure in the period. By definition, fixed overheads should remain the same, regardless of the volume of production and sales. Any difference between budget and actual spending must be due to higher-than-expected or lower-than-expected spending, and can have nothing to do with differences in volume of activity.

The fixed overhead expenditure variance is (Budgeted fixed overhead cost – Actual fixed overhead cost).

3 Sales variances and operating statements

Section overview

- The sales price variance is a measure of the effect on expected contribution of charging a different selling price from the standard selling price.

- The sales volume variance measures the increase or decrease in standard contribution as a result of the actual sales volume being higher or lower than budgeted.

- Operating statements used in a standard marginal costing system show how the combination of variances reconcile the budgeted contribution and the actual contribution for a period.

3.1 Sales variances

Just as it is possible to set predetermined standards for cost, so it is also possible to set predetermined standards for sales: the unit sales price and the sales volume. This enables variances to be calculated to monitor and control the actual sales price and the actual sales volume achieved.

3.1.1 Sales price variance

The **sales price variance** is a measure of the effect on expected contribution of charging a different selling price from the standard selling price. It is calculated as the difference between what the sales revenue should have been for the actual quantity sold, and what it actually was.

3.1.2 Sales volume variance

The **sales volume variance** is the difference between the actual units sold and the budgeted quantity, valued at the standard contribution per unit. In other words, it measures the increase or decrease in standard contribution as a result of the sales volume being higher or lower than budgeted.

Worked example: Calculating sales variances

A company budgets to sell 8,000 units of product J for £12 per unit. The standard variable cost per unit is £7. Actual sales were 7,700 units, at a price of £12.50 per unit.

The sales price variance is calculated as follows.

	£
Sales revenue from 7,700 units should have been (× £12)	92,400
but was (7,700 × £12.50)	96,250
Sales price variance	3,850 (F)

The variance is favourable because the actual price was higher than standard.

The sales volume variance is calculated as follows.

Budgeted sales volume	8,000 units
Actual sales volume	7,700 units
Sales volume variance in units	300 units (A)
× Standard contribution £(12 – 7)	× £5
Sales volume variance	1,500 (A)

The variance is adverse because actual sales volume was less than budgeted.

3.1.3 Using formulae to calculate sales variances

The formulae that you may wish to use to calculate the sales variances are as follows.

Sales price variance	=	(Actual selling price per unit – Standard selling price per unit) × Actual sales quantity
	=	(AP – SP) × AQ
Sales volume variance	=	(Actual sales quantity – Budgeted sales quantity) × Standard contribution per unit
	=	(AQ – BQ) × SC

Worked example: Using formulae to calculate sales variances

Using the data in the last example the formulae would be applied as follows.

Sales price variance	=	(AP – SP) × AQ
	=	(£12.50 – £12.00) × 7,700
	=	£3,850 (F)
Sales volume variance	=	(AQ – BQ) × SC
	=	(7,700 – 8,000) × £(12 – 7)
	=	£1,500 (A)

3.2 Operating statements

So far, we have considered how variances are calculated in a standard marginal costing system without considering how they combine to reconcile the difference between budgeted contribution and actual contribution during a period. This reconciliation is usually presented as a report to senior management at the end of each control period. The report is called an operating statement or statement of variances.

An operating statement might look like this.

OPERATING STATEMENT FOR PERIOD 8

	£
Budgeted contribution	928,000
Sales volume variance	17,320 (A)
Sales price variance	11,830 (F)
Actual sales less standard variable cost of sales	922,510

VARIABLE COST VARIANCES	Favourable £	Adverse £	
Material price	7,120		
Material usage		6,190	
Labour rate		5,340	
Labour efficiency		4,140	
Variable overhead expenditure	4,920		
Variable overhead efficiency		2,870	
Total variable cost variances	12,040	18,540	6,500 (A)
ACTUAL CONTRIBUTION			916,010

	£	
Budgeted fixed overhead	400,470	
Fixed overhead expenditure variance	15,010 (A)	
Actual fixed overhead		415,480
Actual profit		500,530

Note that favourable variances are added to the budgeted contribution and adverse variances are subtracted, in reaching the actual profit figure.

However, in the case of the adverse fixed overhead expenditure variance, this is added to the budgeted expenditure because the actual expenditure was higher than budgeted.

ICAEW

Interactive question 1: Operating statement

[Difficulty level: Intermediate]

NN Co manufactures a single product, the SK. The standard variable cost for this item is as follows.

	£	£
Materials:		
P (8 kg at £0.40 per kg)	3.20	
Q (4 kg at £0.70 per kg)	2.80	
		6.00
Labour (3 hours at £7.50)		22.50
Variable overhead (3 labour hours at £0.50)		1.50
		30.00

Budgeted fixed overhead expenditure is £8,600.

The standard sales price per unit is £40. The budgeted production and sales for period 7 were 3,000 units.

Actual results for period 7 were as follows.

Sales and production	2,800 units
Sales revenue	£113,120

Materials purchased and used:

P	19,000 kg	Cost £7,410
Q	14,000 kg	Cost £10,220

Labour	8,300 hours	Cost £64,740

Variable overhead	£4,067
Fixed overhead	£8,250

Complete the operating statement for period 7 shown below. For the cost variances, make ONE entry (adverse or favourable) for each variance AND enter a zero or a dash in the other column.. For the sales variances, indicate in the box whether they are adverse (A) or favourable (F).

OPERATING STATEMENT FOR PERIOD 7

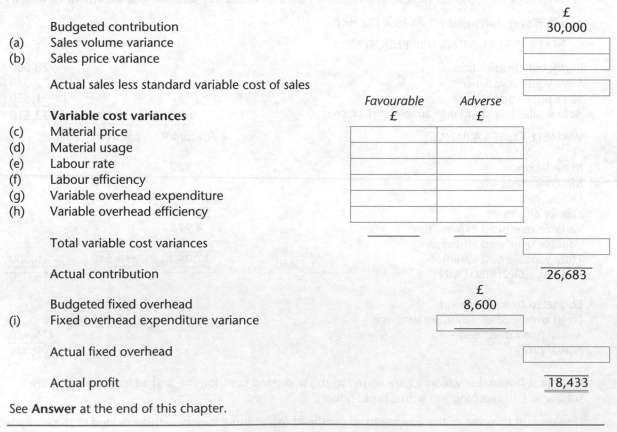

		£
	Budgeted contribution	30,000
(a)	Sales volume variance	
(b)	Sales price variance	
	Actual sales less standard variable cost of sales	

		Favourable £	Adverse £
	Variable cost variances		
(c)	Material price		
(d)	Material usage		
(e)	Labour rate		
(f)	Labour efficiency		
(g)	Variable overhead expenditure		
(h)	Variable overhead efficiency		

	Total variable cost variances	
	Actual contribution	26,683

		£
	Budgeted fixed overhead	8,600
(i)	Fixed overhead expenditure variance	
	Actual fixed overhead	
	Actual profit	18,433

See **Answer** at the end of this chapter.

There are several ways in which an operating statement may be presented. A common format is one which reconciles budgeted profit to actual profit.

Worked example: Reconciling budgeted profit to actual profit

Sydney manufactures one product, and the entire product is sold as soon as it is produced. There are no opening or closing inventories and work in progress is negligible. The standard cost card for the product, a boomerang, is as follows.

STANDARD COST CARD – BOOMERANG

		£
Direct materials	0.5 kg at £4 per kg	2.00
Direct wages	2 hours at £2.00 per hour	4.00
Variable overheads	2 hours at £0.30 per hour	0.60
Fixed overhead	2 hours at £3.70 per hour	7.40
Standard cost		14.00
Standard selling price		20.00

Budgeted output for the month of June year 7 was 5,100 units. Actual results for June year 7 were as follows.

Production of 4,850 units was sold for £95,600.

Materials consumed in production amounted to 2,300 kg at a total cost of £9,800.

Labour hours paid for amounted to 8,500 hours at a cost of £16,800.

Variable overheads amounted to £2,600.

Fixed overheads amounted to £42,300.

Requirement

Complete the table to generate a marginal costing operating statement for the month ended 30 June year 7. Make ONE entry (adverse or favourable) for each variance AND enter a zero or a dash in the other column. Enter the net total of adverse and favourable variances as either a positive number (favourable total) or negative number (adverse total) in the fourth column.

Operating statement for June

	Favourable £	Adverse £	£
Budgeted profit			30,600
Sales volume variance	0	3,350	
Sales price variance	0	1,400	
Cost variances			
Materials price	0	600	
Materials usage	500	0	
Labour rate	200	0	
Labour efficiency	2,400	0	
Variable overhead rate	0	50	
Variable overhead efficiency	360	0	
Fixed overhead expenditure	0	4,560	
Total variances	3,460	9,960	(6,500)
Actual profit			24,100

WORKING

(a) Revenue from 4,850 boomerangs should be (× £20) 97,000
   but was 95,600
   Selling price variance 1,400 (A)

(b)

Budgeted sales volume	5,100 units
Actual sales volume	4,850 units
Sales volume variance in units	250 units (A)
× standard contribution per unit	× £13.40
Sales volume contribution variance in £	£3,350 (A)

(c)

	£
2,300 kg of material should cost (× £4)	9,200
but did cost	9,800
Material price variance	600 (A)

(d)

4,850 boomerangs should use (× 0.5 kg)	2,425 kg
but did use	2,300 kg
Material usage variance in kg	125 kg (F)
× standard cost per kg	× £4
Material usage variance in £	£ 500 (F)

(e)

	£
8,500 hours of labour should cost (× £2)	17,000
but did cost	16,800
Labour rate variance	200 (F)

(f)

4,850 boomerangs should take (× 2 hrs)	9,700 hrs
but did take	8,500 hrs
Labour efficiency variance in hours	1,200 hrs (F)
× standard cost per hour	× £2
Labour efficiency variance in £	£2,400 (F)

(g)

	£
8,500 hours incurring variable o/hd expenditure should cost (× £0.30)	2,550
but did cost	2,600
Variable overhead expenditure variance	50 (A)

(h) Variable overhead efficiency variance in hours is the same as the labour efficiency variance:

1,200 hours (F) × £0.30 per hour	£360 (F)

(i)

	£
Budgeted fixed overhead (5,100 units × 2 hrs × £3.70)	37,740
Actual fixed overhead	42,300
Fixed overhead expenditure variance	4,560 (A)

4 Interpreting variances and deriving actual data from variance detail

Section overview

- There is a wide range of possible reasons for the occurrence of sales and cost variances.

- Individual variances should not be looked at in isolation. It is possible that one variance is inter-related with one or more other variances.

- Variances can be manipulated to derive actual data from standard cost details.

4.1 The reasons for variances

There is a wide range of reasons for the occurrence of adverse or favourable sales and cost variances.

The following list is not exhaustive but it should give you an idea of the type of circumstance that could give rise to each of the variances.

Variance	Favourable	Adverse
Material price	• Unforeseen discounts received • More care taken in purchasing • Material standard price set too high	• Price increase in the market • Careless purchasing • Material standard price set too low
Material usage	• Material used of higher quality than standard • More effective use made of material • Errors in allocating material to jobs	• Defective material • Excessive waste • Theft • Stricter quality control • Errors in allocating material to jobs
Labour rate	• Use of apprentices or other workers at a rate of pay lower than standard	• Wage rate increase • Use of higher grade labour
Labour efficiency	• Output produced more quickly than expected because of work motivation, better quality of equipment or materials, or better methods • Errors in allocating time to jobs	• Lost time in excess of standard allowed • Output lower than standard set because of deliberate restriction, lack of training, or sub-standard material used • Errors in allocating time to jobs
Variable overhead expenditure	• Change in types of overhead or their cost	• Change in types of overhead or their cost
Variable overhead efficiency	• As for labour efficiency (if based on labour hours)	• As for labour efficiency (if based on labour hours)
Fixed overhead expenditure	• Fixed overheads include a wide range of different items of expense. Any of these might be higher or lower than budgeted. For example rent, rates or insurance for the period might be higher or lower than budgeted	
Sales price	• Supply shortages meant customers prepared to pay higher prices • Quantity discounts given to customers were lower than expected • Original standard selling price set too low	• Supply surplus meant customers wished to pay lower price • Quantity discounts given to customers were higher than expected • Original standard selling price set too high
Sales volume	• Efficient sales force • Successful advertising campaign • Potential market was larger than expected • Original budgeted sales were very conservative	• Demotivated sales force • Competitor increased advertising effort • Original budgeted sales were too optimistic

4.2 Inter-relationships between variances

Quite possibly, individual variances should not be looked at in isolation. **One variance might be inter related with another**, and much of it might have occurred only because the other, inter related, variance occurred too.

Here are some examples of inter-related variances.

(a) **Materials price and usage**

It may be decided to purchase cheaper, lower quality materials for a job in order to obtain a favourable price variance, possibly with the consequence that materials wastage is higher and an adverse usage variance occurs. If the cheaper materials are more difficult to handle, there might also be an adverse labour efficiency variance and an adverse variable overhead efficiency variance.

If a decision is made to purchase more expensive materials, which perhaps have a longer service life, the price variance will be adverse but the usage variance might be favourable.

(b) **Labour rate and efficiency**

If employees are paid higher rates for experience and skill, using a highly skilled team to do some work would incur an adverse rate variance, but should also obtain a favourable efficiency variance. In contrast, a favourable rate variance might indicate a larger than expected proportion of inexperienced workers in the workforce, which could result in an adverse labour efficiency variance, and perhaps poor materials handling and high rates of wastage or product rejections (adverse material usage variance).

(c) **Sales price and sales volume**

The inter-relationship between sales price and sales volume variances should (hopefully) be obvious to you. A reduction in the sales price might stimulate bigger sales demand, so that an adverse sales price variance might be offset by a favourable sales volume variance. Similarly, a price rise would give a favourable price variance, but possibly at the cost of a fall in demand and an adverse sales volume variance.

(d) **Cost and sales variances**

(i) If there are favourable cost variances (perhaps cheaper labour or material have been used, say, so that there are favourable labour rate or material price variances), the possible drop in quality of the product could lead to an adverse sales volume variance because customers don't wish to buy the lower quality product.

(ii) If product quality is improved this might result in an adverse cost variance.

- If more expensive material is used (adverse material price variance)

- If labour are more careful in production of the product and hence take longer than standard (adverse labour efficiency variance)

- If more skilled labour is used (adverse labour rate variance)

But the change in quality might result in a favourable sales volume variance because customers want to buy more of the higher-quality product or a favourable sales price variance as a higher price could be charged for the better quality product.

(iii) If costs have risen (resulting in adverse labour rate, material price and variable overhead expenditure variances), the sales price might have to be increased to cover the extra costs. This would result in a favourable sales price variance, but could lead to an adverse sales volume variance.

4.3 Deriving actual data from standard cost details and variances

Variances can be **manipulated** to derive actual data from standard cost details.

Worked example: Deriving actual data

The standard marginal cost card for the TR, one of the products made by P Co, is as follows.

	£
Material 16 kgs × £6 per kg	96
Labour 6 hours × £12 per hour	72
	168

P Co reported the following variances in control period 13 in relation to the TR.

Material price: £18,840 favourable
Material usage: £480 adverse
Labour rate: £10,598 adverse
Labour efficiency: £8,478 favourable
Actual wages cost £171,320. P Co paid £5.50 for each kg of material. There were no opening or closing inventories of the material.

Requirements

Calculate the following.

(a) Actual output
(b) Actual hours worked
(c) Average actual wage rate per hour
(d) Actual number of kilograms purchased and used

Solution

(a)

	£
Total wages cost	171,320
Adjust for variances:	
Labour rate	(10,598)
Labour efficiency	8,478
Standard wages cost	169,200

∴ Actual output   = Total standard cost ÷ unit standard cost
                       = £169,200 ÷ £72
                       = 2,350 units

(b)

	£
Total wages cost	171,320.0
Less rate variance	(10,598.0)
Standard rate for actual hours	160,722.0
÷ Standard rate per hour	÷ £12.0
Actual hours worked	13,393.5 hrs

(c) Average actual wage rate per hour = Actual wages/actual hours = £171,320/13,393.5 = £12.79 per hour.

(d) Number of kgs purchased and used = x

	£
x kgs should have cost (× £6)	6.0x
but did cost (× £5.50)	5.5x
Material price variance	0.5x

∴   £0.5x =   £18,840
∴   x =   37,680 kgs

Alternatively the formula for the material price variance could be used as follows.

Price variance	=	(SP – AP) × AQ
£18,840	=	£(6 – 5.50) × AQ
AQ	=	£18,840 /£0.50
	=	37,680 kgs

CHAPTER 9

Summary and Self-test

Summary

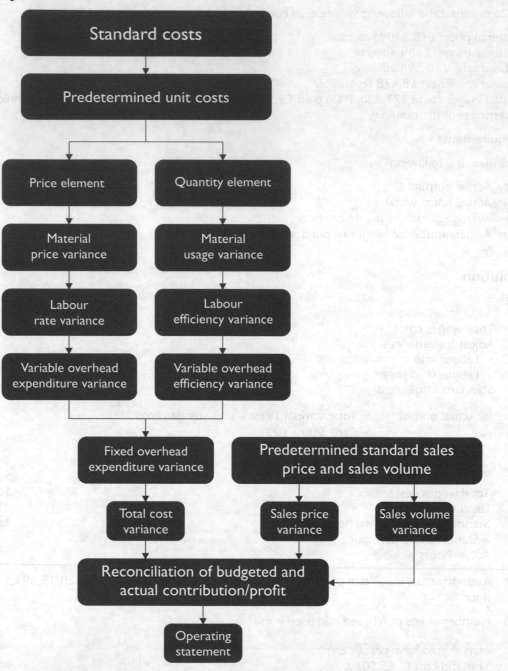

Self-test

Answer the following questions.

1   Gough Ltd manufactures a product with a standard material cost of £11. This is made up as follows.

		£
Material X	2 kgs at £1.00	2
Material Y	6 kgs at £1.50	9
		11

Actual production of 1,010 units required the following material purchases.

Material X	2,200 kgs	£2,530
Material Y	6,080 kgs	£8,512

There were no opening and closing inventories, and materials X and Y are not substitutable.

Using the table identify the total material price variance and whether it is adverse or favourable.

		Adverse	Favourable
A	£150	☐	☐
B	£162	☐	☐
C	£210	☐	☐
D	£278	☐	☐

2   Based on the same data as for question 1, using the table identify the total materials usage variance and whether it is adverse or favourable.

		Adverse	Favourable
A	£150	☐	☐
B	£162	☐	☐
C	£210	☐	☐
D	£278	☐	☐

3   S Limited has extracted the following details from the standard cost card of one of its products.

Labour standard   4.5 hours @ £6.40 per hour

During March, S Limited produced 2,300 units of the product and incurred wages costs of £64,150. The actual hours worked were 11,700.

The labour rate and efficiency variances were:

	Rate (£)	Efficiency (£)
A	10,730 (F)	8,640 (F)
B	10,730 (F)	8,640 (A)
C	10,730 (A)	8,640 (A)
D	10,730 (F)	7,402 (A)

4   The following diagram represents the standard and actual material costs incurred in manufacturing a product.

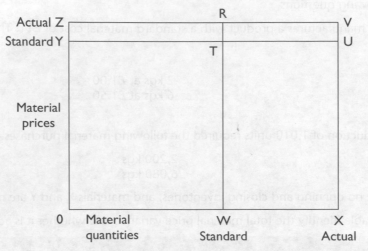

Using the table identify the areas corresponding to the conventional price and usage variances. Tick **one** box for each variance.

	Area			
	WXRV	WXTU	YZVU	YZRT
A Price variance	☐	☐	☐	☐
B Usage variance	☐	☐	☐	☐

5   A firm incurred a total adverse labour variance of £750. The standard pay rate was £7.50 per hour, while the actual pay rate was £8 per hour. The labour rate variance was £2,250. What are the flexed budgeted hours for labour?

A   4,300 hours
B   4,500 hours
C   4,600 hours
D   4,700 hours

6   Using the table identify the most likely labour variance to arise under each of the circumstances described. Tick **one** box for each circumstance.

	Adverse rate	Adverse efficiency	Favourable rate	Favourable efficiency
A Labour more skilled than expected	☐	☐	☐	☐
B More machine breakdowns than expected	☐	☐	☐	☐
C Pay increase less than expected	☐	☐	☐	☐

7   Using the table identify the most likely impact of the following on the fixed overhead expenditure variance. Tick **one** box for each item.

	Adverse	Favourable	No impact
A Volume of activity up marginally	☐	☐	☐
B Supervisors' salaries increase less than expected	☐	☐	☐
C Higher energy consumption	☐	☐	☐

8   The budgeted sales revenue of Thorold Ltd for August was £210,000 with an estimated selling price of £84 and estimated variable cost per unit of £70. Actual sales in August were 2,650 units, amounting to £219,950 revenue with a total resultant profit of £35,775.

Using the table below indicate the monetary value of the sales volume variance and whether it is adverse or favourable.

		Adverse	Favourable
A	£2,025	☐	☐
B	£2,100	☐	☐
C	£12,450	☐	☐
D	£12,600	☐	☐

9   A company had budgeted contribution of £26,700 for the latest period. The variances reported to managers at the end of the period were as follows.

	£
Material price	3,020 (A)
Labour efficiency	310 (A)
Variable overhead efficiency	217 (A)
Variable overhead total	149 (F)
Sales volume	2,700 (F)

The actual contribution for the period was £..

10 The following sales data are available for product P for the last period.

	Budget	Actual
Sales revenue	£69,000	£79,530
Sales volume (units)	4,600	4,820

The sales price variance for the period was:

A   £3,300 (F)
B   £6,900 (F)
C   £7,230 (F)
D   £10,530 (F)

Now, go back to the Learning Objectives in the Introduction. If you are satisfied you have achieved these objectives, please tick them off.

Answer to Interactive question 1

OPERATING STATEMENT FOR PERIOD 7

		£
	Budgeted contribution	30,000
(a)	Sales volume variance	2,000 (A)
(b)	Sales price variance	1,120 (F)
	Actual sales less standard variable cost of sales	29,120

	Variable cost variances	£ Favourable	£ Adverse
(c)	Material price	0	230
(d)	Material usage	0	600
(e)	Labour rate	0	2,490
(f)	Labour efficiency	750	0
(g)	Variable overhead expenditure	83	0
(h)	Variable overhead efficiency	50	0

		£
	Total variable cost variances	2,437 (A)
	Actual contribution	26,683
	Budgeted fixed overhead	8,600
(i)	Fixed overhead expenditure variance	350 (F)
	Actual fixed overhead	8,250
	Actual profit	18,433

Important point. In an exam, read the requirement carefully to make sure that you are entering your answers in the correct format. For example, this type of question may require you to enter zeros in boxes that you don't use. (The reason for this is so that the computer programme can tell whether you have completed the question or not.)

WORKINGS

(a) **Sales volume**

	£
Budgeted sales volume	3,000 units
Actual sales volume	2,800 units
Sales volume variance in units	200 units (A)
× Standard contribution per unit (£(40 – 30))	× £10
Sales volume variance in £	£2,000 (A)

(b) **Sales price**

	£
Revenue from 2,800 units should have been (× £40)	112,000
but was	113,120
Sales price variance	1,120 (F)

(c) **Material price**

	£	£
19,000 kg of P should cost (× £0.40)	7,600	
but did cost	7,410	
Material P price variance		190 (F)
14,000 kg of Q should cost (× £0.70)	9,800	
but did cost	10,220	
Material Q price variance		420 (A)
Total material price variance		230 (A)

(d) **Material usage**

Material P

2,800 units of SK should use (× 8 kgs)	22,400	kgs
but did use	19,000	kgs
Material P usage variance in kgs	3,400	kgs (F)
× Standard price per kg	× £0.40	
Material P usage variance in £	£1,360	(F)

Material Q

2,800 units of SK should use (× 4 kgs)	11,200	kgs
but did use	14,000	kgs
Material Q usage variance in kgs	2,800	kgs (A)
× Standard price per kg	× £0.70	
Material Q usage variance in £	£1,960	(A)
Total material usage variance (£1,960 – £1,360)	£600	(A)

(e) **Labour rate**

	£
8,300 hours of labour should cost (× £7.50)	62,250
but did cost	64,740
Labour rate variance	2,490 (A)

(f) **Labour efficiency**

To make 2,800 units of SK should take (× 3 hrs)	8,400	hrs
but did take	8,300	hrs
Labour variance in hrs	100	hrs (F)
× Standard rate per hour	× £7.50	
Labour efficiency variance in £	£750	(F)

(g) **Variable overhead expenditure**

	£
8,300 worked hours should cost (× £0.50)	4,150
but did cost	4,067
Variable overhead expenditure variance	83 (F)

(h) **Variable overhead efficiency** (same as labour hours)

	£
100 hrs (F) × Standard rate (£0.50)	50 (F)

(i) **Fixed overhead expenditure**

	£
Budgeted expenditure	8,600
Actual expenditure	8,250
Fixed overhead expenditure variance	350 (F)

1 D Favourable

Material X

	£	£
2,200 kgs should cost (× £1.00)	2,200	
but did cost	2,530	
Materials price variance		330 (A)

Material Y

	£	£
6,080 kgs should cost (× £1.50)	9,120	
but did cost	8,512	
Materials price variance		608 (F)
Total materials price variance		278 (F)

2 C Adverse

Material X

	kgs	£
1,010 units produced should use (× 2 kg)	2,020	
but did use	2,200	
Variance in kgs	180 (A)	
× Standard price per kg (× £1.00)		180 (A)

Material Y

	kgs	£
1,010 units produced should use (× 6 kg)	6,060	
but did use	6,080	
Variance in kgs	20 (A)	
× Standard price per kg (× £1.50)		30 (A)
Total materials usage variance		210 (A)

3 B

	£
11,700 hours should cost (× £6.40)	74,880
but did cost	64,150
Labour rate variance	10,730 (F)

2,300 units should take (× 4.5 hrs)	10,350 hrs
but did take	11,700 hrs
Variance in hours	1,350 hrs (A)
× Standard rate per hour	× £6.40
Labour efficiency variance	£8,640 (A)

If you selected options A or C you calculated the correct monetary values of the variances but misinterpreted their direction.

If you selected option D you valued the efficiency variance in hours at the actual rate per hour instead of the standard rate per hour.

4 A = YZVU

The material price variance is based on the actual quantity purchased

B = WXTU

The usage variance is evaluated at the standard price

5   D

The flexed budgeted hours for labour are the standard hours allowed for the actual production.

Labour rate variance	=	Actual hours worked × difference in labour rate
2,250	=	Actual hours worked × (£8.00 – £7.50)
Actual hours worked	=	4,500
Since total labour variance	=	Efficiency variance + rate variance
∴ £750 (A)	=	Efficiency variance + £2,250 (A)
∴ Efficiency variance	=	£1,500 (F)
1,500 (F)	=	Saving in labour hours compared with standard × standard rate per hour
Saving in labour hours	=	£1,500/£7.50
	=	200 hours
∴ Standard hours for actual production	=	4,500 hours worked + 200 hours saved
	=	4,700 hours

6   A   Favourable efficiency. More skilled workers would work at a faster rate

B   Adverse efficiency. Labour hours would still be recorded but there would be no output

C   Favourable rate. The hourly rate of pay would be lower than that used in the standard cost calculation

7   A   No impact. Fixed overhead expenditure would not be affected by a marginal increase in the volume of activity

B   Favourable

C   No impact. Energy costs related to consumption are variable overheads

8   B   Favourable

Budgeted sales volume (£210,000/£84)	2,500 units
Actual sales volume	2,650 units
Sales volume variance in units	150 units (F)
× Standard contribution per unit (£84 – £70)	× £14
Sales volume variance	£2,100 (F)

9   The actual contribution for the period was £26,219

	£
Budgeted contribution	26,700
Variances	
Material price	(3,020)
Labour efficiency	(310)
Variable overhead total	149
(excluding variable overhead efficiency because included within the total variance)	–
Sales volume variance	2,700
Actual contribution	26,219

10 C

Standard sales price per unit	=	£69,000/4,600
	=	£15

	£
4,820 units should sell for (× £15)	72,300
but did sell for	79,530
Sales price variance	7,230 (F)

CHAPTER 10

Breakeven analysis and limiting factor analysis

Introduction

Learning objectives

Tick off

- Calculate the breakeven point, contribution and margin of safety for a given product or service

☐

- Allocate scarce resources to those products and services with the highest contribution per unit of limiting factor

☐

The specific syllabus references for this chapter are: 4a, b.

Syllabus links

You will study the identification and management of limiting factors in more depth in the context of the Business Strategy syllabus.

Examination context

Examination questions about breakeven analysis and limiting factor analysis can be quite complicated but there are strict decision rules which can be applied in every question of this type. For example, unless otherwise stated, the **absolute amount** of expenditure on fixed costs and the variable cost **per unit** remain the same for every level of activity.

Questions on this area of the syllabus will usually involve some calculations.

In the examination, candidates may be required to:

- Calculate the breakeven point, margin of safety and contribution ratio for a product or service
- Calculate the volume of sales or level of activity required to achieve a target profit for the period
- Calculate the effect on profit, breakeven point, etc, of changes in the major decision variables
- Identify the optimum production plan or similar when a resource is in limited supply, and when

  - There is a maximum and/or minimum limit on the demand for individual products or services; and/or

  - It is possible to alleviate the resource restriction by subcontracting work to parties outside the business

This area involves candidates following a logical series of steps (or rules) which must be learned. The most difficult type of question in this area normally involves consideration of the possibility of sub contracting or outsourcing work.

1 Breakeven analysis and contribution

Section overview

- Breakeven analysis or cost-volume-profit (CVP) analysis is the study of the interrelationships between costs, volume and profit at various levels of activity.

- Contribution = selling price less variable costs; profit = contribution less fixed costs.

- The breakeven point occurs when there is neither a profit nor a loss and so fixed costs equal contribution.

- Breakeven point in units = total fixed costs ÷ contribution per unit.

- The contribution ratio is a measure of how much contribution is earned per £1 of sales revenue. It is usually expressed as a percentage.

- Breakeven point (in £) = total fixed costs ÷ contribution ratio.

- The margin of safety is the difference between the budgeted sales volume and the breakeven sales volume. It is sometimes expressed as a percentage of the budgeted sales volume.

- The contribution required for a target profit is equal to the fixed costs plus the target profit.

1.1 Contribution

Breakeven analysis or **cost-volume-profit (CVP) analysis** is the study of the interrelationships between costs, volume and profit at various levels of activity.

Contribution, a concept we encountered in Chapter 4, is fundamental to CVP analysis. As you know, contribution per unit is the difference between the selling price per unit and the variable costs per unit. The **total contribution** from the sales volume for a period can be **compared with the fixed costs** for the period. Any **excess of contribution** is **profit**, any **deficit** of contribution is a **loss**.

1.2 Breakeven point

The management of an organisation usually wishes to know the profit likely to be made if the aimed for production or activity and sales for the year are achieved. Management may also be interested to know the activity level at which there is neither profit nor loss. This is known as the **breakeven point**.

The breakeven point (BEP) can be calculated as

Breakeven point = Number of units of sale required to breakeven

$$= \frac{\text{Total fixed costs}}{\text{Contribution per unit}}$$

$$= \frac{\text{Contribution required to breakeven}}{\text{Contribution per unit}}$$

Worked example: Breakeven point

Expected sales	10,000 units at £8 = £80,000
Variable cost	£5 per unit
Fixed costs	£21,000

Requirement

Compute the breakeven point.

CHAPTER

10

Solution

The contribution per unit is £(8 – 5)	=	£3	
Contribution required to break even	=	fixed costs = £21,000	
Breakeven point (BEP)	=	£21,000 ÷ £3	
	=	7,000 units	
In revenue, BEP	=	(7,000 × £8) = £56,000	

Sales above £56,000 will result in profit of £3 per unit of additional sales and sales below £56,000 will mean a loss of £3 per unit for each unit by which sales fall short of 7,000 units. In other words, profit will improve or worsen per unit of sales by the level of contribution per unit.

	7,000 units £		7,001 units £
Revenue	56,000		56,008
Less variable costs	35,000		35,005
Contribution	21,000		21,003
Less fixed costs	21,000		21,000
Profit	0	(= breakeven)	3

1.3 The contribution ratio

The **contribution ratio** is a measure of how much contribution is earned from each £1 of sales revenue.

An alternative way of calculating the breakeven point to give an answer in terms of sales revenue and using the contribution ratio is as follows.

Breakeven point	=	**Sales revenue** required to break even
	=	$\dfrac{\text{Contribution required to break even}}{\text{Contribution ratio}}$
	=	$\dfrac{\text{Fixed costs}}{\text{Contribution ratio}}$

Worked example: Contribution ratio

Using the data in the last worked example the contribution ratio is $\dfrac{£3}{£8}$ = 37.5%

Breakeven is where sales revenue equals $\dfrac{£21,000}{0.375}$ = £56,000. At a price of £8 per unit, this represents 7,000 units of sales, as calculated earlier.

Interactive question 1: Contribution ratio   [Difficulty level: Easy]

The contribution ratio of product W is 20%. IB, the manufacturer of product W, wishes to make a contribution of £50,000 towards fixed costs.

If the selling price is £10 per unit, the number of units of W that must be sold is [   ].

See **Answer** at the end of this chapter.

1.4 The margin of safety

As well as being interested in the breakeven point, management may also be interested in the amount by which actual sales can fall below anticipated sales without a loss being incurred. This is the **margin of safety**.

The **margin of safety** is the difference in units between the budgeted or expected sales volume and the breakeven sales volume. It is sometimes expressed as a percentage of the budgeted sales volume. Alternatively the margin of safety can be expressed as the difference between the budgeted sales revenue and breakeven sales revenue, expressed as a percentage of the budgeted sales revenue.

Worked example: Margin of safety

Mal de Mer Co makes and sells a product which has a variable cost of £30 and which sells for £40. Budgeted fixed costs are £70,000 and budgeted sales are 8,000 units.

Requirement

Calculate the breakeven point and the margin of safety.

Solution

(a) Breakeven point $= \dfrac{\text{Total fixed costs}}{\text{Contribution per unit}} = \dfrac{£70,000}{£(40-30)}$

$= 7,000$ units

(b) Margin of safety $= 8,000 - 7,000$ units $= 1,000$ units

which may be expressed as $\dfrac{1,000 \text{ units}}{8,000 \text{ units}} \times 100\% = 12\frac{1}{2}\%$ of budget

(c) The margin of safety indicates to management that actual sales can fall short of budget by 1,000 units or 12½% before the breakeven point is reached and no profit is made.

1.5 Cost-volume-profit analysis and profit targets

Once the selling price and cost structure have been established for a product or service it is possible to manipulate the data to provide a variety of information for management decisions.

Worked example: CVP analysis

Butterfingers Company makes a product which has a variable cost of £7 per unit.

Requirement

If fixed costs are £63,000 per annum, calculate the selling price per unit if the company wishes to break even with a sales volume of 12,000 units.

Solution

		£
Contribution required to breakeven (= fixed costs)	=	£63,000
Volume of sales	=	12,000 units
Required contribution per unit	= £63,000 ÷ 12,000 =	5.25
Variable cost per unit	=	7.00
Required sales price per unit	=	12.25

Worked example: Target profits

RB Co makes and sells a single product, for which variable costs are as follows.

	£ per unit
Materials	10
Labour	8
Production overhead	6
	24

The sales price is £30 per unit, and fixed costs per annum are £68,000. The company wishes to make a profit of £16,000 per annum.

Requirement

Determine the sales required to achieve this profit.

Solution

Since the contribution earned in a period is literally the contribution towards fixed costs and profit, in order to achieve a certain target profit the contribution required is equal to the fixed costs plus the target profit.

Required contribution = fixed costs + profit = £68,000 + £16,000 = £84,000

Required sales can be calculated in one of two ways.

(a) $\dfrac{\text{Required contribution}}{\text{Contribution per unit}}$ = $\dfrac{£84,000}{£(30-24)}$ = 14,000 units, or £420,000 in revenue

(b) $\dfrac{\text{Required contribution}}{\text{Contribution ratio}}$ = $\dfrac{£84,000}{20\%\,^*}$ = £420,000 of revenue, or 14,000 units.

* Contribution ratio = $\dfrac{£30-£24}{£30}$ = $\dfrac{£6}{£30}$ = 0.2 = 20%.

Interactive question 2: Target profits   [Difficulty level: Easy]

SLB Limited wishes to sell 14,000 units of its product, which has a variable cost of £15 to make and sell. Fixed costs are £47,000 and the required profit is £23,000.

The required sales price per unit is £ ⬚ .

See **Answer** at the end of this chapter.

1.5.1 Variations on breakeven and profit target calculations

You may come across variations on breakeven and profit target calculations in which you will be expected to consider the effect of altering the selling price, variable cost per unit or fixed cost.

Worked example: Change in selling price

Stomer Cakes Ltd bake and sell a single type of cake. The variable cost of production is £0.15 per cake and the current sales price is £0.25 per cake. Fixed costs are £2,600 per month, and the annual profit for the company at the current sales volume is £36,000. The volume of sales demand is constant throughout the year.

The sales manager wishes to raise the sales price to £0.29 per cake, but considers that a price rise will result in some loss of sales.

Requirement

Ascertain the volume of sales required each month to maintain current profitability, if the selling price is raised to £0.29.

Solution

The volume of sales required is one which would leave total profit the same as before, ie £3,000 per month. Required profit should be converted into required contribution, as follows.

	£
Monthly fixed costs	2,600
Monthly profit required	3,000
Current monthly contribution	5,600

The volume of sales required after the price rise will be an amount which earns a contribution of £5,600 per month, the same as before. The contribution per cake at a sales price of £0.29 would be (£0.29 – £0.15) = £0.14.

$$\text{Required sales} = \frac{\text{Required contribution}}{\text{Contribution per unit}} = \frac{£5,600}{£0.14} = 40,000 \text{ cakes per month}$$

Worked example: Change in production costs

Close Brickett Ltd makes a product which has a variable production cost of £8 and a variable selling cost of £2 per unit. Fixed costs are £40,000 per annum, the sales price per unit is £18, and the current volume of output and sales is 6,000 units.

The company is considering whether to hire an improved machine for production. Annual hire costs would be £10,000 and it is expected that the variable cost of production would fall to £6 per unit.

Requirements

(a) Determine the number of units that must be produced and sold to achieve the same profit as is currently earned, if the machine is hired.

(b) Calculate the annual profit with the machine if output and sales remain at 6,000 units per annum.

Solution

(a) The current unit contribution is £(18 – (8 + 2)) = £8

	£
Current contribution (6,000 × £8)	48,000
Less current fixed costs	40,000
Current profit	8,000

With the new machine fixed costs will increase by £10,000 to £50,000 per annum. The variable cost per unit will reduce to £(6 + 2) = £8, and the contribution per unit will increase to £10.

	£
Required profit (as currently earned)	8,000
Fixed costs	50,000
Required contribution	58,000

	£
Contribution per unit	£10
Sales required to earn £8,000 profit = £58,000/£10 =	5,800 units

(b) If sales are 6,000 units

	£
Profit at 5,800 units of sale (see (a))	8,000
Contribution from sale of extra 200 units (× £10)	2,000
Profit at 6,000 units of sale	10,000

2 Breakeven charts

Section overview

- A breakeven chart is a chart that indicates the profit or loss at different levels of sales volume within a limited range.

- A traditional breakeven chart has a line for sales revenue, for fixed costs and for total costs.

- The breakeven point is at the intersection of the sales line and the total costs line.

- A contribution breakeven chart depicts variable costs, so that contribution can be read directly from the chart.

- Despite the usefulness of breakeven analysis, the technique has some serious limitations.

2.1 Breakeven charts

The breakeven point can be determined graphically using a **breakeven chart**. A **breakeven chart** is a chart that indicates the profit or loss at different levels of sales volume within a limited range.

A breakeven chart has the following axes.

- A **horizontal** axis showing the **sales/output** (in value or units)
- A **vertical axis** showing £ for **sales revenues** and **costs**

2.2 Lines on a breakeven chart

The following lines are drawn on the breakeven chart.

(a) The **sales line**

- Starts at the origin
- Ends at the point signifying expected sales volume and sales value

(b) The **fixed costs line**

- Runs parallel to the horizontal axis
- Meets the vertical axis at a point which represents the value of total fixed costs

(c) The **total costs line**

- Starts where the fixed costs line meets the vertical axis

- Ends at the point which represents anticipated sales volume on the horizontal axis and the total costs of anticipated sales on the vertical axis

The **breakeven point** is the **intersection** of the **sales line** and the **total costs line**.

The distance between the **breakeven point** and the **expected (or budgeted) sales**, in units, indicates the **margin of safety** at that level of sales.

Worked example: A breakeven chart

The budgeted annual output of a factory is 120,000 units. The fixed overheads amount to £40,000 and the variable costs are 50p per unit. The sales price is £1 per unit.

Requirement

Construct a breakeven chart showing the current breakeven point and profit earned up to the present maximum capacity of 120,000 units.

Solution

We begin the construction of the breakeven chart by calculating the profit at the budgeted annual output.

	£
Sales (120,000 units)	120,000
Variable costs	60,000
Contribution	60,000
Fixed costs	40,000
Profit	20,000

The breakeven chart is shown on the following page.

The chart is drawn as follows.

(a) The **vertical axis** represents **money** (costs and revenue) and the **horizontal axis** represents the **level of activity** (production and sales).

(b) The fixed costs are represented by a **straight line parallel to the horizontal axis** (in our example, at £40,000).

(c) The **variable costs** are added 'on top of' fixed costs, to give **total costs**. It is assumed that fixed costs are the same in total and variable costs are the same per unit at all levels of output.

The line of costs is therefore a straight line and only two points need to be plotted and joined up. Perhaps the two most convenient points to plot are total costs at zero output, and total costs at the budgeted output and sales.

- At zero output, costs are equal to the amount of fixed costs only, £40,000, since there are no variable costs.

- At the budgeted output of 120,000 units, total costs are £100,000.

	£
Fixed costs	40,000
Variable costs 120,000 × 50p	60,000
Total costs	100,000

(d) The sales line is also drawn by plotting two points and joining them up.

- At zero sales, revenue is nil.
- At the budgeted output and sales of 120,000 units, revenue is £120,000.

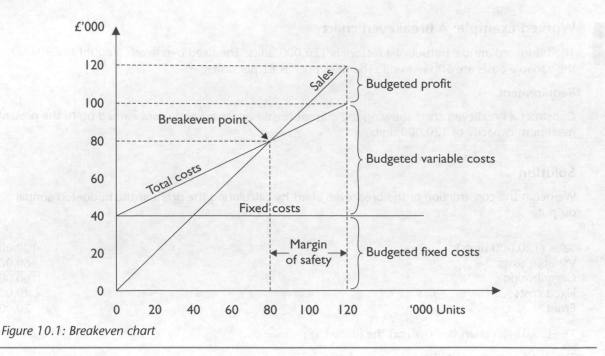

Figure 10.1: Breakeven chart

2.3 Interpreting the breakeven chart

The breakeven point is where total costs are matched exactly by total revenue. From the chart, this can be seen to occur at output and sales of 80,000 units, when revenue and costs are both £80,000. This breakeven point can be calculated as:

$$\frac{\text{Required contribution (= fixed costs)}}{\text{Contribution per unit}} = \frac{£40,000}{£0.50 \text{ per unit}} = 80,000 \text{ units}$$

The margin of safety can be seen on the chart as the difference between the budgeted level of activity and the breakeven level.

2.4 The contribution breakeven chart

The main problem with the traditional breakeven chart is that it is not possible to read contribution directly from the chart.

The contribution breakeven chart remedies this by **drawing the variable cost line instead of the fixed cost line**. This line will always run parallel to the total cost line. A contribution breakeven chart for the last worked example would include the variable cost line passing through the origin and the total variable cost of £60,000 for 120,000 units. The contribution breakeven chart is shown on the next page.

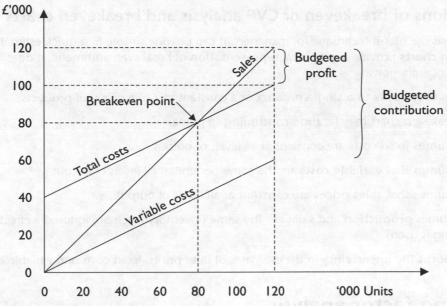

Figure 10.2: Contribution breakeven chart

If you look back at the traditional breakeven chart shown in Figure 10.1 you will see that the breakeven point is the same, but that the budgeted contribution can now be read more easily from the chart.

Interactive question 3: Breakeven chart   [Difficulty level: Easy]

Match the following labels to (a), (b), (c) and (d) marked on the breakeven chart below.

| Budgeted fixed costs | Margin of safety | Budgeted profit | Budgeted variable costs |

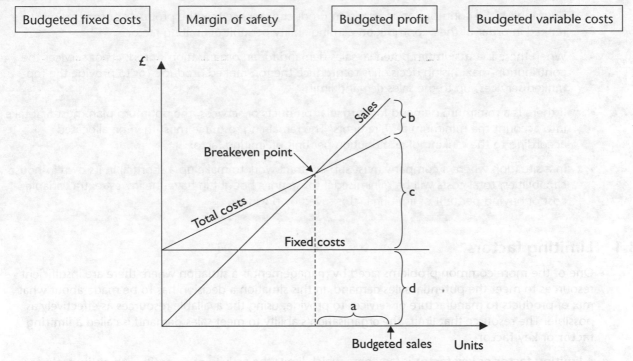

See **Answer** at the end of this chapter.

2.5 Limitations of breakeven or CVP analysis and breakeven charts

CVP analysis is a useful technique for managers. It can provide **simple** and **quick** estimates, and **breakeven charts** provide a **graphical representation** of breakeven arithmetic. It does, however, have a number of limitations.

- It **can only apply to a single product** or a constant mix of a group of products.

- A breakeven chart may be **time-consuming** to prepare.

- It **assumes** fixed costs are constant at all levels of output.

- It **assumes** that **variable costs** are the **same** per unit at all levels of output.

- It **assumes** that **sales prices** are **constant** at all levels of output.

- It assumes **production** and **sales** are the **same** (inventory levels are ignored – effectively marginal costing is used).

- It **ignores** the **uncertainty** in the estimates of sales prices, fixed costs and variable cost per unit.

3 Limiting factor analysis

Section overview

- A limiting factor is anything which limits the activity of an entity.

- If a specific resource is a limiting factor, contribution will be maximised by earning the highest possible contribution per unit of limiting factor.

- To establish the contribution-maximising product or service mix the products or services must be ranked in order of their contribution-earning ability per unit of limiting factor.

- When there is a maximum potential sales demand for an organisation's products or services the contribution-maximising decision is to produce the top-ranked products (or to provide the top-ranked services) up to the sales demand limit.

- If there is a minimum demand for particular products or services, the optimum plan must first take into account the minimum requirements. The remaining resource must then be allocated according to the ranking of contribution per unit of limiting factor.

- In a situation where a company must sub-contract work to make up a shortfall in its own in-house capabilities, total costs will be minimised if those units bought in have the lowest extra variable cost of buying per unit of limiting factor saved by buying.

3.1 Limiting factors

One of the more common problems faced by management is a situation where there are insufficient resources to meet the potential sales demand. In this situation a decision has to be made about what mix of products to manufacture or services to provide, using the available resources as effectively as possible. The resource that limits the organisation's ability to meet sales demand is called a **limiting factor** or **key factor**.

A **limiting factor** or **key factor** is 'anything which limits the activity of an entity'. An entity seeks to optimise the benefit it obtains from the limiting factor. Examples are a shortage of supply of a resource or a restriction on sales demand at a particular price.

A **limiting factor** could be sales if there is a limit to sales demand but any one of the organisation's resources (labour, materials and so on) may be insufficient to meet the level of production demanded.

It is assumed in limiting factor analysis that management wishes to maximise profit and that since there is no change in the fixed cost incurred **profit will be maximised when contribution is maximised**.

3.2 Limiting factor situations

For example if grade A labour is the limiting factor, contribution will be maximised by earning the highest contribution from each hour of grade A labour worked.

The limiting factor decision therefore involves the determination of **the contribution earned by each different product or service from each unit of the limiting factor.**

Worked example: Limiting factor

AB Ltd makes two products, the Ay and the Be. Unit variable costs are as follows.

	Ay £	Be £
Materials	1	3
Labour (£9 per hour)	18	9
Overhead	1	1
	20	13

The sales price per unit is £26 per Ay and £17 per Be. During July 20X2 the available labour is limited to 8,000 hours. Sales demand in July is expected to be 3,000 units for Ays and 5,000 units for Bes.

Requirement

Determine the profit-maximising production mix, assuming that monthly fixed costs are £20,000, and that no inventories are held.

Solution

Step 1
Confirm that the limiting factor is something other than sales demand.

	Ays	Bes	Total
Labour hours per unit	2 hrs	1 hr	
Sales demand	3,000 units	5,000 units	
Labour hours needed	6,000 hrs	5,000 hrs	11,000 hrs
Labour hours available			8,000 hrs
Shortfall			3,000 hrs

Labour is the limiting factor on production

Step 2
Identify the contribution earned by each product per unit of limiting factor, that is per labour hour worked.

	Ays £	Bes £
Sales price	26	17
Variable cost	20	13
Unit contribution	6	4
Labour hours per unit	2 hrs	1 hr
Contribution per labour hour (= unit of limiting factor)	£3	£4

Although Ays have a higher unit contribution than Bes, two Bes can be made in the time it takes to make one Ay. Because labour is in short supply it is more profitable to make Bes than Ays.

Step 3
Determine the **optimum production plan**. Sufficient Bes will be made to meet the full sales demand, and the remaining labour hours available will then be used to make Ays.

Product	Demand	Hours required	Hours available	Priority of manufacture
Bes	5,000	5,000	5,000	1st
Ays	3,000	6,000	3,000 (bal)	2nd
		11,000	8,000	

Product	Units	Hours needed	Contribution per hour £	Total £
Bes	5,000	5,000	4	20,000
Ays	1,500	3,000	3	9,000
		8,000		29,000
Less fixed costs				20,000
Profit				9,000

Interactive question 4: Limiting factors [Difficulty level: Easy]

LF Ltd makes a single product for which the standard cost details are as follows.

	£
Variable material (£3 per kg)	12
Variable labour (£8 per hour)	72
Production overhead	48
Total production cost	132

Demand for next period will be 20,000 units. No inventories are held and only 75,000 kg of material and 190,000 hours of labour will be available.

Indicate, by placing ticks where relevant in the table below, which resource or resources represent a limiting factor for LF Ltd.

	Limiting factor	Not a limiting factor
Materials	☐	☐
Labour	☐	☐

See **Answer** at the end of this chapter.

Interactive question 5: Limiting factor analysis [Difficulty level: Intermediate]

POV Ltd manufactures three products – X, Y and Z – that use the same machines. The budgeted income statements for the three products are as follows.

	X £'000	Y £'000	Z £'000
Sales	1,000	1,125	625
Variable material and labour costs	(500)	(563)	(438)
Variable overheads	(250)	(187)	(62)
Fixed overheads	(200)	(315)	(130)
Profit/(loss)	50	60	(5)
Annual sales demand (units)	5,000	7,500	2,500
Machine hours per unit	20	21	26

However, after the budget had been formulated, an unforeseen condition has meant that during the next period the available machine capacity has been limited to 296,500 hours.

(a) The shortfall in available machine hours for next period is .... hours

(b) The contribution earned per machine hour used on product X is £ ....
The contribution earned per machine hour used on product Y is £ ....
The contribution earned per machine hour used on product Z is £ ....

(c) The number of units of each product that should be manufactured next period is:

(i) Product X............... units
(ii) Product Y.............. units
(iii) Product Z............... units

See **Answer** at the end of this chapter.

3.3 Limiting factor analysis and restricted freedom of action

In certain circumstances an organisation faced with a limiting factor on production and sales **might not be able to produce the profit-maximising product mix** because the mix and/or volume of products that can be produced and sold is also restricted by a factor other than a scarce resource.

(a) A contract to supply a certain number of products to a customer which cannot be cancelled.

(b) Production/sales of a minimum quantity of one or more products to **provide a complete product range and/or to maintain customer goodwill**.

(c) Maintenance of a **certain market share** of one or more products.

In each of these cases, the organisation might have to **produce more of a particular product or products than the level established by ranking** according to contribution per unit of limiting factor.

If an organisation has to **produce more of a particular product or products than the level established by ranking** according to contribution per unit of limiting factor, the products should be ranked in the normal way but the optimum production plan must first take into account the minimum production requirements. The remaining resource must then be allocated according to the ranking.

Worked example: Restricted freedom of action

Harvey is currently preparing its budget for the year ending 30 September 20X2. The company manufactures and sells three products, Beta, Delta and Gamma.

The unit selling price and cost structure of each product is budgeted as follows.

	Beta £	Delta £	Gamma £
Selling price	100	124	32
Variable costs:			
Labour	24	48	6
Materials	26	7	8
Overhead	10	5	6
	60	60	20

The labour rate is budgeted at £6 per hour, and fixed costs at £1,300,000 per annum. The company has a maximum production capacity of 228,000 labour hours.

A meeting of the board of directors has been convened to discuss the budget and to resolve the problem as to the quantity of each product which should be made and sold. The sales director presented the results of a recent market survey which reveals that market demand for the company's products will be as follows.

Product	Units
Beta	24,000
Delta	12,000
Gamma	60,000

The production director proposes that since Gamma only contributes £12 per unit, the product should no longer be produced, and the surplus capacity transferred to produce additional quantities of Beta and Delta. The sales director does not agree with the proposal. Gamma is considered necessary to complement the product range and to maintain customer goodwill. If Gamma is not offered, the sales director believes that sales of Beta and Delta will be seriously affected. After further discussion the board decided that a minimum of 10,000 units of each product should be produced. The remaining production capacity would then be allocated so as to achieve the maximum profit possible.

Requirement

Prepare a budget statement which clearly shows the maximum profit which could be achieved in the year ending 30 September 20X2.

Solution

Step 1

Ascertain whether labour hours are a scarce resource

	Units demanded	Labour hours per unit	Total labour hours
Beta	24,000	4 (£24/£6)	96,000
Delta	12,000	8 (£48/£6)	96,000
Gamma	60,000	1 (£6/£6)	60,000
			252,000

Labour hours are a limiting factor.

Step 2

Rank the products

Since only 228,000 hours are available we need to establish which product earns the greatest contribution per labour hour.

	Beta	Delta	Gamma
Contribution per unit	£40	£64	£12
Labour hours	4	8	1
Contribution per labour hour	£10	£8	£12
Ranking	2nd	3rd	1st

Step 3

Determine a production plan

The optimum production plan must take into account the requirement that 10,000 units of each product are produced, and then allocate the remaining hours according to the above ranking.

		Hours
Beta	10,000 units × 4 hours	40,000
Delta	10,000 units × 8 hours	80,000
Gamma	10,000 units × 1 hour	10,000
		130,000
Gamma	50,000 units × 1 hour (full demand)	50,000
Beta	12,000 units × 4 hours (balance)	48,000
		228,000

Step 4

Draw up a budget.

BUDGET STATEMENT

	£
Contribution	
Beta (22,000 units × £40)	880,000
Delta (10,000 units × £64)	640,000
Gamma (60,000 units × £12)	720,000
Total contribution	2,240,000
Fixed costs	1,300,000
Profit	940,000

3.4 Make or buy decisions and scarce resources

An organisation might **want to do more things than it has the resources for**, and so its alternatives would be as follows.

(a) Make the best use of the available resources and ignore the opportunities to buy help from outside.

(b) Combine internal resources with subcontracting externally so as to do more and increase profitability.

Buying help from outside is justifiable if it adds to profits. A further decision is then required on how to split the work between internal and external effort. What parts of the work should be given to suppliers or subcontractors so as to maximise profitability?

In a situation where a company must **subcontract work to make up a shortfall in its own in-house capabilities**, its total costs will be minimised if those units bought have the lowest extra variable cost of buying per unit of scarce resource saved by buying.

Worked example: Make or buy decisions with scarce resources

MM manufactures three components, S, A and T using the same machines for each and assembles them into a single product. The budget for the next year calls for the production and assembly of 4,000 of each component. The variable production cost per unit of the final product is as follows.

	Machine hours	Variable cost £
1 unit of S	3	20
1 unit of A	2	36
1 unit of T	4	24
Assembly		100

Only 24,000 hours of machine time will be available during the year, and a subcontractor has quoted the following unit prices for supplying components: S £29; A £40; T £34.

Requirement

Advise MM on its most profitable plan.

Solution

The organisation's budget calls for 36,000 hours of machine time, if all the components are to be produced in-house. Only 24,000 hours are available, and so there is a shortfall of 12,000 hours of machine time, which is therefore a limiting factor. The shortage can be overcome by subcontracting the equivalent of 12,000 machine hours' output to the subcontractor.

The assembly costs are not relevant costs because they are not affected by the decision.

The decision rule is to **minimise the extra variable costs of subcontracting per unit of scarce resource saved** (that is, per machine hour saved).

	S £	A £	T £
Variable cost of making	20	36	24
Variable cost of buying	29	40	34
Extra variable cost of buying	9	4	10
Machine hours saved by buying	3 hrs	2 hrs	4 hrs
Extra variable cost of buying per hour saved	£3	£2	£2.50

This analysis shows that it is **cheaper to buy A than to buy T** and it is **most expensive to buy S**. The **priority for making** the components in-house will be in the **reverse order**: S, then T, then A. There are enough machine hours to make all 4,000 units of S (12,000 hours) and to produce 3,000 units of T (another 12,000 hours). 12,000 hours' production of T and A must be subcontracted.

The cost-minimising and so profit-maximising make and buy schedule is as follows.

Component		Machine hours used/saved	Number of units	Unit variable cost £	Total variable cost £
Make:	S	12,000	4,000	20	80,000
	T	12,000	3,000	24	72,000
		24,000			152,000
Buy:	T	4,000	1,000	34	34,000
	A	8,000	4,000	40	160,000
		12,000			
Total variable cost of components, excluding assembly costs					346,000

Interactive question 6: Make or buy and limiting factors   [Difficulty level: Exam standard]

TW manufactures two products, the D and the E, using the same material for each. Annual demand for the D is 9,000 units, while demand for the E is 12,000 units. The variable production cost per unit of the D is £10, and that of the E £15. The D requires 3.5 kgs of raw material per unit, the E requires 8 kgs of raw material per unit. Supply of raw material will be limited to 87,500 kgs during the year.

A sub contractor has quoted prices of £17 per unit for the D and £25 per unit for the E to supply the product. How many of each product should TW manufacture in order to maximise profits?

Requirement

Fill in the boxes in the sentence below.

TW should manufacture ⬚ units of D and ⬚ units of E to maximise profits.

See **Answer** at the end of this chapter.

Summary

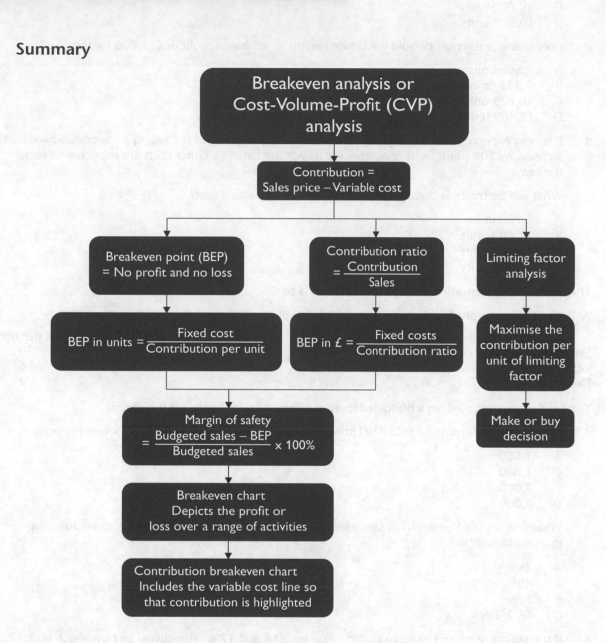

Breakeven analysis or Cost-Volume-Profit (CVP) analysis

Contribution = Sales price − Variable cost

Breakeven point (BEP) = No profit and no loss

Contribution ratio = Contribution / Sales

Limiting factor analysis

BEP in units = Fixed cost / Contribution per unit

BEP in £ = Fixed costs / Contribution ratio

Maximise the contribution per unit of limiting factor

Margin of safety = (Budgeted sales − BEP) / Budgeted sales × 100%

Make or buy decision

Breakeven chart
Depicts the profit or loss over a range of activities

Contribution breakeven chart
Includes the variable cost line so that contribution is highlighted

Self-test

Answer the following questions.

The following information relates to questions 1 to 3.

Information concerning K Limited's single product is as follows.

	£ per unit
Selling price	6.00
Variable production cost	1.20
Variable selling cost	0.40
Fixed production cost	4.00
Fixed selling cost	0.80

Budgeted production and sales for the year are 10,000 units.

1   What is the company's breakeven point, to the nearest whole unit?

    A   8,000 units
    B   8,333 units
    C   10,000 units
    D   10,909 units

2   How many units must be sold if K Limited wants to achieve a profit of £11,000 for the year?

    A   2,500 units
    B   9,833 units
    C   10,625 units
    D   13,409 units

3   It is now expected that the variable production cost per unit and the selling price per unit will each increase by 10%, and fixed production costs will rise by 25%. Other costs are expected to remain the same.

    What will be the new breakeven point, to the nearest whole unit?

    A   8,788 units
    B   11,600 units
    C   11,885 units
    D   12,397 units

The following information relates to questions 4 to 6.

W Limited sells one product for which data is given below:

	£ per unit
Selling price	10
Variable cost	6
Fixed cost	2

The fixed costs are based on a budgeted level of activity of 5,000 units for the period.

4   How many units must be sold if W Limited wishes to earn a profit of £6,000 for one period?

    A   1,500
    B   1,600
    C   4,000
    D   8,000

5   What is W Limited's margin of safety for the budget period if fixed costs prove to be 20% higher than budgeted?

    A   29%
    B   40%
    C   50%
    D   66 2/3%

6   If the selling price and variable cost increase by 20% and 12% respectively by how much must sales volume change compared with the original budgeted level in order to achieve the original budgeted profit for the period?

    A   24.2% decrease
    B   24.2% increase
    C   39.4% decrease
    D   39.4% increase

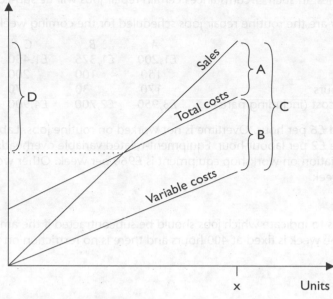

In the above breakeven chart, the contribution at level of activity x can be read as:

A Distance A
B Distance B
C Distance C
D Distance D

8 R Limited manufactures three products, the selling price and cost details of which are given below.

	Product P £	Product Q £	Product R £
Selling price per unit	150	190	190
Costs per unit			
Variable materials (£5/kg)	20	10	30
Variable labour (£8/hour)	32	48	40
Variable overhead	16	24	20
Fixed overhead	48	72	60

In a period when materials are restricted in supply, the most and least profitable uses of materials are:

	Most profitable	Least profitable
A	R	P
B	Q	R
C	Q	P
D	R	Q

9 JJ makes two products, the K and the L. The K sells for £50 per unit, the L for £70 per unit. The variable cost per unit of the K is £35, that of the L £40. Each unit of K uses 2 kgs of raw material. Each unit of L uses 3 kgs of material.

In the forthcoming period the availability of raw material is limited to 2,000 kgs. JJ is contracted to supply 500 units of K. Maximum demand for the L is 250 units. Demand for the K is unlimited.

What is the profit-maximising product mix?

	K	L
A	250 units	625 units
B	1,250 units	750 units
C	625 units	250 units
D	750 units	1,250 units

10   B has insufficient workshop capacity to carry out all the repair work currently required on its fleet of delivery vehicles. In such circumstances certain repair jobs will be sub-contracted to local garages.

Set out below are the routine repair jobs scheduled for the coming week.

Job	A	B	C	D	E	F
Cost of parts	£1,200	£1,375	£1,450	£500	£375	£690
Labour hours	150	100	200	50	150	100
Equipment hours	170	30	70	30	70	70
Sub-contract cost (including parts)	£3,950	£2,700	£4,900	£1,800	£2,700	£2,400

Labour is paid £6 per hour. Overtime is not worked on routine jobs. Labour-related variable overheads are £2 per labour hour. Equipment-related variable overheads are £1 per equipment-hour. Depreciation on workshop equipment is £960 per week. Other workshop fixed overheads are £1,540 per week.

Requirement

Tick the boxes to indicate which jobs should be subcontracted if the amount of workshop labour available in the week is fixed at 400 hours and there is no restriction on equipment availability.

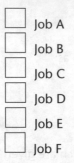

☐   Job A

☐   Job B

☐   Job C

☐   Job D

☐   Job E

☐   Job F

Now, go back to the Learning Objectives in the Introduction. If you are satisfied you have achieved these objectives, please tick them off.

Answer to Interactive question 1

The number of units that must be sold is $\boxed{25{,}000}$

WORKINGS

$$\frac{\text{Required contribution}}{\text{Contribution ratio}} = \frac{£50{,}000}{20\%} = £250{,}000$$

∴ Number of units = £250,000 ÷ £10 = 25,000.

Answer to Interactive question 2

The required sales price per unit is £ $\boxed{20}$

WORKINGS

Required contribution	=	fixed costs plus profit
	=	£47,000 + £23,000
	=	£70,000
Required sales		14,000 units
Required contribution per unit	=	£70,000/14,000 = £5 per unit

	£
Required contribution per unit sold	5
Variable cost per unit	15
Required sales price per unit	20

Answer to Interactive question 3

(a)   = Margin of safety
(b)   = Budgeted profit
(c)   = Budgeted variable costs
(d)   = Budgeted fixed costs

Answer to Interactive question 4

	Limiting factor	Not a limiting factor
Materials	✓	
Labour		✓

Material required   =   20,000 units × (£12/£3)   =   80,000 kg

Material is therefore a limiting factor, since 75,000 kg are available.

Labour required   =   20,000 units × (£72/£8)   =   180,000 hours

Labour is not a limiting factor, since 190,000 labour hours are available.

Answer to Interactive question 5

(a) The shortfall in available machine hours for next period is $\boxed{26{,}000}$ hours.

WORKINGS

Machine hours required to satisfy annual sales demand:

		Hours
Product X	5,000 units × 20 hrs	100,000
Product Y	7,500 units × 21 hrs	157,500
Product Z	2,500 units × 26 hrs	65,000
Total machine hours required		322,500
Machine hours available		296,500
Shortfall in available machine hours		26,000

(b) The contribution earned per machine hour used on product X is £ $\boxed{2.50}$

The contribution earned per machine hour used on product Y is £ $\boxed{2.38}$

The contribution earned per machine hour used on product Z is £ $\boxed{1.92}$

WORKINGS

	X £'000	Y £'000	Z £'000
Sales revenue	1,000	1,125	625
Variable material and labour costs	(500)	(563)	(438)
Variable overheads	(250)	(187)	(62)
Contribution	250	375	125
Contribution per unit	£50	£50	£50
Contribution per machine hour	£2.50	£2.38	£1.92

(c) (i)   Product X $\boxed{5{,}000}$ units

(ii)   Product Y $\boxed{7{,}500}$ units

(iii)   Product Z $\boxed{1{,}500}$ units

WORKINGS

Ranking	Product	Demand units	Hours required	Hours available	Production units
1st	X	5,000 (× 20)	100,000	100,000	5,000
2nd	Y	7,500 (× 21)	157,500	157,500	7,500
3rd	Z	2,500 (× 26)	65,000	39,000*	1,500
				296,500	

* Balance (296,500 – 100,000 – 157,500)

Answer to Interactive question 6

TW should manufacture $\boxed{9{,}000}$ units of D and $\boxed{7{,}000}$ units of E.

WORKINGS

	D £ per unit	E £ per unit
Variable cost of making	10	15
Variable cost of buying	17	25
Extra variable cost of buying	7	10
Raw material saved by buying	3.5 kgs	8 kgs
Extra variable cost of buying per kg saved	£2	£1.25
Priority for internal manufacture	1	2

Production plan

		Material used kgs
∴ Make D	(9,000 × 3.5 kgs)	31,500
E	(7,000 × 8 kgs)	56,000
		87,500

The remaining 5,000 units of E should be purchased from the sub contractor.

1   D   Breakeven point

$$= \frac{\text{Fixed costs}}{\text{Contribution per unit}}$$

$$= \frac{10,000 \times (\pounds 4.00 + \pounds 0.80)}{(\pounds 6.00 - (\pounds 1.20 + \pounds 0.40))} = \frac{\pounds 48,000}{\pounds 4.40} = 10,909 \text{ units}$$

If you selected option A you divided the fixed cost by the selling price, but the **selling price also has to cover the variable cost.** Option B ignores the selling costs, but these are costs that **must be covered before the breakeven point is reached.** Option C is the budgeted sales volume, which happens to be below the breakeven point.

2   D   Contribution required for target profit   = Fixed costs + Profit

                                                 = £48,000 + £11,000

                                               = £59,000

∴ Contribution per unit (from question 1)   = £4.40

∴ Sales units required $= \dfrac{\pounds 59,000}{\pounds 4.40} = 13,409 \text{ units}$

If you selected option A you divided the required profit by the contribution per unit, but the fixed costs must be covered before any profit can be earned. If you selected option B you identified correctly the contribution required for the target profit, but you then divided by the selling price per unit instead of the contribution per unit. Option C ignores the selling costs, which must be covered before a profit can be earned.

3   C

	£ per unit
New selling price (£6 × 1.1)	6.60
New variable cost (£1.20 × 1.1) + £0.40	1.72
Revised contribution per unit	4.88
New fixed costs (£40,000 × 1.25) + £8,000	£58,000

$$\text{Revised breakeven point} = \frac{\pounds 58,000}{\pounds 4.88} = 11,885 \text{ units}$$

If you selected option A you divided the fixed cost by the selling price, but the **selling price also has to cover the variable cost.** Option B fails to allow for the increase in variable production cost and option D increases all of the costs by the percentages given, rather than the production costs only.

4   C

	£
Target profit	6,000
Fixed costs (5,000 × £2)	10,000
Target contribution	16,000
Contribution per unit (£10 – £6)	£4
Units required to achieve target profit = $\dfrac{\pounds 16,000}{\pounds 4}$ =	4,000

If you selected option A you divided £6,000 target profit by the £4 contribution per unit, but **the fixed costs must be covered before any profit can be earned.** If you selected option B you divided by the selling price, but the variable costs must also be taken into account. If you selected option D you divided by the profit per unit instead of the contribution per unit, but the fixed costs are taken into account in the calculation of the target contribution.

5   B

Fixed costs (£10,000 × 120%)	£12,000

Units required now to break even = $\dfrac{£12,000}{£4 \text{ (contribution)}}$ =   3,000

Budgeted units of sales	5,000
Margin of safety (units)	2,000

In percentage terms, margin of safety = $\dfrac{2,000}{5,000}$ × 100% = 40%

Option A increases the **variable** cost by 20% and option C increases the **activity** by 20%. If you selected option D you calculated the margin of safety as a percentage of the breakeven volume, but it should be **expressed as a percentage of budgeted sales.**

6   A

	£
Original budgeted profit:	
Contribution (5,000 × £4)	20,000
Fixed costs	10,000
Profit	10,000

	£ per unit
New sales price (£10 × 1.20)	12.00
New variable cost (£6 × 1.12)	6.72
New contribution	5.28

Contribution required (as above)	£20,000

Sales volume now needed = $\dfrac{£20,000}{£5.28}$ =   3,788 units

This is 1,212 units or 24.24% less than the original budgeted level of 5,000 units of sales.

If you selected option B you identified the correct percentage change but you misinterpreted it as a required increase. If you selected options C or D you took £6,000 as your figure for the original budgeted profit. However, the budgeted profit would be based on the budgeted level of activity of 5,000 units for the period.

7   C   Contribution at level of activity x = Sales value less variable costs, which is indicated by distance C. Distance A indicates the profit at activity x, B indicates the fixed costs and D indicates the margin of safety in terms of sales value.

8   B

	Product P	Product Q	Product R
Contribution per unit	£82	£108	£100
Kgs required per unit	4	2	6
Contribution per kg of material	£20.50	£54	£16.67
Ranking	2	1	3

Therefore Q is the most profitable and R is the least profitable.

If you selected option A you ranked the products according to their profit per unit, but this takes no account of the **limiting factor** and is distorted by the fixed costs.

9 C

	K	L
Contribution per unit	£15	£30
Contribution per unit of limiting factor	£15/2 = £7.50	£30/3 = £10
Ranking	2	1

	Raw materials used kg
Contracted supply of K (500 × 2 kg)	1,000
Meet demand for L (250 × 3 kg)	750
Remainder of resource for K (125 × 2 kg)	250
	2,000

10 Jobs B, E and F should be subcontracted

WORKING 1

	A	B	C	D	E	F
Additional cost of subcontracting (W2)	£1,380	£495	£1,780	£870	£1,055	£840
Labour hours required	150	100	200	50	150	100
Cost per labour hour saved by subcontracting	£9.20	£4.95	£8.90	£17.40	£7.03	£8.40
Ranking of jobs to subcontract	5	1*	4	6	2*	3*

* Subcontracted jobs

As labour capacity is restricted to 400 hours per week there is only enough capacity for jobs C, A and D. Jobs B, E and F should therefore be subcontracted as they have the lowest incremental cost per labour hour saved.

WORKING 2

	A £	B £	C £	D £	E £	F £
Cost of doing work in-house						
Parts	1,200	1,375	1,450	500	375	690
Labour (labour hours × £6 per hour)	900	600	1,200	300	900	600
Labour-related overhead (labour hours × £2 per hour)	300	200	400	100	300	200
Equipment-related overhead (equipment hours × £1 per hour)	170	30	70	30	70	70
Total cost of doing work in-house	2,570	2,205	3,120	930	1,645	1,560
Cost of subcontracting (including parts)	3,950	2,700	4,900	1,800	2,700	2,400
Additional cost of subcontracting	1,380	495	1,780	870	1,055	840

CHAPTER 11

Investment appraisal techniques

Introduction
Examination context
Topic List
Summary and Self-test
Answers to Interactive questions
Answers to Self-test

Learning objectives

- Calculate the net present value, internal rate of return, payback period or accounting rate of return for a given project

- Identify the advantages and disadvantages of the investment appraisal techniques specified above

The specific syllabus references for this chapter are: 4c, d.

Syllabus links

You will be using the techniques you learn in this chapter when you study the Financial Management syllabus. In that syllabus you will explore further the investment decision-making process and associated issues.

Examination context

Since most of this part of your syllabus is concerned with calculation techniques you can expect to encounter predominately numerical questions about these topics.

In the examination, candidates may be required to:

- Calculate the net present value, internal rate of return, payback period or accounting rate of return from data supplied

- Interpret information about the net present value, internal rate of return, payback or accounting rate of return for a project or projects

- Demonstrate an understanding of the advantages and disadvantages of the investment appraisal techniques specified above

- Manipulate simple data involving annuities, perpetuities and non-conventional cash flows

- Demonstrate an understanding of the derivation and meaning of the net terminal value of a project

While most of the questions in this area of the syllabus will be numerical (where such issues as the timing of cash flows will be critical) it is vital to understand what each of the techniques involves (and their weaknesses) in order to be able to tackle narrative questions.

1 Making investment appraisal decisions

Section overview

- A typical model for investment decision making has a number of distinct stages.

- These stages are typically: the origination of proposals, project screening, analysis and acceptance, and monitoring and review.

1.1 The investment decision-making process

You will study the investment decision-making process in more detail in your Financial Management syllabus so we will review the process in outline only here, to set the financial investment appraisal techniques in context.

A typical model for investment decision making has a number of distinct stages.

- **Origination of proposals.** It has been suggested that good ideas for investment are likely to occur in environments in which staff feel free to present and develop ideas. Some alternatives will be rejected early on. Others will be more thoroughly evaluated.

- **Project screening.** Before a detailed financial analysis is undertaken a qualitative evaluation of the project will be made. For example, questions will be asked such as whether the project 'fits' with the organisation's long-term objectives and whether all possible alternatives have been considered. Only if the project passes this initial screening will more detailed financial analysis begin.

- **Analysis and acceptance.** This will include a financial analysis, using the organisation's preferred investment appraisal techniques. You will be studying the most common techniques in the remainder of this chapter. Qualitative issues will also be considered before a decision is made whether to proceed and the project is implemented.

- **Monitoring and review.** During the project's progress it will be necessary to ensure that capital spending does not exceed the amount authorised, that the implementation of the project is not delayed and that the anticipated benefits are eventually obtained.

2 The payback method

Section overview

- The payback period is the time it takes for a project's net cash inflows to equal the initial cash investment.

- The payback period is often used as an initial screening process.

- If a project's payback period is shorter than a defined maximum period then the project should be evaluated further using a more sophisticated project appraisal technique.

- A major disadvantage is that the timing of cash flows within the payback period are ignored and therefore no account is taken of the time value of money.

2.1 The payback period

Definition

Payback: is defined by The Chartered Institute of Management Accountants as 'The time required for the cash inflows from a capital investment project to equal the initial cash outflow(s)'.

Payback is often used as a **'first screening method'**. By this, we mean that when a capital investment project is being subjected to financial appraisal, the first question to ask is: 'How long will it take to pay back its cost?' The organisation might have a target payback, and so it would reject a capital project unless its payback period was less than that target payback period.

However, a project should not be evaluated on the basis of payback alone. Payback should be a **first** screening process, and if a project gets through the payback test, it ought **then to be evaluated with a more sophisticated project appraisal technique,** such as those presented later in this chapter.

You should note that when payback is calculated, we use **profits before depreciation** in the calculation, because we are trying to estimate the *cash* returns from a project and profit before depreciation is likely to be a **rough approximation of cash flows**.

2.2 Why is payback alone an inadequate project appraisal technique?

Look at the figures below for two mutually exclusive projects (this means that only one of them can be undertaken).

	Project P £	Project Q £
Capital cost of asset	60,000	60,000
Profits before depreciation		
Year 1	20,000	50,000
Year 2	30,000	20,000
Year 3	40,000	5,000
Year 4	50,000	5,000
Year 5	60,000	5,000

Project P pays back in year 3 (one quarter of the way through year 3). Project Q pays back half way through year 2. **Using payback alone** to judge projects, **project Q would be preferred. But the returns from project P total £200,000 over its life and are much higher than the returns from project Q which totals just £85,000.**

Worked example: Payback period

An asset costing £120,000 is to be depreciated over ten years to a nil residual value. Profits after depreciation for the first five years are as follows.

Year	£
1	12,000
2	17,000
3	28,000
4	37,000
5	8,000

Requirement

Calculate the payback period to the nearest month.

Solution

Cash flows, ie profits before depreciation should be used.

Year	Profit after depreciation £'000	Depreciation £'000	Cash flow £'000	Cumulative cash flow £'000
1	12	12	24	24
2	17	12	29	53
3	28	12	40	93
4	37	12	49	142
5	8	12	20	162

$$\therefore \text{ Payback period } = 3 \text{ years} + \left(\frac{(120 - 93)}{49} \times 12 \text{ months} \right)$$

$$= 3 \text{ years } 7 \text{ months}$$

2.3 Disadvantages of the payback method

There are a number of serious drawbacks to the payback method.

- It **ignores the timing of cash flows** within the payback period.

- It also ignores the cash flows after the end of the payback period and therefore the total project return.

- It **ignores the time value of money** (a concept incorporated into more sophisticated appraisal methods). This means that it does not take account of the fact that £1 today is worth more than £1 in one year's time. This is because an investor who has £1 today can either consume it immediately or alternatively can invest it at the prevailing interest rate, say 10%, to get a return of £1.10 in a year's time.

There are also other disadvantages.

- The method is **unable to distinguish between projects with the same payback period**.

- The **choice of any cut-off payback period** by an organisation is **arbitrary**.

- It may lead to excessive **investment in short-term projects**.

- It takes account of the risk of the timing of cash flows but **does not take account of the variability of those cash flows**.

2.4 Advantages of the payback method

The use of the payback method does have advantages, especially as an initial screening device.

- A long payback means **capital is tied up**.
- Focus on early payback can **enhance liquidity**.
- **Investment risk is increased** if payback is longer.
- **Shorter-term forecasts** are likely to be **more reliable**.
- The calculation is **quick** and **simple**.
- Payback is an **easily understood** concept.

3 The accounting rate of return method

Section overview

- The Accounting Rate of Return (ARR) expresses the average accounting profit as a percentage of the capital outlay.

- The capital outlay (the denominator in the ARR calculation) may be expressed as the initial investment or as the average investment in the project.

- The decision rule is that projects with an ARR above a defined minimum are acceptable; the greater the ARR, the more desirable the project.

- The main advantage of the ARR is that it is simple to calculate and understand. However it does have a number of major disadvantages.

- The main disadvantage of the ARR is that it does not take account of the timing of the profits from a project.

3.1 Calculating the accounting rate of return

The accounting rate of return (ARR) method of appraising a project involves estimating the accounting rate of return that a project should yield. If it exceeds a target rate of return then the project is acceptable.

There are two different ways of calculating the ARR.

$$\text{ARR} = \frac{\text{Average annual accounting profit}}{\text{Initial investment}} \times 100\%$$

$$\text{ARR} = \frac{\text{Average annual accounting profit}}{\text{Average investment}} \times 100\%$$

The average investment is calculated as $\frac{1}{2}$ (initial investment + final or scrap value).

An examination question will always make it clear whether you are to calculate the ARR based on the average investment or based on the initial investment.

Note that this is the only appraisal method that we will be studying that uses accounting profits instead of cash flow.

Worked example: The accounting rate of return

A project involves the immediate purchase of plant at a cost of £110,000. It would generate annual profits before depreciation of £24,000 for five years. Scrap value will be £10,000 at the end of the fifth year.

Requirement

Calculate the ARR using the initial and average investment.

Solution

(a) **Using initial investment**

$$\text{Average profit} = \frac{\text{Profits before depreciation} - \text{Depreciation}}{5}$$

$$= \frac{(£24,000 \times 5) - (£110,000 - £10,000)}{5}$$

$$= £4,000 \text{ p.a.}$$

$$\text{ARR} = \frac{£4,000}{£110,000} \times 100\% \qquad = 3.6\%$$

(b) **Using average investment**

$$\frac{£4,000}{£(110,000 + 10,000)/2} \times 100\% \qquad = 6.7\%$$

3.2 The ARR and the comparison of mutually exclusive projects

The ARR method of capital investment appraisal can also be used to compare two or more projects which are mutually exclusive. The project with the highest ARR would be selected (provided that the expected ARR is higher than the company's target ARR).

Interactive question 1: The ARR and mutually exclusive projects [Difficulty level: Intermediate]

Arrow wants to buy a new item of equipment. Two models of equipment are available, one with a slightly higher capacity and greater reliability than the other. The expected costs and profits of each item are as follows.

	Equipment item X	Equipment item Y
Capital cost	£100,000	£175,000
Life	5 years	5 years
Profits before depreciation	£	£
Year 1	50,000	50,000
Year 2	50,000	50,000
Year 3	30,000	60,000
Year 4	20,000	60,000
Year 5	10,000	60,000
Disposal value for equipment	20,000	25,000

ARR is measured as the average annual profits divided by the average investment.

Fill in the boxes below to determine which equipment item should be purchased, if the company's target ARR is 25%.

	Item X £	Item Y £
Total profit over life of equipment:		
before depreciation		
after depreciation		
Average annual accounting profit		
Average investment		
ARR, based on average investment	%	%

The equipment that should be purchased is item ☐.

See **Answer** at the end of this chapter.

3.3 The advantages and disadvantages of the ARR method of project appraisal

The ARR method has the serious **disadvantage** that it **does not take account of the timing of the profits from a project**. Whenever capital is invested in a project, money is tied up until the project begins to earn profits which pay back the investment. Money tied up in one project cannot be invested anywhere else until the profits come in. Management should be aware of the benefits of early repayments from an investment, which will provide the money for other investments.

There are a number of other **disadvantages**.

* It is **based on accounting profits** rather than cash flows, which are **subject to a number of different accounting policies**.

* It is a **relative measure** rather than an absolute measure and hence **takes no account of the size of the investment**.

* **It takes no account of the length of the project.**

* Like the payback method, **it ignores the time value of money**.

  There are, however, **advantages** to the ARR method

* It is quick and **simple** to calculate.

* It involves a **familiar concept** of a percentage return.

* Accounting profits can be **easily calculated from financial statements**.

* It **looks at the entire project life**.

- Managers and investors are accustomed to thinking in terms of profit, and so an appraisal method which **employs profit** may be more **easily understood.**

- It allows more than one project to be compared.

4 The net present value method

Section overview

- The terminal value of an investment is its value at some point in the future, including an allowance for interest.

- Discounting converts a sum of money receivable or payable in the future to its present value, which is the cash equivalent now of the future value.

- Discounted cash flow (DCF) techniques discount all the forecast cash flows of an investment proposal to determine their present value.

- The net present value (NPV) of a project is the difference between its projected discounted cash inflows and discounted cash outflows.

- The decision rule is to accept a project with a positive NPV.

- An annuity is a constant cash flow for a number of years.

- The net terminal value (NTV) is the cash surplus remaining at the end of a project after taking account of interest and capital payments.

- One of the principal advantages of the DCF appraisal method is that it takes account of the time value of money.

- The payback method can be combined with DCF to calculate a discounted payback period.

- A perpetuity is a constant cash flow forever. The present value of a perpetuity is $\frac{£a}{r}$, where a is the constant annual amount and r is the discount rate.

4.1 Compounding: calculating the terminal value

Suppose that a company has £10,000 to invest, and wants to earn a return of 10% (compound interest*) on its investments. This means that if the £10,000 could be invested at 10%, the value of the investment with interest would build up as follows.

(a) After 1 year   £10,000 × (1.10) = £11,000
(b) After 2 years £10,000 × (1.10)² = £12,100
(c) After 3 years £10,000 × (1.10)³ = £13,310

and so on.

* This means that interest is earned each year on the previous years' interest.

This is **compounding**. The formula for the future value or terminal value of an investment plus accumulated interest after n time periods is **V = X(1 + r)ⁿ**

where   V is the future value or terminal value of the investment with interest

X is the initial or 'present' value of the investment

r is the compound rate of return per time period, expressed as a decimal (so 10% = 0.10, 5% = 0.05 and so on)

n is the number of time periods.

Usually r is an **annual rate** of return and n is the number of **years**.

Worked example: Terminal value

What is the terminal value of £200 invested today at an interest rate of 7% per annum in ten years' time?

Solution

Terminal value = £200 × $(1.07)^{10}$ = £393

Terminal values can cause difficulties when trying to compare or choose between projects because:

- The projects may not end on the same future date (or may not end at all).

- Decision makers are more likely to be interested in the effect of the project on shareholder wealth now, rather than in the future.

It is therefore more common to look at present values. The present value of a future sum shows what that future sum is worth today. This is in effect the reverse of compounding.

4.2 Discounting

Discounting starts with the future value (a sum of money receivable or payable at a future date), and converts the future value to a **present value**, which is the cash equivalent now of the future value.

For example, if a company expects to earn a (compound) rate of return of 10% on its investments, how much would it need to invest now to have the following investments?

(a) £11,000 after 1 year
(b) £12,100 after 2 years
(c) £13,310 after 3 years

The answer is £10,000 in each case, and we can calculate it by discounting.

The **discounting formula** to calculate the present value (X) of a future sum of money (V) at the end of n time periods is $X = V/(1+r)^n$

(a) After 1 year, £11,000/1.10 = £10,000
(b) After 2 years, £12,100/1.10^2 = £10,000
(c) After 3 years, £13,310/1.10^3 = £10,000

The **timing of cash flows is taken into account by discounting them**. The effect of discounting is to **give a bigger value per £1 for cash flows that occur earlier**: £1 earned after one year will be worth more than £1 earned after two years, which in turn will be worth more than £1 earned after five years, and so on.

The discount rate (r) used when calculating the present value is the relevant interest rate (or cost of capital) to the entity in question. In the exam this will always be made clear.

4.2.1 Discount factors

In the calculations above we were converting each cash flow into its present value by effectively multiplying by a **discount factor**. This discount factor is calculated as $1/(1 + r)^n$.

The calculations could be presented as follows.

	Multiply by 10% discount factor	Present value £
After 1 year £11,000	× 1/1.10	10,000
After 2 years £12,100	× 1/$(1.10)^2$	10,000
After 3 years £13,310	× 1/$(1.10)^3$	10,000

Interactive question 2: Present value calculation   [Difficulty level: Intermediate]

Spender expects the cash inflow from an investment to be £40,000 after two years and another £30,000 after three years. Its target rate of return is 12%.

Use the table below to calculate the present value of these future returns.

Year	Cash flow £	Multiplied by 12% discount factor	Present value £
2			
3			
Total present value			

See **Answer** at the end of this chapter.

4.3   Net present value (NPV)

Discounted cash flow (DCF) techniques are used in calculating the net present value of a series of cash flows. This measures the change in shareholder wealth now as a result of accepting a project.

NPV = present value of cash inflows **less** present value of cash outflows

- If the **NPV is positive**, it means that the cash inflows from a project will yield a return in excess of the cost of capital, and so the **project should be undertaken** if the cost of capital is the organisation's target rate of return.

- If the **NPV is negative**, it means that the cash inflows from a project will yield a return below the cost of capital, and so the **project should not be undertaken** if the cost of capital is the organisation's target rate of return.

- If the **NPV is exactly zero**, the cash inflows from a project will yield a return which is exactly the same as the cost of capital, and so if the cost of capital is the organisation's target rate of return, the **project will have a neutral impact on shareholder wealth and therefore would not be worth undertaking because of the inherent risks in any project.**

Worked example: NPV

Slogger has a cost of capital of 15% and is considering a capital investment project, where the estimated cash flows are as follows.

Year	Cash flow £
0 (ie now)	(100,000)
1	60,000
2	80,000
3	40,000
4	30,000

Requirement

Calculate the NPV of the project, and assess whether it should be undertaken.

Solution

Year	Cash flow	Discount factor	Present value
	£	15%	£
0	(100,000)	1.000	(100,000)
1	60,000	$1/1.15 = 0.870$	52,200
2	80,000	$1/1.15^2 = 0.756$	60,480
3	40,000	$1/1.15^3 = 0.658$	26,320
4	30,000	$1/1.15^4 = 0.572$	17,160
		NPV =	56,160

Point to note

The discount factor for any cash flow 'now' (time 0) is always 1, whatever the cost of capital.

The **present value (PV) of cash inflows exceeds the PV of cash outflows** by £56,160, which means that the project will earn a discounted cash flow (DCF) yield in excess of 15%. It should therefore be undertaken.

4.4 Timing of cash flows: conventions used in DCF

Discounting reduces the value of future cash flows to a present value equivalent and so is clearly concerned with the timing of the cash flows. As a general rule, the following guidelines may be applied.

- A **cash outlay to be incurred at the beginning of an investment project ('now') occurs in time 0.** The **present value of £1 now, in time 0, is £1** regardless of the value of the discount rate r.

- A **cash flow** which occurs **during the course of a time period** is **assumed to occur** all at once at the **end of the time period** (at the end of the year). Receipts of £10,000 during time period 1 are therefore taken to occur at the end of time period 1.

- A **cash flow** which occurs **at the beginning of a time period** is **taken to occur at the end of the previous time period**. Therefore a cash outlay of £5,000 at the beginning of time period 2 is taken to occur at the end of time period 1.

4.5 Cash flows, not accounting profits

It is important to remember that DCF techniques are based on the **cash flows** of a project, **not the accounting profits**. Like the payback technique of investment appraisal, DCF is concerned with liquidity, not profitability. Cash flows are considered because they show the costs and benefits of a project when they actually occur. For example, the capital cost of a project will be the original cash outlay, and not the notional cost of depreciation which is used to spread the capital cost over the asset's life in the financial accounts.

4.6 Discount tables for the PV of £1

Instead of having to calculate the discount factor every time we can use **tables**. Discount tables for the present value of £1, for a range of **integer** values of r and n, are **shown in the third column of the discount table in the Appendix at the back of this Study Manual. These tables will be provided in the exam.**

4.7 Annuities

An annuity is a series of constant cash flows for a number of years. For example, a college might enter into a contract to provide training courses for a firm for a fixed annual fee of £30,000 payable at the end of each of the next three years. This would be a three year annuity.

Worked example: Calculating the present value of an annuity

In the example of the college training course, the present value of the fees, assuming a 20% cost of capital, could be calculated as follows.

Year	Cash flow £	Present value factor 20%	Present value of cash values £
1	30,000	0.833	24,990
2	30,000	0.694	20,820
3	30,000	0.579	17,370
		2.106	63,180

Where there is a **constant cash flow from year to year** (in this case £30,000 per annum for years 1–3) it is quicker to calculate the present value by adding together the discount factors for the individual years. These total factors could be described as 'same cash flow per annum' factors, **'cumulative present value' factors** or **'annuity' factors**. They are **shown in the final column of the discount tables in the Appendix at the back of this Study Manual** (2.106, for example, is in the final column for 20% per annum and the row for year 3).

The calculation could then be performed in one step:

£30,000 × 2.106 = £63,180

4.8 Net terminal value

Net terminal value (NTV) is the cash surplus remaining at the end of a project after taking account of interest and capital repayments.

The NTV discounted at the cost of capital will give the NPV of the project.

Worked example: The net terminal value

A project has the following cash flows.

Year	£
0	(5,000)
1	3,000
2	2,600
3	6,200

The project has an NPV of £4,531 at the company's cost of capital of 10% (workings not shown).

Requirement

Calculate the net terminal value of the project.

Solution

The net terminal value can be determined directly from the NPV, or by calculating the cash surplus at the end of the project.

Assume that the £5,000 for the project is borrowed at an annual interest rate of 10% and that cash flows from the project are used to repay the loan.

	£
Loan balance outstanding at beginning of project	5,000
Interest in year 1 at 10%	500
Repaid at end of year 1	(3,000)
Balance outstanding at end of year 1	2,500
Interest year 2	250
Repaid year 2	(2,600)
Balance outstanding year 2	150
Interest year 3	15
Repaid year 3	(6,200)
Cash surplus at end of project	6,035

The net terminal value is £6,035.

Check

NPV = £6,035 × 0.751 (10% discount factor for year 3) = £4,532

Allowing for the rounding errors caused by three figure discount tables, this is the correct figure for the NPV.

4.9 Advantages of NPV

The advantages of NPV are as follows.

- It is directly linked to the assumed objective of maximising shareholder wealth as it measures, in absolute (£) terms, the effect of taking on the project now, ie year 0.

- It considers the time value of money, ie the further away the cash flow the less it is worth in present terms.

- It considers all relevant cash flows, so that it is unaffected by the accounting policies which cloud profit-based investment appraisal techniques such as ARR.

- Risk can be incorporated into decision making by adjusting the company's discount rate.

- It provides clear, unambiguous decisions, ie if the NPV is positive, accept; if it is negative, reject.

Interactive question 3: Non-standard discount factors   [Difficulty level: Intermediate]

A project has the following forecast cash flows.

Year	£
0	(280,000)
1	149,000
2	128,000
3	84,000
4	70,000

Using two decimal places in all discount factors, complete the following table to calculate the net present value of the project at a cost of capital of 16.5%.

Year	Cash flow £	16.5% discount factor	Present value £
0			
1			
2			
3			
4			
Net present value			

See **Answer** at the end of this chapter.

4.10 The time value of money

DCF is a project appraisal technique that is based on the concept of the time value of money, that £1 earned or spent sooner is worth more than £1 earned or spent later. Various reasons could be suggested as to **why a present £1 is worth more than a future £1**.

- **Uncertainty.** The business world is full of risk and uncertainty, and although there might be the promise of money to come in the future, it can never be certain that the money will be received until it has actually been paid. This is an important argument, and risk and uncertainty must always

ICAEW

be considered in investment appraisal. But this argument does not explain why the discounted cash flow technique should be used to reflect the time value of money.

- **Inflation.** Because of inflation it is common sense that £1 now is worth more than £1 in the future. It is important, however, that the problem of inflation should not confuse the meaning of DCF, and the following points should be noted.

    - If there were no inflation at all, discounted cash flow techniques would still be used for investment appraisal

    - Inflation, for the moment, has been completely ignored

    - It is obviously necessary to allow for inflation

- **An individual attaches more weight to current pleasures than to future ones, and would rather have £1 to spend now than £1 in a year's time**. Individuals have the choice of consuming or investing their wealth and so the return from projects must be sufficient to persuade individuals to prefer to invest now. Discounting is a measure of this time preference.

- Money is invested now to make profits (more money or wealth) in the future. **Discounted cash flow techniques** can therefore be used to **measure** either of two things.

    - **What alternative uses of the money would earn (NPV method)** (assuming that money can be invested elsewhere at the cost of capital)

    - **What the money is expected to earn (IRR method** – to be covered in the next section of this chapter)

4.11 Advantages of DCF methods of appraisal

Taking account of the time value of money (by discounting) is one of the principal advantages of the DCF appraisal method. Other advantages include the following.

- The method uses all cash flows relating to the project.
- It allows for the timing of the cash flows.
- There are universally accepted methods of calculating the NPV and IRR.

4.12 A comparison of the ROI and NPV methods

In Chapter 8 we saw that managers are often judged on the return on investment (ROI) of their division or responsibility centre which is very similar in principle to the ARR. Managers will only want to **invest in projects that increase divisional ROI** but on occasion such a strategy **may not correspond** with the **decision** that would be arrived at if **NPV** were used to appraise the investment.

For example, suppose that Division M is considering an investment of £200,000 which will provide a net cash inflow (before depreciation) of £78,000 each year for the four years of its life. It is group policy that investments must show a minimum return of 15%.

As the working below shows, using net book value (NBV) at the start of each year and depreciating on a straight line basis to a nil residual value, in year 1 the ROI would be below the target rate of return of 15%. If management were to take a **short-term view** of the situation, the **investment would be rejected if** the ROI measure were to be **used**, despite the fact that the investment's **NPV is positive** and that in **years 2 to 4** the **ROI** is **greater** than the **target** rate of return.

	Years			
	1	*2*	*3*	*4*
	£	£	£	£
NBV of investment at start of year	200,000	150,000	100,000	50,000
Cash flow (before depreciation)	78,000	78,000	78,000	78,000
Less depreciation	(50,000)	(50,000)	(50,000)	(50,000)
Net profit	28,000	28,000	28,000	28,000
ROI	14.00%	18.67%	28.00%	56.00%

Net present value = – £200,000 + (£78,000 × 2.855) = £22,690.

4.13 Discounted payback

The payback method can be combined with DCF to calculate a **discounted payback period**.

The **discounted payback period (DPP)** is the time it will take before a project's cumulative NPV turns from being negative to being positive.

Worked example: Discounted payback

If we have a cost of capital of 10% and a project with the cash flows shown below, we can calculate a discounted payback period.

Year	Cash flow £	Discount factor 10%	Present value £	Cumulative NPV £
0	(100,000)	1.000	(100,000)	(100,000)
1	30,000	0.909	27,270	(72,730)
2	50,000	0.826	41,300	(31,430)
3	40,000	0.751	30,040	(1,390)
4	30,000	0.683	20,490	19,100
5	20,000	0.621	12,420	31,520
		NPV =	31,520	

The DPP is early in year 4.

A company can set a target DPP, and choose not to undertake any projects with a DPP in excess of a certain number of years, say five years.

4.13.1 Advantages and disadvantages of discounted payback period

The approach has **all the perceived advantages of the payback period** method of investment appraisal: it is easy to understand and calculate, and it provides a focus on liquidity where this is relevant. In addition, however, it **also takes into account the time value of money**. It therefore bridges the gap between the theoretically superior NPV method and the regular payback period method.

Because the DPP approach takes the time value of money into consideration, it **produces a longer payback period** than the non-discounted payback approach, and **takes into account more of the project's cash flows**.

Another advantage it has over traditional payback is that it has a **clear accept-or-reject criterion**. Using payback, acceptance of a project depends on an arbitrarily determined cut-off time. Using DPP, a project is acceptable if it pays back within its lifetime (because it has a positive NPV).

DPP still shares one disadvantage with the payback period method: **cash flows which occur after the payback period are ignored** (although as the DPP is longer than the payback period, fewer of these are ignored).

4.14 The discount rate

Throughout our study of DCF techniques we have been using the same discount rate across all years of the project under consideration, on the assumption that the cost of capital will remain the same over the life of the project. There are a range of factors that influence the cost of capital, however, including inflation and interest rates, and these can fluctuate widely over fairly short periods of time. An organisation may therefore wish to **use different discount rates at different points over the life of a project** to reflect this. This is **possible if NPV and discounted payback methods of appraisal are being used**, but IRR (see Section 5) and ARR methods are based on a single rate.

Another problem is **deciding on the correct rate in the first place**. This is difficult enough in year one of a project's life, but even more problematic five years later, say, because of economic changes and so on.

4.15 Other aspects of discounting

Now that we have learned about the basics of the discounted cash flow technique we can move on to consider some of the complications that might arise.

4.15.1 Delayed annuities

A company may take out a loan, agreeing to repay it in equal annual instalments (ie an annuity) but starting at the end of year 2, so that the first cash flow does not occur until after year 1. As annuity factor tables work on the assumption that the first cash flow occurs at the end of year 1, care will be needed when using the tables. Remember that if an annuity factor from the table is used, the present value of the annuity stream is being found one period before the first annuity flow, so further discounting will be needed to find the present value at year 0.

4.15.2 Annuities in advance

When, for example, a firm leases vans for its business, the lease payments are usually paid in advance, ie the first cash flow occurs in year 0. This is a combination of a normal annuity starting at year 1 plus an extra sum now which does not need to be discounted.

Worked example: Annuities in advance and delayed annuities

What is the present value of £1,000 received annually for five years if the first receipt is:

(a) In one year's time?
(b) Now?
(c) In three years' time?

Use a discount rate of 15%.

Solution

(a) Present value   = £1,000 × annuity factor for five years at 15%

                              = £1,000 × 3.352 = £3,352

(b) Only the cash flows at the end of years 1 to 4 need discounting.

     Present value   = £1,000 received now + (£1,000 × annuity factor for four years at 15%)

                              = £1,000 + (£1,000 × 2.855)

                              = £3,855

(c) This can be solved in two possible ways.

     (i)   Present value   = £1,000 × (annuity factor for seven years – annuity factor for two years)

           This leaves the cash flows for years 3, 4, 5, 6 and 7 being discounted.

                              = £1,000 × (4.160 – 1.626)

                              = £2,534

     (ii) Present value of annuity at end of year two   = £1,000 × 3.352

                              = £3,352

           Now this must be discounted again to bring it back to the present value at year 0 (now).

           Present value   = £3,352 × PV factor for year 2 at 15%

                              = £3,352 × 0.756

                              = £2,534

4.15.3 Annual cash flows in perpetuity

A perpetuity is an equal annual cash flow forever, ie an annuity that lasts forever.

The present value of a perpetuity of £a per annum forever is calculated as $\frac{£a}{r}$, where r is the annual discount rate. This formula finds the present value of the perpetuity stream one year before the first cash flow.

Worked example: Perpetuities

(a) What is the present value of £3,000 received in one year's time and forever if the annual interest rate is 10%?

(b) What would be the present value if the first receipt is in four years' time?

Solution

(a) Present value   = £3,000/0.10

                       = £30,000

(b) Present value one year before the first cash flow = at end of year 3

                                       = £3,000/0.10

                                       = £30,000

Present value at year 0   = £3,000 × year 3 10% discount factor

                                       = £30,000 × 0.751

                                       = £22,530

4.15.4 Changing discount rates

If the discount rate changes over time the net present value is calculated as follows

	Year 0	Year 1	Year 2	
NPV =	outflow	+ inflow/(1+r_1)	+ inflow/(1+r_1)(1+r_2)	etc

Where r_1 = interest rate for year 1

             r_2 = interest rate for year 2

Worked example: Changing discount rates

A project's estimated cash flows are as follows.

	Year 0 £m	Year 1 £m	Year 2 £m
Cash flow	(10)	6	8

Calculate the NPV if the cost of capital is 10% for the first year and 20% for the second year.

Solution

$$NPV = (£10m) + \frac{£6m}{1.10} + \frac{£8m}{1.10 \times 1.20} = £1.52m$$

5 The internal rate of return method

Section overview

- The internal rate of return (IRR) is the DCF rate of return that a project is expected to achieve. It is the discount rate at which the NPV is zero.

- If the IRR exceeds a target rate of return, the project would be worth undertaking.

- The IRR can be estimated from a graph of the project's NPV profile. The IRR can be read from the graph at the point on the horizontal axis where the NPV is zero.

- The IRR interpolation formula is $IRR = a + \dfrac{NPVa}{NPVa - NPVb}(b - a)$

- The IRR method has a number of disadvantages compared with the NPV method.

    - It ignores the relative size of the investments

    - There are problems with its use when a project has non-conventional cash flows or when deciding between mutually exclusive projects

    - Discount rates which differ over the life of a project cannot be incorporated into IRR calculations

5.1 The internal rate of return

Another discounted cash flow (DCF) technique for appraising capital projects involves calculating the **internal rate of return (IRR)**. The IRR is a relative measure (%) in contrast to the absolute (£) measure resulting from NPV calculations.

The IRR is the DCF rate of return (DCF yield) that a project is expected to achieve, in other words the discount rate at which the NPV is zero.

If the IRR exceeds a target rate of return, the project would be worth undertaking.

5.2 Graphical approach

The easiest way to estimate the IRR of a project is to **find the project's NPV at a number of costs of capital** and **sketch a graph of NPV against discount rate**. The graph can be used to estimate the **discount rate at which the NPV is equal to zero (the point where the curve cuts the axis)**.

Worked example: Graphical approach

A project might have the following NPVs at the following discount rates.

Discount rate	NPV
%	£
5	5,300
10	700
15	(1,500)
20	(3,200)

This could be sketched on a graph as follows.

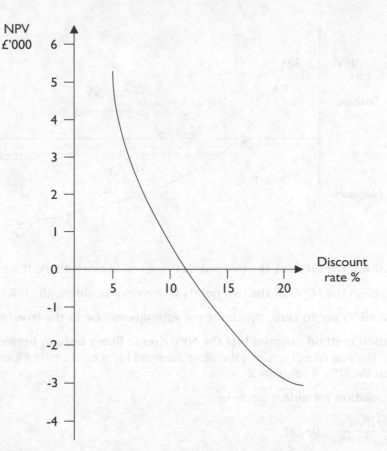

The IRR can be estimated as 13%. The NPV should then be recalculated using this interest rate. The resulting NPV should be equal to, or very near, zero. If it is not, additional NPVs at different discount rates should be calculated, the graph resketched and a more accurate IRR determined.

5.3 Interpolation method

If we are appraising a 'typical' capital project, with a negative cash flow at the start of the project, and positive net cash flows afterwards up to the end of the project, we could draw a graph of the project's NPV at different costs of capital. It would look like this.

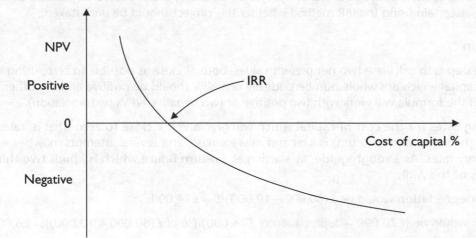

If we determine a **cost of capital where the NPV is (slightly) positive, and another cost of capital where it is (slightly) negative,** we can **estimate the IRR – where the NPV is zero – by drawing a straight line between the two points** on the graph that we have calculated.

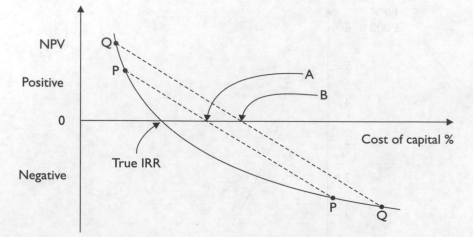

- If we **establish the NPVs at the two points P**, we would estimate the **IRR** to be at point A.

- If we **establish the NPVs at the two points Q**, we would estimate the **IRR** to be at point B.

The **closer our NPVs are to zero, the closer our estimate will be to the true IRR**.

The **interpolation method assumes that the NPV rises in linear fashion between the two NPVs close to zero**. The real rate of return is therefore assumed to be on a straight line between the two points at which the NPV is calculated.

The **IRR interpolation formula** to apply is:

$$IRR = a + \frac{NPVa}{NPVa - NPVb}(b - a)$$

where   a is the first discount rate giving NPVa

b is the second discount rate giving NPVb

Worked example: The IRR method and interpolation

A company is trying to decide whether to buy a machine for £80,000 which will save costs of £20,000 per annum for five years and which will have a resale value of £10,000 at the end of year 5.

Requirement

If it is the company's policy to undertake projects only if they are expected to yield a DCF return of 10% or more, ascertain using the IRR method whether this project should be undertaken.

Solution

The first step is to calculate two net present values, both as close as possible to zero, using rates for the cost of capital which are whole numbers. Ideally one NPV should be positive and the other negative although the formula will work with two positive or two negative NPVs (extrapolation).

Choosing rates for the cost of capital which will give an NPV close to zero (that is, rates which are close to the actual rate of return) is a hit and miss exercise, and several attempts may be needed to find satisfactory rates. **As a rough guide**, try starting at a **return figure which is about two thirds or three quarters of the ARR**.

Annual depreciation would be £(80,000 – 10,000)/5 = £14,000.

The **ARR** would be (£20,000 – depreciation of £14,000)/(½ of £(80,000 + 10,000)) = £6,000/£45,000 = 13.3%.

Two thirds of this is 8.9% and so we can start by trying 9%. The discounted tables do not provide discount factors for an interest rate of 9% therefore we need to calculate our own factors.

Using the formula provided at the top of the final column in the tables

PV of an annuity $= \dfrac{1}{r}\left[1-\dfrac{1}{(1+r)^n}\right]$

PV factor for 5 years at 9% $= \dfrac{1}{0.09}\left[1-\dfrac{1}{(1.09)^5}\right]$

                                     $= 3.89$

PV factor at 9% for year 5 $= \dfrac{1}{(1.09)^5}$

                                     $= 0.65$

We can use these factors to discount the cash flows.

Try 9%

Year	Cash flow	PV factor	PV of cash flow
	£	9%	£
0	(80,000)	1.00	(80,000)
1 – 5	20,000	3.89	77,800
5	10,000	0.65	6,500
		NPV	4,300

This is **fairly close to zero**. It is also **positive**, which means that the **internal rate of return** is **more than 9%**. We can use 9% as one of our two NPVs close to zero, although for greater accuracy, we should try 10% or even 11% to find an NPV even closer to zero if we can. As a guess, it might be worth trying 12% next, to see what the NPV is. Again we will need to calculate our own discount factors.

PV factor for 5 years at 12% $= \dfrac{1}{0.12}\left[1-\dfrac{1}{(1.12)^5}\right]$

                                     $= 3.605$

PV factor at 12% for year 5 $= \dfrac{1}{(1.12)^5} = 0.567$

Try 12%

Year	Cash flow	PV factor	PV of cash flow
	£	12%	£
0	(80,000)	1.000	(80,000)
1 – 5	20,000	3.605	72,100
5	10,000	0.567	5,670
		NPV	(2,230)

This is **fairly close to zero** and **negative**. The **internal rate of return** is therefore **greater than 9%** (positive NPV of £4,300) but **less than 12%** (negative NPV of £2,230).

Note. If the first NPV is positive, choose a higher rate for the next calculation to get a negative NPV. If the first NPV is negative, choose a lower rate for the next calculation.

So $\text{IRR} = 9 + \left[\dfrac{4,300}{4,300+2,230}\times(12-9)\right]\% = 10.98\%$, say 11%

If it is company policy to undertake investments which are expected to yield 10% or more, this project would be undertaken. An alternative approach would be to calculate the NPV at 10%. As it would be positive it would tell us that the IRR is greater than 10% and therefore the project should be accepted.

Interactive question 4: IRR [Difficulty level: Intermediate]

Calculate the IRR of the project below and complete the box at the end of the question.

Time		£
0	Investment	(4,000)
1	Receipts	1,200
2	Receipts	1,410
3	Receipts	1,875
4	Receipts	1,150

The project IRR is [   ] %

See **Answer** at the end of this chapter.

5.4 NPV and IRR compared

The IRR method has a number of advantages and disadvantages when compared with the NPV method.

5.4.1 Advantages of IRR method

- The main advantage is that the information it provides is more **easily understood** by managers, especially non financial managers. 'The project will be expected to have an initial capital outlay of £100,000, and to earn a yield of 25%. This is in excess of the target yield of 15% for investments' is easier to understand than 'The project will cost £100,000 and have an NPV of £30,000 when discounted at the minimum required rate of 15%'.

- A **discount rate does not have to be specified** before the IRR can be calculated. A hurdle discount rate is simply required which is then compared with the IRR.

5.4.2 Disadvantages of IRR method

- If managers were given information about both **ARR and IRR**, it might be easy to get their relative **meaning and significance mixed up**.

- It **ignores the relative size of investments**. Both projects below have an IRR of 18%.

	Project A £	Project B £
Cost, year 0	350,000	35,000
Annual savings, years 1–6	100,000	10,000

Clearly, project A is bigger (ten times as big) and so more 'profitable' but if the only information on which the projects were judged were to be their IRR of 18%, project B would be made to seem just as beneficial as project A, which is not the case.

- **When discount rates are expected to differ over the life of the project, such variations can be incorporated easily into NPV calculations, but not into IRR calculations.**

- There are **problems** with using the IRR **when the project has non-conventional cash flows** (see Section 5.5) or when **deciding between mutually exclusive projects** (see Section 5.6).

5.5 Non-conventional cash flows

The projects we have considered so far have had **conventional or normal cash flows (an initial cash outflow followed by a series of inflows)** and in such circumstances the NPV and IRR methods give the same accept or reject decision. When flows vary from this they are termed non-conventional. The following project has non-conventional cash flows.

Year	Project X £'000
0	(1,900)
1	4,590
2	(2,735)

Project X has two IRRs as shown by the diagram which follows.

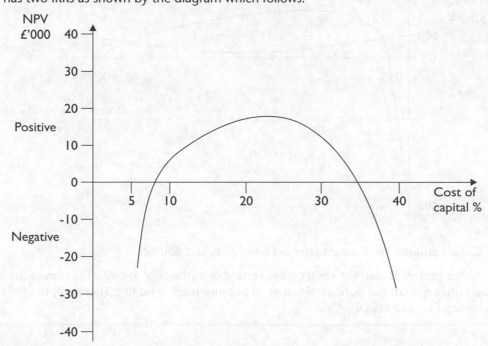

Suppose that the required rate of return on project X is 10% but that the IRR of 7% is used to decide whether to accept or reject the project. The project would be rejected since it appears that it can only yield 7%. The diagram shows, however, that **between rates of 7% and 35% the project should be accepted**. Using the IRR of 35% would produce the correct decision to accept the project. **Lack of knowledge of multiple IRRs** could therefore lead to serious **errors in the decision** of whether to accept or reject a project.

In general, if the sign of the net cash flow changes in successive periods (inflow to outflow or *vice versa*), it is possible for the calculations to produce **up to as many IRRs as there are sign changes**.

The use of the **IRR** is therefore **not recommended** in circumstances in which there are **non-conventional cash flow patterns** (unless the decision maker is aware of the existence of multiple IRRs). The NPV method, on the other hand, gives clear, unambiguous results whatever the cash flow pattern.

Before moving on to the worked example you might like to check that the IRRs of project X are indeed 7% and 35%. Apply the relevant discount factors to the project cash flows and on both occasions you should arrive at an NPV of approximately zero.

Worked example: Sketching an NPV graph with non-conventional cash flows

Two projects have estimated cash flows as follows.

	Year 0 £	Year 1 £	Year 2 £	IRR
Project C	(4,000)	25,000	(25,000)	25% & 400%
Project D	1,000	(1,600)	1,200	–

To clear up the confusion about whether the projects are acceptable when using IRR draw a graph. To find the starting point on the vertical axis find the NPV at 0% (ie add up the cash flows).

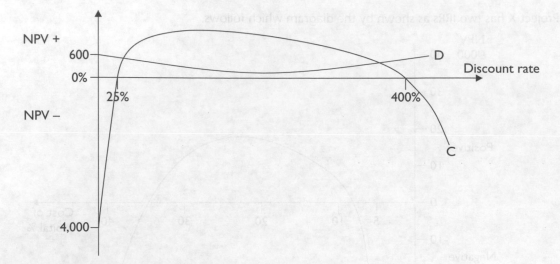

Project C is acceptable for discount rates between 25% and 400%.

The graph for project D starts at +600 on the vertical axis (the NPV at 0% = the sum of the cash flows). The graph does not cut the horizontal axis at all because there is no IRR. Therefore, the IRR decision rule cannot be used for project D.

5.6 Mutually exclusive projects

The IRR and NPV methods can give conflicting rankings when assessing which project should be given priority. Let us suppose that a company with a cost of capital of 16% is considering two mutually exclusive options, option A and option B. The cash flows for each are as follows.

Year		Option A £	Option B £
0	Capital outlay	(10,200)	(35,250)
1	Net cash inflow	6,000	18,000
2	Net cash inflow	5,000	15,000
3	Net cash inflow	3,000	15,000

The NPV of each project is calculated below. Use the formula $\dfrac{1}{(1+r)^n}$ to calculate the discount factors.

		Option A		Option B	
Year	Discount factor	Cash flow	Present value	Cash flow	Present value
	16%	£	£	£	£
0	1.000	(10,200)	(10,200)	(35,250)	(35,250)
1	0.862	6,000	5,172	18,000	15,516
2	0.743	5,000	3,715	15,000	11,145
3	0.641	3,000	1,923	15,000	9,615
			NPV = + 610		NPV = + 1,026

The **IRR of option A is 20%**, while the **IRR of option B is only 18%** (workings not shown).

On a **comparison of NPVs, option B would be preferred**, but on a **comparison of IRRs, option A would be preferred**.

The preference should go to option B because with the higher NPV it creates more wealth than option A.

Interactive question 5: Sketching NPV profiles   [Difficulty level: Intermediate]

Use the working table below to deduce the data required to sketch the NPV profiles of projects A and B on the scales provided. At what discount rate do the two projects earn the same NPV?

Project	Cash flows Year 0 £	Year 1 £	IRR	NPV at 0% £	NPV at 10% £	NPV at 30% £
A	(1,000)	1,250	25%			
B	(100)	140	40%			

Sketch of the NPV profiles

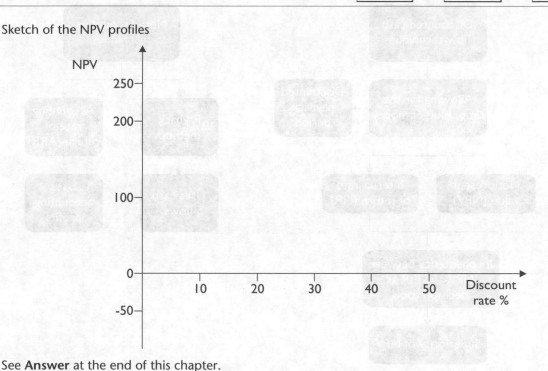

See **Answer** at the end of this chapter.

5.7 Reinvestment assumption

An assumption underlying the NPV method is that any net cash inflows generated during the life of the project **will be reinvested elsewhere at the cost of capital** (that is, the discount rate). The IRR method, on the other hand, assumes these cash flows **can be reinvested elsewhere to earn a return equal to the IRR of the original project**.

In the example in Section 5.6, the NPV method assumes that the cash inflows of £6,000, £5,000 and £3,000 for option A will be reinvested at the cost of capital of 16% whereas the IRR method assumes they will be reinvested at 20%. If the IRR is considerably higher than the cost of capital this is an unlikely assumption. In theory, a firm will have accepted all projects which provide a return in excess of the cost of capital and any other funds which become available can only be reinvested at the cost of capital. (This is the assumption implied in the NPV rule.) If the assumption is not valid **the IRR method overestimates the real return**.

Summary

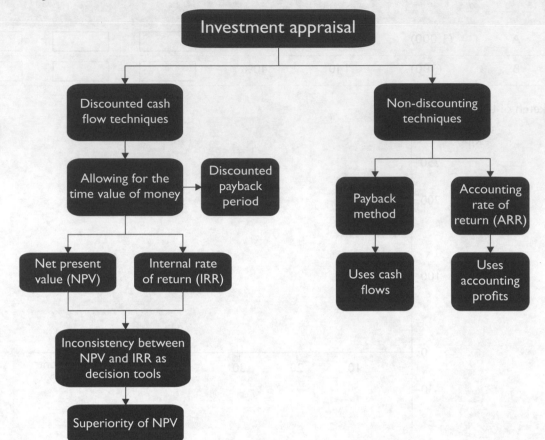

Self-test

Answer the following questions.

1   The payback period takes some account of the time value of money by

A   Placing greatest value on £1 receivable in the first year and progressively less on £1 received in each subsequent year

B   Placing least value on £1 receivable in the first year and progressively more on £1 received in each subsequent year

C   Placing the same value on £1 receivable up to the payback period and no value on subsequent receipts

D   Placing the same value on each £1 receivable over the life of a project

2   A project has the following cash flows.

Year	£
0	(40,000)
1	15,000
2	15,000
3	15,000
4	15,000

If the company were to discover that the cash inflow in year 4 had been overestimated, what would be the effect on the project's internal rate of return (IRR) and payback period if the error were corrected?

	IRR	Payback period
A	Decrease	No change
B	Decrease	Increase
C	Increase	No change
D	Increase	Increase

3   A project requires an initial investment in equipment of £100,000 and will produce eight equal annual cash flows of £40,000. The investment has no scrap value and straight line depreciation is used.

What are the payback period and accounting rate of return (ARR), based on the initial investment?

	Payback	ARR
A	2 years 6 months	27.5%
B	2 years 6 months	40%
C	3 years 6 months	27.5%
D	3 years 6 months	40%

4   £50,000 is to be spent on a machine having a life of five years and a residual value of £5,000. Operating cash inflows will be the same each year, except for year 1 when the figure will be £6,000. The accounting rate of return on the initial investment has been calculated at 30% pa.

What is the payback period?

A   2.75 years
B   2.55 years
C   2.54 years
D   2.33 years

5   A firm has two projects available. Project 1 has two internal rates of return of 15% and 30%, and project 2 has two internal rates of return of 10% and 20%. At a zero discount rate project 1 has a positive NPV and project 2 has a negative NPV. The appropriate discount rate for both projects is 25%.

Which of the following decisions about projects 1 and 2 should be taken?

	Project 1	Project 2
A	Accept	Accept
B	Accept	Reject
C	Reject	Accept
D	Reject	Reject

6   A project has a normal pattern of cash flows (ie an initial outflow followed by several years of inflows).

What would be the effects of an increase in the company's cost of capital on the internal rate of return (IRR) of the project and its payback period?

	IRR	Payback period
A	Increase	Increase
B	Increase	No change
C	No change	Increase
D	No change	No change

7   Which TWO of the following statements in relation to the use of IRR as an investment appraisal method are incorrect?

A   It always establishes if a single project is worthwhile ☐

B   It always establishes which of several projects to accept ☐

C   It ignores the relative size of the investment ☐

8   Consider the following graph.

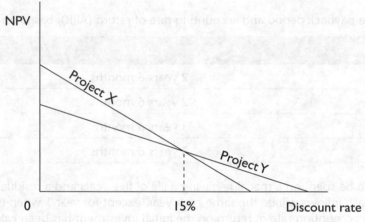

Which of the following statements is true?

A   Project Y has a higher internal rate of return than project X

B   At a discount rate of less than 15%, project Y is preferred to project X

C   Project X is preferred to project Y irrespective of the discount rate

D   Project Y is preferred to project X irrespective of the discount rate

9   A firm is evaluating the following four mutually-exclusive projects. All four projects involve the same initial outlay and have positive net present values. The projects generate the following cash inflows during their lives:

	Year 1 £	Year 2 £	Year 3 £	Year 4 £
Project A	500	400	600	300
Project B	300	600	500	400
Project C	500	300	600	400
Project D	300	500	600	400

Which project should be chosen?

A   Project A
B   Project B
C   Project C
D   Project D

10　An investment of £100,000 now is expected to generate equal annual cash flows to perpetuity of £15,000 pa, commencing in five years' time.

　　If the discount rate is 10% pa, what is the net present value of the investment (to the nearest £10)?

　　A　– £15,330
　　B　– £6,860
　　C　+ £2,450
　　D　+ £50,000

Now, go back to the Learning Objectives in the Introduction. If you are satisfied you have achieved these objectives, please tick them off.

Answer to Interactive question 1

The equipment that should be purchased is item ⊠ .

	Item X £	Item Y £
Total profit over life of equipment:		
before depreciation	160,000	280,000
after depreciation	80,000	130,000
Average annual accounting profit	16,000	26,000
Average investment = (capital cost + disposal value)/2	60,000	100,000
ARR, based on average investment	26.7%	26%

Both projects would earn a return in excess of 25%, but since **item X would earn a bigger ARR, it would be preferred to item Y**, even though the profits from Y would be higher by an average of £10,000 a year.

Answer to Interactive question 2

Year	Cash flow £	Multiplied by 12% discount factor	Present value £
2	40,000	$\dfrac{1}{(1.12)^2} = 0.797$	31,880
3	30,000	$\dfrac{1}{(1.12)^3} = 0.712$	21,360
Total present value			53,240

Answer to Interactive question 3

Year	Cash flow £	16.5% discount factor	Present value £
0	(280,000)	1.00	(280,000)
1	149,000	$\dfrac{1}{(1.165)} = 0.86$	128,140
2	128,000	$\dfrac{1}{(1.165)^2} = 0.74$	94,720
3	84,000	$\dfrac{1}{(1.165)^3} = 0.63$	52,920
4	70,000	$\dfrac{1}{(1.165)^4} = 0.54$	37,800
Net present value			33,580

Answer to Interactive question 4

The project IRR is ⬚ 15% .

The **total receipts** are £5,635 giving a **total profit** of £1,635 and **average profits** of £409. The **average investment** is £2,000. The **ARR** is £409 ÷ £2,000 = 20%. **Two thirds of the ARR** is approximately 14%. The **initial estimate of the IRR** that we shall try is therefore **14%**.

		Try 14%		Try 16%	
Time	Cash flow	Discount factor 14%	PV £	Discount factor 16%	PV £
	£				
0	(4,000)	1.000	(4,000)	1.000	(4,000)
1	1,200	0.877	1,052	0.862	1,034
2	1,410	0.769	1,084	0.743	1,048
3	1,875	0.675	1,266	0.641	1,202
4	1,150	0.592	681	0.552	635
		NPV	83	NPV	(81)

The **IRR must be less than 16%, but higher than 14%**. The NPVs at these two costs of capital will be used to estimate the IRR.

Using the **interpolation formula**

$$IRR = 14\% + \left(\frac{83}{83 + 81} \times (16\% - 14\%) \right) = 15.01\%$$

The IRR is, in fact, exactly 15%.

Answer to Interactive question 5

Project	Cash flows		IRR	NPV at 0%	NPV at 10%	NPV at 30%
	Year 0 £	Year 1 £		£	£	£
A	(1,000)	1,250	25%	250	136	(38)
B	(100)	140	40%	40	27	8

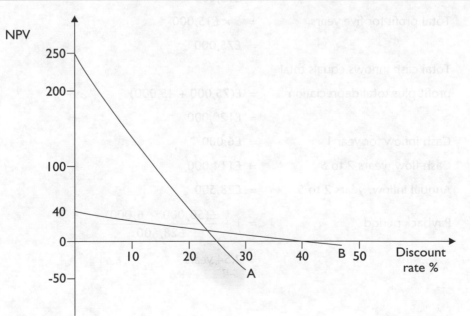

The two projects earn the same NPV at the point where the lines intersect, which is at a discount rate of approximately 23%.

1   C   Statement A describes how DCF methods account for the time of money. Statement B is the reverse of statement A and is incorrect because it is not taking account of the time value of money at all.

Statement D is incorrect because the payback method ignores cash flows after the payback period.

2   A   The payback period is not affected because the year 4 cash flow occurs after the payback period, however the IRR would be reduced because of the lower cash inflow in year 4.

3   A   Payback period $= \dfrac{£100,000}{£40,000}$

= 2.5 years

Annual depreciation $= \dfrac{£100,000}{8}$

= £12,500

Annual profit = £40,000 – £12,500

= £27,500

ARR $= \dfrac{£27,500}{£100,000} \times 100\%$

= 27.5%

4   C   ARR $= \dfrac{\text{Average profit}}{\text{Initial investment}} \times 100$

0.3 $= \dfrac{\text{Average profit}}{£50,000}$

Average profit = 0.3 × £50,000

= £15,000

Total profit for five years = 5 × £15,000

= £75,000

Total cash inflows equals total

profit plus total depreciation = £(75,000 + 45,000)

= £120,000

Cash inflow for year 1 = £6,000

Cash flow, years 2 to 5 = £114,000

Annual inflow, years 2 to 5 = £28,500

Payback period $= 1 + \dfrac{£(50,000 - 6,000)}{£28,500}$

= 2.54 years

5   D   The NPV profiles can be sketched as follows.

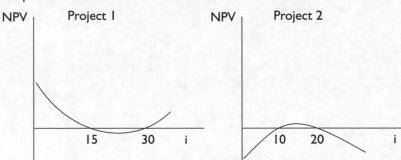

At a discount rate of 25%, both projects have a negative NPV therefore they should be rejected.

6   D   Both the internal rate of return and the payback period are independent of the cost of capital.

7   A, B

A is not true because IRR cannot be used to assess projects that do not have an IRR.

B is not true because NPV is used for mutually exclusive projects.

8   A   Statement A is correct because the NPV profile of project Y crosses the horizontal axis at a higher discount rate than that for project X.

Statement B is incorrect because at discount rates less than 15% project X has a higher NPV and is therefore preferred.

Statements C and D are incorrect because at discount rates less than 15% project X is preferred, whereas at rates greater than 15% project Y is preferred.

9   A   By a comparison of the cash flows A is better than C (it gives the same inflows in year 1 and year 3, but returns £100 higher in year 2 and £100 lower in year 4).

B is also better than D (same flows in years 1 and 4, but returns £100 more in year 2, and £100 less in year 3).

By a similar argument A is better than B; therefore A is the preferred project.

10   C $-£100,000 + \left(\dfrac{£15,000}{0.1} \right) \times 0.683$ (year 4 factor at 10%) = £2,450

ICAEW

APPENDIX

Discount tables

APPENDIX

Discount tables

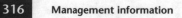

316   **Management information**

DISCOUNT TABLES

Interest rate p.a. r	Number of years n	Present value of £1 receivable at the end of n years $\dfrac{1}{(1+r)^n}$	Present value of £1 receivable at the end of each of n years $\dfrac{1}{r}\left[1-\dfrac{1}{(1+r)^n}\right]$
1%	1	0.990	0.990
	2	0.980	1.970
	3	0.971	2.941
	4	0.961	3.902
	5	0.951	4.853
	6	0.942	5.795
	7	0.933	6.728
	8	0.923	7.652
	9	0.914	8.566
	10	0.905	9.471
5%	1	0.952	0.952
	2	0.907	1.859
	3	0.864	2.723
	4	0.823	3.546
	5	0.784	4.329
	6	0.746	5.076
	7	0.711	5.786
	8	0.677	6.463
	9	0.645	7.108
	10	0.614	7.722
10%	1	0.909	0.909
	2	0.826	1.736
	3	0.751	2.487
	4	0.683	3.170
	5	0.621	3.791
	6	0.564	4.355
	7	0.513	4.868
	8	0.467	5.335
	9	0.424	5.759
	10	0.386	6.145
15%	1	0.870	0.870
	2	0.756	1.626
	3	0.658	2.283
	4	0.572	2.855
	5	0.497	3.352
	6	0.432	3.784
	7	0.376	4.160
	8	0.327	4.487
	9	0.284	4.772
	10	0.247	5.019
20%	1	0.833	0.833
	2	0.694	1.528
	3	0.579	2.106
	4	0.482	2.589
	5	0.402	2.991
	6	0.335	3.326
	7	0.279	3.605
	8	0.233	3.837
	9	0.194	4.031
	10	0.162	4.192

Glossary of terms

Absorption costing	The direct (or prime) cost of an item plus a fair share of the indirect (overhead) costs. Also called full costing.
Accounting rate of return	A measure of the expected average annual accounting profits from an investment expressed as a percentage of the value of that investment. Either the initial or average value of the investment can be used. Also called return on investment (ROI) or return on capital employed (ROCE).
Activity based budgeting (ABB)	An approach to budgeting which uses cost drivers as a basis for preparing budgets.
Activity based costing (ABC)	An alternative to traditional absorption costing where overheads are related to output using multiple cost drivers (activities which cause the overheads).
Allocation	The process by which overheads are charged directly to cost centres.
Annuity	A constant annual cash flow, for a number of years.
Apportionment	A procedure where indirect (overhead) costs are spread fairly between cost centres.
Avoidable costs	Costs which would not be incurred if the activity to which they relate did not exist.
Balanced scorecard approach	An approach to the provision of information to management to assist strategic policy formulation and achievement. It emphasises the need to provide the user with a set of information which addresses all relevant areas of performance in an objective and unbiased fashion. The information provided may include both financial and non-financial elements, and cover areas such as profitability, customer satisfaction, internal efficiency and learning and growth.
Batch costing	A costing method applied where a group (batch) of identical items is treated as a cost unit. The cost per item = total batch cost ÷ number of items in the batch.
Blanket absorption rate	An absorption rate used throughout a factory for all products irrespective of the department in which they were produced.
Bottom-up budgeting	See participative budgeting.
Breakeven analysis	See cost-volume-profit analysis.
Breakeven point	Number of units sold at which neither a profit nor a loss is made.
Budget	A quantitative statement, for a defined period of time, which may include planned revenues, expenses, assets, liabilities and cash flows.
Budget manual	A collection of instructions governing the responsibilities of persons and the procedures, forms and records relating to the preparation and use of budgetary data.
Budget slack	Deliberately underestimating revenues or overestimating costs in order to ensure that achieving the budget is easy.
Capital expenditure	Expenditure which results in the acquisition of long-term assets or an improvement in their earning capacity.
Cash budget	A statement in which estimated future cash receipts and payments are tabulated in such a way as to show the forecast cash balance of a business at defined intervals.
Cash operating cycle	The period of time which elapses between the point at which cash begins to be spent on the production of a product and the collection of cash from the customer who purchases it.
Coefficient of correlation r	Measures the degree to which one variable is related to another.

Coefficient of determination r^2	The square of the correlation coefficient, r^2. This measures the amount of the total variation in the value of one variable that can be explained by variations in the value of the other variable.
Contract costing	A form of specific order costing where costs are attributed to contracts.
Contribution	The difference between the selling price and all of the variable costs of a product.
Controllable costs	Items of expenditure which can be directly influenced by a given manager within a given time span.
Cost behaviour	The way in which costs are affected by changes in the level of activity where 'activity' can be volume of output, number of production runs etc.
Cost centre	Any part of an organisation which incurs costs.
Cost driver	Something which causes costs to change eg volume of output, number of production runs etc.
Cost object	Something (eg product, service, activity) in relation to which costs are determined.
Cost plus pricing	A desired profit mark-up is added to total costs to arrive at the selling price.
Cost pool	A grouping of costs relating to a particular activity in an activity-based costing system.
Cost unit	A unit of product or service in relation to which costs are ascertained.
Cost-volume-profit (CVP) analysis	An analysis of costs, volume and profit at various levels of activity. Also known as break-even analysis.
Cumulative weighted average pricing	An inventory valuation method that calculates a weighted average cost from both opening inventory and units introduced in the current period. The average is calculated whenever a new delivery occurs.
Current ratio	Current assets ÷ current liabilities.
Curvilinear correlation	A relationship between variables which appears as a curve when drawn on a graph.
Decentralisation	When managers of divisions have freedom to make certain decisions relating to their division (as opposed to decisions being made centrally by a head office).
Development costs	The costs incurred between the decision to produce a new or improved product and the commencement of full manufacture of the product.
Differential cost	The difference in total cost between alternatives.
Direct cost	A cost that can be traced in full to the product, service, or department that is incurring the cost.
Direct labour cost	The specific costs of the workforce used to make a product or provide a service. Direct labour costs are established by measuring the time taken for a job, or the time taken in 'direct production work'.
Direct labour efficiency variance	The difference between the hours that should have been worked for the number of units actually produced, and the actual number of hours worked, valued at the standard labour rate per hour.
Direct labour rate variance	The difference between the standard cost and the actual cost for the actual number of hours paid for.
Direct labour total variance	The difference between what the output actually cost and what it should have cost, in terms of labour.
Direct material costs	The costs of materials that are known to have been used in making and selling a product, or providing a service.

ICAEW

Direct material price variance	The difference between the standard cost and the actual cost for the actual quantity of material used or purchased.
Direct material total variance	The difference between what the output actually cost and what it should have cost, in terms of material used.
Direct material usage variance	The difference between the standard quantity of materials that should have been used for the number of units actually produced, and the actual quantity of materials used, valued at the standard cost per unit of material.
Discounted cash flow	Converting future sums of money to their present value, which is the cash equivalent now of those future sums.
Discounted payback method	How long it will take for a project to pay back the capital outlay on a discounted cash flow basis.
Economic order quantity (EOQ)	The order quantity which minimises inventory costs. The EOQ can be calculated using a table, graph or formula.
Extrapolation	Predicting costs at activity levels outside the relevant range.
Factoring organisation	Takes over the management of the trade debts owed to its client (a business customer) on the client's behalf. The factor company collects the debts and provides an immediate cash advance of a proportion of the money it is due to collect.
FIFO (first in, first out)	A method of pricing materials based on the cost of the oldest units held regardless of the sequence in which the issue of the materials takes place.
Financing costs	Costs incurred to finance a business such as loan interest.
Fixed budget	A budget which is set for a single activity level.
Fixed cost	A cost which is incurred for a particular period of time and which, within certain activity levels (the relevant range), is unaffected by changes in the level of activity.
Fixed overhead expenditure variance	The difference between the budgeted fixed overhead expenditure and actual fixed overhead expenditure.
Flexible budget	A budget which, by recognising different cost behaviour patterns, is designed to change as volume of activity changes.
Full cost-plus pricing	A method of determining the sales price by calculating the full (absorption) cost of the product and adding a percentage mark-up for profit.
Functional budgets	The budgets for the various functions of the business eg production, marketing, sales, purchasing budgets.
Goal congruence	When individuals' goals and company goals coincide.
Incremental budgeting	Basing this year's budget on last year's budget with adjustments for changes and inflation.
Imposed budget	A budget set without allowing the budget holder to participate in the budgeting process.
Indirect cost or overhead	A cost that is incurred in the course of making a product, providing a service or running a department, but which cannot be traced directly and in full to the product, service or department.
International Accounting Standard 2 (IAS 2)	States that the cost of all inventories should comprise those costs which have been incurred in the normal course of business in bringing the inventories to their 'present location and condition'.
Internal rate of return (IRR)	The discount rate at which a project has a zero NPV.
Investment centre	A section of an organisation whose manager has some say in investment policy in their area of operations as well as being responsible for costs and

	revenues.
Invoice discounting	The purchase (by the provider of the discounting service) of a company's trade debts, at a discount. Invoice discounting enables a company to raise finance based on their expected invoice receipts. The invoice discounter does not take over the administration of the client's sales ledger so the client remains in control of debt collection.
Job costing	The costing method used where work is undertaken to customers' special requirements and each order is of comparatively short duration.
Just-in-time (JIT)	A system whose objective is to produce or to procure products or components as they are required by a customer or for use, rather than for inventory. A JIT system is a 'pull' system, which responds to demand, in contrast to a 'push' system, in which inventories act as buffers between the different elements of the system, such as purchasing, production and sales.
Just-in-time production	A system which is driven by demand for finished products whereby each component on a production line is produced only when needed for the next stage.
Just-in-time purchasing	A system in which material purchases are contracted so that the receipt and usage of material coincide to the maximum extent possible.
Life cycle costing	A costing method that takes into account the costs and revenues of a product over its entire life span.
LIFO (last in, first out)	A method of pricing materials based on the cost of the newest units held regardless of the sequence in which the issue of the materials takes place.
Limiting factor	Anything which limits the activity of a company.
Linear regression analysis	A technique for estimating the equation of a line of best fit.
Liquidity	How quickly an asset can be converted to cash determines its liquidity. Cash is the most liquid asset.
Management accounting systems	Provide information specifically for the use of managers within an organisation.
Management by exception	Only paying attention to results that are substantially different from expected.
Management control	The process by which managers assure that resources are obtained and used effectively and efficiently in the accomplishment of the organisation's objectives
Margin of safety	The difference in units between the budgeted sales volume and the breakeven sales volume. It is sometimes expressed as a percentage of the budgeted sales volume.
Marginal cost	The variable cost of one unit of product or service.
Mutually exclusive	If two events are mutually exclusive, it means that they cannot occur at the same time.
Net present value	The sum of the present value of the benefits (revenues or savings) from an investment, less the present value of expenditures. Uses discounted cash flows (see above).
Operating statement	A regular report for management of actual costs and revenues, usually showing variances from budget.
Opportunity cost	The value of the benefit sacrificed when one course of action is chosen in preference to an alternative.
Outsourcing	The use of external suppliers as a source of finished products, components or services. This is also known as contract manufacturing or sub-contracting.

ICAEW

Overhead absorption	The process whereby overhead costs allocated and apportioned to production cost centres (in traditional costing systems) or cost pools (in activity based costing systems) are added to unit, job or batch costs. Overhead absorption is sometimes called overhead recovery.
Participative budgeting	Budgeting style which allows all budget holders to participate in setting their own budget.
Payback period	The time required for the cash inflows from a capital investment project to equal the cash outflows.
Period cost	A cost relating to a period of time.
Perpetuity	A constant annual cash flow that continues forever (a perpetual annuity).
Prime costs	The sum of all the direct costs.
Principal budget factor	The budgeted factor which limits the activities of an organisation.
Process costing	A form of costing applicable to continuous processes where process costs are attributed to the number of units produced.
Production costs	The costs which are incurred by the sequence of operations beginning with the supply of raw materials, and ending with the completion of the product ready for warehousing as a finished goods item.
Profit centre	Any section of an organisation, for example, a division of a company, which earns revenue and incurs costs. The profitability of the section can therefore be measured.
Quick ratio	Current assets less inventories ÷ current liabilities
Residual income (RI)	Profit less a notional interest charge for invested capital.
Residual value	The disposal value of equipment at the end of its life, or its disposal cost.
Responsibility accounting	A system of accounting that makes revenues and costs the responsibility of particular managers so that the performance of each part of the organisation can be monitored and assessed.
Responsibility centre	A section of an organisation that is headed by a manager who has direct responsibility for its performance.
Return on capital employed (ROCE)	Also called **Return on investment (ROI)**. Is calculated as (profit/capital employed) x 100% and shows how much profit has been made in relation to the amount of resources invested.
Revenue centre	A section of an organisation which creates revenue but has no responsibility for production. A sales department is an example.
Revenue expenditure	Expenditure which is incurred for the purpose of the trade of the business or to maintain the existing earning capacity of non-current assets.
Rolling budget	A budget continually updated to add a new budget period as the most recent one has finished.
Sales price variance	A measure of the effect on expected profit of a different selling price to standard selling price. It is calculated as the difference between what the sales revenue should have been for the actual quantity sold, and what it actually was.
Sales volume variance	The difference between the actual units sold and the budgeted (planned) quantity, valued at the standard contribution per unit. In other words, it measures the increase or decrease in standard contribution as a result of the sales volume being higher or lower than budgeted (planned).
Scrap	Discarded material having some value.
Selling costs	Sometimes known as marketing costs, are the costs of creating demand for products and securing firm orders from customers.

Semi-variable/mixed cost	A cost which contains both fixed and variable components and so is partly affected by changes in the level of activity.
Sensitivity analysis	Assesses how sensitive a budget is to changes in the budget assumptions.
Step fixed cost	A cost that is fixed for a certain range of activity but increases to a new fixed level once a critical level of activity is reached.
Target costing approach	A process that begins with the development of a product concept and then determination of the price customers would be willing to pay for that concept. The desired profit margin is deducted from the price, leaving a figure that represents total cost. This is the target cost.
Time value of money	Recognises that £1 today is worth more than £1 at a future time, because money can be reinvested today to earn more money over time.
Top down budget	See imposed budget.
Total quality management	A philosophy that means that quality management is the aim of every part of the organisation. The aim is to 'get it right first time' which means that there is a striving for continuous improvement in order to eliminate faulty work and prevent mistakes.
Transfer price	The amount charged by one part of an organisation for the provision of goods or services to another part of the same organisation.
Variable cost	A cost which varies with the level of activity.
Variable production overhead efficiency variance	The difference between the hours that should have been worked and those actually worked, evaluated at the standard variable overhead rate per hour.
Variable production overhead expenditure variance	The difference between the amount of variable production overhead that should have been incurred in the actual hours worked, and the actual amount of variable production overhead incurred.
Variable production overhead total variance	The difference between what the output actually cost and what it should have cost, in terms of variable overheads.
Variance	The difference between a planned, budgeted, or standard cost and the actual cost incurred.
Working capital	Current assets less current liabilities (the value of raw materials, work-in-progress, finished goods inventories, accounts receivable and cash less accounts payable and overdraft).
Zero-based budgeting (ZBB)	Involves preparing a budget for each cost centre from a zero base. Every item of expenditure has to be justified in its entirety in order to be included in the next year's budget.

ICAEW

Index

Notes